PACIFIC SWEEP

Other Books by William N. Hess

FIGHTING MUSTANG

THE ALLIED ACES OF WORLD WAR II

THE AMERICAN ACES OF WORLD WAR II AND KOREA

SLYBIRD: THE 353RD FIGHTER GROUP

ON ESCORT AND GROUND ATTACK
(with Kenn C. Rust)

CHECKERTAIL CLAN: THE 325TH FIGHTER

GROUP IN NORTH AFRICA AND ITALY
(with Ernest R. McDowell)

PACIFIC SWEEP

THE 5th and 13th FIGHTER COMMANDS
IN WORLD WAR II

William N. Hess

DOUBLEDAY & COMPANY, INC.

Garden City, New York

1974

ISBN: 0-385-07579-0
Library of Congress Catalog Card Number: 74-4649

ACKNOWLEDGMENTS

Many people have helped me put this story together over the past two years. My sincere thanks to former 5th Fighter Command personnel; W. K. "Kenny" Giroux, Bob DeHaven, Marvin Grant, Jim Watkins, James Haislip, Hubert Hendrix, Richard Tansing, and Curtis Ehlert for their recollections, suggestions, and invaluable knowledge. A special thanks to the 80th Fighter Squadron Association, which made its invaluable records and photos available.

My heartfelt thanks to Stanley M. Ulanoff and Harold Kuebler for their encouragement and efforts in making this book possible.

As usual, Margo Kennedy and the staff at Aerospace Studies Institute were wonderful in making all the many official files available to me.

The dank and dampness of the Pacific made suitable photos hard to come by, but the above-listed 5th Fighter Command people plus Ernie McDowell, Yasuho Izawa, Tom Mitchell, Arthur Wox, Dick Hill, Colonel Charles King, and the Book and Magazine Branch of the Office of the Secretary of Defense solved this problem. My deepest appreciation to my photo developer and printer, John Bardwell, for the excellence of the many copy prints utilized.

As always, my thanks to my wife, Ann, who has suffered through another phase of the war in the air.

CONTENTS

INTRODUCTION

This is the story of the U. S. Army Air Force fighter pilots who flew in the South and Southwest Pacific in World War II. Theirs is not a story of glamor and glory of the war in the air. These men fought a war not only against the Japanese but against the sea, the jungle, disease, insects, and at times just plain boredom.

It all began with a handful of pilots flying inferior aircraft in the Philippine Islands in 1941. After their first day of war they were called on to not only defend but to carry out a large portion of what little aerial offense the Americans could muster.

After the fall of the Philippines came another last-ditch stand on the island of Java in the Netherlands East Indies. Once more a little band of fighter pilots did battle in the skies in another episode of the "too little and too late" efforts that marked the Allied defeats in the Far East in 1942.

In early 1942 the Curtiss P-40s and the Bell P-39s of the Far East Air Force stood firm in their defense of northern Australia and New Guinea. Their gallant stand against the victory-inspired and numerically superior Japanese was one of the few bright spots in a very dark period of history for the Allied cause.

When the Americans began the long road back north from Guadalcanal in August of 1942, the fighter pilots of the Army Air Force were right there along with their fellow Marine Corps and Navy pilots slugging it out to hold the embattled island. When American forces moved to seize the balance of the Solomon Islands, the men of 13th Fighter Command were in the thick of things.

In the Southwest Pacific the story of the 5th Fighter Command was that of progressive moves up the coast of New Guinea to places like Dobodura, Nadjab, Gusap, and Biak. Each move saw the command grown larger and stronger and more proficient in its task of shooting Japanese aircraft from the skies and making his bases unlivable through the use of repeated bombing and strafing attacks.

Both commands would join in 1944 on the return to the Philippine Islands, whence their predecessors had departed in defeat in 1942. Following victory in the Philippines, all units of 5th and 13th fighter commands were slated to move north to the Ryukyu Islands for the invasion of Japan. The dropping of the atomic bombs made the final offensive step unnecessary.

I have tried to tell in these pages the largely untold story of these gallant pilots and their devoted ground crews whose job it was to defeat the Japanese in the air. I say "largely untold," for the majority of the official records and unofficial diaries that provided the basis for this book had languished long untouched in the historical archives and in nearly forgotten footlockers of various individuals. For the early days in the Philippine Islands and Java there exist only the statements taken from the men who fought and survived to make their way to Australia to fight again.

The jungle bases of the South and Southwest Pacific were not favorite places with news correspondents. They had no comfortable officers' clubs, lovely ladies just off the base, nor historic cities in their proximity, as did their counterparts in Europe. Theirs was a world of moldy tents, jungle mud, and absolutely no place to go. For obvious reasons the majority of the wartime news releases concerning the men of these commands were dispatched by their own public relations men where there happened to be one assigned.

These men of the 5th and 13th fighter commands defeated the Japanese in the skies with a minimum of personnel and often with inferior aircraft. What they lacked in men and equipment they made up for in skill and sheer guts.

I

THE PHILIPPINES

On the afternoon of November 20, 1941, a convoy of 3 ships slipped into Manila Bay. This convoy consisted of the S.S. *Coolidge*, the U.S.A.T. *Winfield S. Scott,* and the heavy cruiser *Louisville.* The *Coolidge* docked at Pier 7, the longest pier at Manila, and the men aboard grumbled for some 3 hours before they were allowed to disembark.

Aboard the *Coolidge* were 15 pilots of the 21st Pursuit Squadron and 16 pilots of the 34th Pursuit Squadron. These were the last reinforcing fighter pilots who would arrive in the Philippines before hostilities with Japan commenced. The young pilots were of the opinion that new Curtiss P-40s would be awaiting them at Nichols Field, but on their arrival they found that they were to be relegated worn-out Seversky P-35s that had been cast off by the 3rd, 17th, and 20th pursuit squadrons. These older units had been equipped with P-40s during the summer of 1941 and had been undergoing intensive gunnery training at the airfield at Iba, which was located some 90 miles northwest of Manila on the west coast of Luzon.

Lieutenant William E. Dyess' 21st Squadron flew the old P-35s from Nichols Field until December 4, when they received brand-new P-40Es from the air depot. Their obsolete aircraft were then passed along to the 34th Squadron, under the command of Lieutenant Samuel W. Marrett.

In view of the tense international situation that existed between the United States and Japan, all units in the Philippines had been placed on alert since the fifteenth of November. All pursuit aircraft were fueled, armed, and on constant alert 24 hours each day with all pilots available on 30 minutes' notice. All of the squadrons were undergoing intensive interception exercises in conjunction with the bombers at Clark Field.

On November 27, 1941, General Douglas MacArthur, commander of the U. S. Army Forces in the Far East, received a message at his Manila headquarters from General George C. Marshall, U. S. Army Chief of Staff, informing him that for all practical purposes the negotiations between the Japanese Government and the United States appeared to be terminated. MacArthur was authorized to take such reconnaissance and other measures as he deemed necessary for the defense of the Philippines, but he was warned at the same time not to take any overt hostile action. If war was to come the Japanese would make the first move.

On the eve of war Major General Lewis H. Brereton, commander of the recently designated Far East Air Force, headquartered at Nielson Field just south of Manila, took stock of his forces, which were meager to say the least.

The 5th Bomber Command, which was headed by Colonel Eugene L. Eubank, was composed of the 19th and 27th bombardment groups. The ground echelon of the 27th Bombardment Group had arrived, but its air echelon, equipped with Douglas A-24 dive bombers, had not arrived, and upon the outbreak of war would be diverted to Australia.

In view of the international crisis, 2 squadrons numbering 16 B-17s of the 19th Bombardment Group had been deployed to Del Monte Airfield on the island of Mindanao. The 2 remaining squadrons, composed of 19 B-17s, remained at Clark Field near Manila.

The strength of the 5th Interceptor Command, which was commanded by Brigadier General Henry B. Clagett, was reported by Major Orin L. Grover, commanding officer of the 24th Pursuit Group, as follows:

a. 3rd Pursuit Squadron, equipped with 18 P-40Es under the command of Lieutenant Henry G. Thorne.
b. 17th Pursuit Squadron, equipped with 18 P-40Es under the command of Lieutenant Boyd D. Wagner.
c. 20th Pursuit Squadron, equipped with 18 P-40Bs under the command of Lieutenant J. H. Moore.
d. 21st Pursuit Squadron, equipped with 18 P-40Es under the command of Lieutenant W. E. Dyess.
e. 34th Pursuit Squadron, equipped with 18 P-35s under the command of Lieutenant S. H. Marrett.

The 20th Pursuit Squadron was based at Clark Field along with the 2 squadrons of B-17 Flying Fortresses of the 19th Bombardment Group. The 34th Pursuit Squadron was based at Del Carmen, 14 miles south of Clark Field. The primary fighter base at Nichols Field was located south of Manila and housed the 17th and 21st pursuit squadrons. Only a single squadron, the 3rd, was based at the advanced field at Iba.

The 2nd Observation Squadron, equipped with O-46 and O-52-type aircraft plus a smattering of obsolete Douglas B-18 bombers and training-type aircraft, made up the balance of the Far East Air Force.

To augment the American forces, there was the infant Philippine Air Force, which was composed of a handful of obsolete Boeing P-26A fighters and Martin B-10 bombers.

The air warning system for the Philippines was grossly inadequate. One radar set was in operation at Iba and another set was in the process of being installed 60 miles west of Aparri. A third set was en route to Legaspi for installation. The brunt of the air warning system was dependent on Philippine air watchers and a very inefficient and ineffectual telephone system. Delay in time between the spotting and plotting on the board at 5th Interceptor headquarters at Manila ranged from 5 to 25 minutes.

Time had not permitted the fighter units to become proficient in their aircraft. The 21st Squadron had only received its 18th

P-40E aircraft on the afternoon of December 7. The P-35s that had been turned over to the 34th Squadron were obsolete and in dire need of engine change and machine gun replacement.

This was the dilemma that faced Major General Lewis Brereton on the evening of December 7, 1941.

Since early 1941, the Japanese had begun to build up their forces on the island of Formosa. On the eve of war, the Japanese Navy alone had amassed a total of 184 Zero fighters, 192 land-based attack bombers, and 24 flying boats. This force was supplemented by 150 to 175 first-line combat aircraft of the Japanese Army Air Force. Never before had an American military force faced such overwhelming odds.

Due to the international date line, the war came to the Philippines a day later than in Hawaii and the mainland United States. In the wee hours of the morning of December 8, 1941, the operator manning the radar screen at Iba noted a number of incoming blips on his set that could only have one meaning. A large force of enemy aircraft was approaching. Lieutenant Henry Thorne and his squadron manned their P-40s immediately and took off into the darkness to intercept.

The radar operator could give the fighter pilots a course to bear but could not provide them with an altitude for interception. The P-40s continued to climb into the night until they reached their limitation of 15,000 feet. Alas, there was not even oxygen available for the American aircraft.

The radar set showed that an interception of sorts had been made, for on the instrument screen the converging blips met, but in the air the P-40 pilots made no sighting. Undoubtedly, the enemy aircraft had been far above them. Strangely, the Japanese formation turned and went back toward the island of Formosa. The Americans returned to their base at Iba.

At 3:30 A.M. the commercial radio station at Manila picked up a broadcast stating that Pearl Harbor, Hawaii, had been bombed by the Japanese. This information remained unconfirmed until official confirmation was given to the 24th Pursuit Group by

General MacArthur's headquarters at 4:45 A.M. An official statement was released at 5:30 A.M. that Pearl Harbor had been attacked and that a state of war existed between the United States and the Empire of Japan.

The 20th Pursuit Squadron got its P-40s off at 8 A.M. to patrol the area of Rosales to intercept any flights of Japanese aircraft that might be heading down over the Lingayen Gulf. The 17th Squadron at Nichols Field took off to patrol over Clark Field while the 4-engine Flying Fortresses took to the air as a precautionary move against getting caught on the ground during a bombardment of the base. Ironically, this move on the part of the bombers was to result in their ultimate destruction.

The Japanese bombed the radio station at Aparri and the town of Baguio far to the north and turned back. No interception was made by the American fighters, and both fighter squadrons and the bombers were on the ground at Clark Field at 10:45 A.M.

The 3rd Squadron at Iba had remained under constant alert since their early-morning mission. At 11:30 A.M. the radar picked up a large formation, and the P-40s scrambled once more. Immediately communications were awry. In the confusion "B" Flight, under Lieutenant Woolery, became separated from the rest of the squadron, so "B" Flight set course for Manila, where they expected to get further orders from headquarters of the 24th Pursuit Group at Neilson Field.

Nothing happened for the first few minutes over Manila, and then a call came in that sounded like, "bandits over Clark," so the P-40s pushed throttles wide open and sped northward. Upon arrival everything looked normal, so the flight set course back for Iba in order to refuel.

As the flight began to let down over the coast, they sighted a freighter going full speed and a PT boat zigzagging like mad. The P-40 pilots were mystified by these actions, but still noted no other aircraft, so they went in to land. Lieutenant Andrew Krieger was bringing up the rear of the flight, so he proceeded to circle and cover the landing. Lieutenant Woolery's plane touched down and the others were on their final approach when the field went up in a violent explosion.

Krieger gave his plane full throttle and climbed upward, craning his neck to try to sight the enemy. Finally he saw them, a precise formation of some 54 bombers directly over the field at approximately 28,000 feet. Swarms of Japanese fighters buzzed around them as they let their bombs rain down upon Iba.

Krieger leveled off at 10,000 feet and circled back over the field. This time he sighted what he thought was a squadron of P-35s in a Lufbery circle getting ready to land. Then as he pulled up through the smoke he saw the Japanese insignia on the wings. Immediately, Krieger put in a call for assistance on the radio and dove to the attack.

The capabilities of the Zero fighter were unknown to the young American pilot, and he promptly got 3 of them on his tail when he tried to tack onto the tail of a Zero in front of him. Krieger had time for a single short burst and then went into the most violent maneuvers he knew. Somehow he managed to shake his opponents and make it back to the field at Rosales before he ran out of gas.

Six P-40s of the 21st Squadron took to the air at 11:40 A.M. to patrol over Clark Field, while the fighters there were being refueled and the bombers were made ready for a mission against the Japanese bases on Formosa. Two of the brand-new P-40s had to return to Nichols Field with engine trouble, so only 4 aircraft arrived to patrol the area over Clark. All was serene upon their arrival, so when a formation of aircraft was sighted over the mountains to the west, they flew out to join them. Clark Field was left completely undefended.

The Japanese Navy Air Force had originally planned to strike the Philippines early in the morning. Their primary targets were Iba and Clark Field, while the Army Air Force had been assigned the targets at Aparri and Baguio. Heavy ground fog had prevented the Navy aircraft from becoming airborne, while the Army fields were clear. This resulted in the early-morning raids on the targets at Aparri and Baguio with no strikes being made on the primary air field targets on Luzon.

When the 54 Betty bombers of the Japanese Navy I Air Corps and 34 Zero fighters of the Tainan Air Corps did get off for Clark Field, they felt sure that all hope of surprise was gone and that all available fighter aircraft would be in the air to meet them. They could hardly believe their eyes when they sighted their target.

As the 2 Japanese "V" formations crossed the mountains at an altitude of 18,000 feet, their crews looked down and saw the nucleus of American airpower in the Philippines lined wingtip to wingtip on the field below. The Betty bombers bore down and the first formation was almost to their release line before the alarm was given at Clark Field.

The pilots of the 20th Squadron jumped into their aircraft and raced desperately to become airborne. Only 4 P-40s, led by Lieutenant J. H. Moore, managed to get off before the bomb pattern walked its path of destruction over the balance of the squadron.

The P-40s were hardly off the ground before they encountered their first Zeros. Lieutenant Randall Keator shot one down almost at once to score the first victory over the Philippines. Lieutenant Moore was able to down 2 more before the combat was broken off.

The 4 members of the flight from the 21st now returned to join in the fray, but became split when 1 member developed engine trouble and 1 disappeared. The 2 remaining, Lieutenants Grashio and Williams, tangled with a pack of Zeros but only picked up a few holes in their own aircraft for their trouble.

The 34th Squadron pilots at Del Carmen saw the smoke rising from Clark Field and took off in their P-35s without orders to intercept. Two Zeros were encountered at the base of the cloud ceiling at 6,000 feet, but these were driven off. Lieutenant Marrett's guns failed to operate so he returned to base, and Lieutenant Ben S. Brown took over the squadron.

"I took the squadron over," said Brown, "and proceeded to Clark Field at about 8,000 feet, where we were engaged by 4 Zeros. They were very aggressive and cocky and came right into us. Upon going into the attack I got a shot in at 90 degrees' deflection and got 1 Zero. The fight continued in a seesaw manner, and due to the inexperience of the pilots and lack of gunnery training no more Zeros were shot down."

In these early fights the Americans had no idea how maneuverable the Japanese Zero was, and those who tried to dogfight them ran into trouble immediately. The diving and mutual support tactics that would be employed successfully later were being learned the hard way.

Six planes from "C" Flight of the 3rd Squadron got into the fight when they caught a bunch of Zeros strafing. Although the P-40s were very low on fuel, they pressed the attack, and 1 of them ran out of gas during combat and the pilot had to bail out. Two more P-40s were lost in this action, but not before Lieutenant Herb Ellis had downed 3 Zeros. Ellis chased another Zero into a cloud before he discovered that his tail surfaces were on fire. This necessitated a high-speed bail out at low altitude, but Ellis made it to the ground safely.

All of the B-17s that were caught on the field at Clark were destroyed, along with the P-40s of the 20th Squadron. Even the old B-18s, B-10s, and other obsolete craft were victims of the devastating bombing and strafing of the Japanese.

The initial blow inflicted by the enemy had cut the strength of the Far East Air Force in half. Only 17 B-17s of the original 19th Bomb Group remained. Fifty-five of the P-40s had been destroyed on the ground or in the air. Only 16 of the obsolete P-35s had survived the first day of war.

The depleted 3rd Squadron was split between the 17th Squadron, which moved up to Clark Field, and the 21st Squadron, which remained at Nichols. These aircraft, in addition to the P-35s of the 34th Squadron, flew constant patrols on December 9, but no enemy opposition was encountered.

During the night reports began to trickle in telling of large Japanese invasion convoys headed for the coasts of northern Luzon. Plans for bombing attacks on Formosa were shelved, and B-17s of the 19th Bombardment Group plus the 17th and 34th Pursuit Squadrons made preparations to hit convoys on the morning of December 10. The Flying Fortresses had come up from Mindanao to fill the gap created by the losses of December 8.

Before dawn the next morning Lieutenant Grant Mahoney of the 3rd Pursuit Squadron revved up his P-40 and took off into the darkness. Despite heavy weather he was able to locate the Japanese convoy off Vigan and brought back valuable information regarding the course of the ships, their number and size.

At 6 A.M. 5 Flying Fortresses took off loaded with 100-pound demolition bombs to attack the transports. A few hits were scored by the bombers when the P-40s of the 17th Squadron came down from their top cover position. Down on the deck the P-40s went bombing and strafing the landing barges with good effect. After expending their ammunition the P-40s pulled up and headed home, but 2 of their number experienced engine failure, and their pilots were forced to bail out on the return trip.

The P-35s of the 34th Squadron had flown up to Del Carmen to stage for the mission and were airborne with 16 planes in 2 flights. However, the mission was more than the worn engines of most of the aircraft could take, and one by one the pilots were forced to return to base. By the time the target was reached there were only 7 planes left in the formation.

The P-35 carried only 2 .30-caliber and 2 .50-caliber machine guns, but Lieutenant Sam Marrett didn't hesitate in taking his little force down to attack the landing barges and transports off the beach at Vigan. Marrett concentrated on a 10,000-ton transport and flew continuous strafing passes against the vessel despite intense antiaircraft fire. On his last pass he apparently hit the ship's magazine. As Marrett started to pull up from his dive the ship exploded. A wing tore off Marrett's little pursuit craft and it spun into the sea.

Regardless of the sacrifices of the strafers, initial Japanese landings were effected not only at Vigan, but in the Aparri area on the northern tip of the island of Luzon.

The six survivors of the 34th Squadron made it back to Del Carmen, where they landed and taxied into line with the 8 P-35s that had been forced to abort the mission. No sooner had the pilots climbed out of the cockpits and begun to walk away when 12 Japanese Zeros swept over with guns blazing. After the Zeros had finished their attack, the bulk of the airplanes of the 34th Squadron could be written off the strength of the rapidly diminishing Far East Air Force.

The strafing attack at Del Carmen caused the P-40s of the 17th and 21st pursuit squadrons to be scrambled at approximately 12:30 P.M. Some of the American fighter pilots managed to catch the Zeros in the area, and 4 of the Zeros were shot down.

These P-40s had been in the air for some time and their fuel was running low when the main attack of the day was directed against Clark Field and Manila. The Japanese bombers came in 3 formations of 27 each at approximately 20,000 feet. They were well escorted by more than 40 Zero fighter planes. Now the Americans, with gas tanks that were nearly dry, were faced with intercepting the enemy or running for home in a vain hope that they could refuel and catch the bombers on the bombers' way home. There was no hesitation. The P-40s attacked.

The greatest air battle that was to take place over the Phillippines in 1941 was under way. Dogfights took place all over the sky, and the P-40s were scattered over a wide area as they sought to break through the numerically superior defenses to get to the bombers. Once more the Americans tried to maneuver with the Zeros and again the Americans wound up with the enemy craft on their tails. By diving away most of the P-40s managed to escape, but 3 American pilots were killed and 8 others had to crash-land or bail out. Some of these instances were due to lack of fuel, however.

The Japanese bombers stayed up out of reach and dropped their bombs very effectively on the Manila docks. Unmolested, they continued on toward Nichols Field and the Navy base at Cavite. Nichols was heavily bombed and for all practical purposes was put out of the war. Cavite was wiped out. The entire works of shipyards, warehouses, quarters, and all were destroyed by the heavy bombardment.

On the night of December 10, only 30 pursuit planes remained to make up the fighter force of the Far East Air Force. Eight of these were worn-out Seversky P-35s.

Orders came down that there would be no further interception missions for the fighter planes. Those that remained would be used for observation and reconnaissance duties. The Japanese were free to bomb targets in the Philippines at will.

The little Philippine Air Force made a valiant effort to intercept the Japanese on December 10. Captain Jesus A. Villamor led 3 P-26s against the bombers raiding Zablan. Lieutenant José Gozar attacked 1 of the bombers, and when his guns jammed he attempted to ram the aircraft. The enemy bomber broke and ran, and the little Philippine pursuit plane was unable to overtake it.

Two days later, Villamor led 6 of his P-26s against the Japanese bombers once more. This time he was successful in downing 1 of them before Zeros interceded and the fight scattered all over the sky. The P-26 was no match for the Zero, and the Philippine pilots were lucky to get out with the loss of only 2 of their planes and 1 pilot. This encounter ended the interception career of the Philippine Air Force.

The reconnaissance and observation missions that the American fighter pilots were assigned were usually carried out in pairs, but there were many times when a lone aircraft had to venture out against insurmountable odds. The mission of Lieutenant Boyd D. "Buzz" Wagner on the morning of December 11 is an excellent example.

Wagner took off from Clark Field to make a reconnaissance patrol of the Aparri area. Just north of the airfield he was jumped by 5 Zeros. Wagner had learned that by diving his P-40 and taking it down to the deck he could outrun the vaunted Zero, so this is exactly what he did.

Only 2 of the enemy fighters pursued him, but this duo hung on after him like grim death. Wagner suddenly chopped his throttle, and the onrushing Zeros whipped right past him. Now the tables were reversed, and Wagner was on their tails. Before they were able to take evasive action, Wagner sent them both down in flames.

Turning back, the P-40 pilot came in across the airfield at Aparri and caught the Japanese flatfooted. Twelve enemy aircraft were sitting on the field in neat alignment. When his strafing pass was completed, 5 of them were burning. Wagner then returned to Clark Field with his report.

Wagner was assigned another important mission on the morning of December 16 when he, Lieutenant Russell M. Church, Jr., and Lieutenant Allison W. Strauss were briefed to attack 25 new Japanese aircraft that had been reported on the airstrip at Vigan. The main Japanese landing force had established its beachhead at Vigan on the tenth, and as their troops moved to the south, they were beginning to build up their air strength in the area.

The 3 aircraft came in on the airfield from the sea just as dawn was breaking. Strauss provided top cover, while Wagner and Church went down to bomb and strafe the field. Both of the P-40s carried 6 30-pound fragmentation bombs, 3 slung under each wing. Wagner went down first, let go his bombs, and came out unscathed.

When Church started his bombing run the enemy forces were fully alerted and the sky was full of anti-aircraft fire. Church took a hit in the engine of his aircraft, and it burst into flames. At this point the P-40 pilot could have pulled up and made his way to possible safety, but he didn't waver. Right down the line he went with machine guns blazing, and then his bombs went away right on target. Now the P-40 was blazing from stem to stern. Church never pulled up but continued on course until he crashed to his death about a mile from the strip.

Wagner went back down on the field like an angry hornet and made 5 strafing passes across the field. One Zero tried to get off the ground, but Wagner shot it down as soon as it got its wheels off the ground. When Wagner pulled up to join Strauss and set course for home, 10 of the Japanese planes had been destroyed.

On December 22 the Japanese made 2 further invasion landings in the Lingayen Gulf area. The American and Philippine ground troops were completely outnumbered and overwhelmed, and all that they could do was fight a delaying action. So few aircraft were left that what little opposition the Far East Air Force was able to put up did little to delay the onrushing enemy hordes.

The pursuit squadrons did oppose the landings on the twenty-second, and during this mission Lieutenant Wagner took a 20mm hit in his windshield. The shattered glass filled his face and chest with splinters. The tenacious young fighter pilot, who had become America's first Pacific ace, would see no more action in the Philippines.

The enemy made another landing at Atimonan, only 75 miles southeast of Manila, on December 23. The following day the Americans managed to get 12 P-40s and 6 P-35s up to attack the 40 transports in Lopez Bay. Fragmentation bombs were dropped and many strafing runs were made with good results, but the fighters once more took heavy punishment. Two of the P-35s were so badly damaged that they crashed on the way home.

By noon on Christmas Eve the Japanese advance from the north had become a direct threat to Clark Field, so the handful of fighter planes that were left moved to the new airstrip at Lubao, which was located just north of Manila Bay. This strip was utilized until New Year's Day of 1942, when the surviving aircraft were moved onto Bataan.

On December 31 the first contingent of fighter pilots had been evacuated from the Philippines in one of the Philippine Air Lines' Beechcrafts. Two days later a second contingent was flown out. The Beechcrafts were in poor condition and the route south was under constant surveillance by enemy planes, but both flights managed to make Darwin, Australia, safely. From there the pilots were flown to Brisbane.

The fate of the Philippines was sealed. It had been decided in Washington that Germany was the most prominent enemy of the Allies, now that the United States had also declared war against Germany and Italy. The majority of men and equipment would be sent to Europe. Those who remained in the Philippines would fight a holding action as long as they were able, and what few of them who could be evacuated would get out. The rest would fight on until they were overwhelmed by the Japanese.

All American and Philippine forces were withdrawn to Bataan Peninsula for their final stand. Air Force personnel whose aircraft were gone or had never arrived became provisional infantry. The remaining heavy bombers operated out of the island of Mindanao until the end.

As the fighter planes dwindled they still flew valuable reconnaissance missions from the strip on Bataan and opposed the enemy gallantly until the last. One of the pilots who stayed was Lieutenant Ben S. Brown. This is his description of some of the outstanding efforts made by these pilots in the closing days of the Philippine campaign.

"General MacArthur ordered a photo ship to take pictures of gun emplacements on Cavite. Captain Jesus Villamor volunteered to fly an old O-1 biplane, which had been equipped as a photo plane. Five P-40s were ordered to escort Captain Villamor over the target. I led the flight which consisted of myself, Lieutenant David Obert, Lieutenant Earl Stone, Lieutenant John Posten, and Lieutenant Stinson. We flew the mission over the target area at an altitude of 17,000 feet, the photo plane being at 15,000. After the mission was completed we turned toward the field and were called by ground radio and told that 8 Zeros were waiting for us at 8,000 feet. We went under the Zeros in order to get the photo ship back safely and then tried to climb back up to fight the Zeros. During the ensuing fight all 8 Zeros were shot down and upon attempting to elude a Zero, Lieutenant Stone was going in and out of the clouds and flew into a cloud which enveloped the top of Bataan Mountain, thus crashing into the side of it. He was the only casualty of the flight."

Captain W. E. Dyess assumed command of the "Bastard Outfit" on Bataan in March of 1942. A few days afterward word was received that the Japanese were bringing in 2 tankers and other ships into Subic Bay. When this information was received, General H. H. George ordered that the ships be destroyed.

"Dyess took his P-40 named *Kibosh*," said Lieutenant Ben Brown, "and stuck a 500-pound demolition bomb under the belly and took off to destroy the ships, accompanied by 3 other planes, who were to do the strafing. This was the first time under actual combat conditions that a P-40 carried a 500-pound bomb. The bomb release was made from Chevrolet valve springs. Although I was Dyess' relief pilot, he still made 4 shuttle hops, refusing to let me fly in his place. At the end of the day Dyess had sunk 1 tanker, beached another tanker, sank 4 motor launches and strafed troops and harbor installations."

After this brilliant performance by Dyess the fighter missions were restricted to reconnaissance work and supply drops to guerrilla bands. When there were no more planes serviceable, the remaining pilots and their ground crews joined several hundred other Air Corps men as provisional infantry. In April and May of 1942 the Americans on Bataan and Corregidor surrendered to the Japanese.

II

JAVA

By the end of December 1941, the Japanese advance was progressing so well in the Philippines that their forces began to strike deeper into the South Pacific area. Landings had been made in Borneo as a part of their encirclement of the Netherlands East Indies. Hong Kong had already fallen, and assembly had begun of their forces for the drive south through Burma to conquer Rangoon and Singapore. The battle for Malaya and the Netherlands East Indies had begun.

The Dutch had constructed excellent airbases in the Indies, but possessed only 150 aircraft, all of which were obsolete. They had a few Martin B-10 bombers and a number of slow, stubby Brewster Buffalo fighters and some Curtiss Hawk 75 interceptors, which were vastly inferior to the Japanese Zero.

The Second and Third Japanese fleets were free of their duties in the Philippines and were making preparations for the move south. The 23rd Air Flotilla was in position at Saigon. Japanese plans called for an eastern invasion of Manado, Kendari, and Makasar in the Celebes, while a western task force moved against Tarakan, Balikpapan, and Bandjermasin on the eastern coast of Borneo. Another force would move to occupy the strategic outpost of Rabaul in New Britain.

Major General George H. Brett arrived in Australia on December 31, 1941, to assume command of all U. S. Army forces there, while Major General Lewis H. Brereton remained in command of the remnants of the Far East Air Force. Both of these commanders and their units were placed under the jurisdiction of General Sir Archibald Wavell, supreme commander of American, British, Dutch, Australian Area (to become more commonly known as ABDA) on January 15, 1942.

When General Brereton was appointed to command all American tactical forces in ABDA on January 17, Brigadier General Julian Barnes assumed command of the American base facilities in Australia.

By late December of 1941 the Americans had amassed a force of 18 P-40s and 52 Douglas A-24s at Brisbane. Moving down to join them were 14 B-17s of the 19th Bombardment Group, which had been evacuated from Del Monte in the Philippines. The ground echelon of the 7th Bombardment Group had arrived at Brisbane from the United States, and these men were pressed into duty assembling the crated P-40s that were being rushed into the theater.

In order to strike at the Japanese moving into new bases in the southern island of the Philippines and Borneo, General Brereton ordered 10 of the Flying Fortresses of the 19th Bombardment Group up to Java in early January. Colonel Eugene L. Eubank wasted no time in getting his small force into action. Eight of the B-17s staged through Samarinda in Borneo to bomb enemy warships in Davao Gulf on January 4. The following day they returned to their base at Malang.

These bombers were joined on January 15 when the first reinforcements from the 7th Bombardment Group arrived at Malang. Six B-17s and 4 LB-30s (an export version of the Consolidated B-24 that had been built for the Royal Air Force) arrived to mark the first new heavy bombers to enter the combat zone since the outbreak of hostilities. A few of the aircraft of the 7th Group would be ferried from the United States to Australia by way of Hawaii, but most of the unit's aircraft took the long route; South America, Africa, the Middle East, and India to Java.

The veteran fighter pilots from the Philippines set to in January

1942 to organize new squadrons for duty in Java. As the campaign in the Netherlands East Indies progressed, 5 provisional pursuit squadrons were formed utilizing the pilots with combat experience as leaders of the newcomers, many of whom had arrived as part of the 35th Pursuit Group. All but one of the provisional squadrons would bear the designation of the old fighter squadrons of the 24th Pursuit Group, which had ceased to exist in the Philippines. In order formed, these provisional squadrons were the 17th, 20th, 3rd, 33rd, and 13th.

The 17th Pursuit Squadron (Provisional) came into being on January 14, 1942, at Brisbane, Australia. Only 17 P-40Es were available from a shipment that had arrived from the United States on December 22. Major Charles A. Sprague was given command of the unit whose nucleus was composed of 12 veterans of the Philippines. Four of the more promising pilots were selected from the casual pool to round out the squadron.

Just to get the P-40s from Brisbane to Java entailed a pioneering feat. The combat echelon of the squadron split into 2 flights and departed on the first leg of its journey on January 16. The first 9 aircraft were led by Captain P. I. "Pappy" Gunn in a twin-engine Beechcraft, and the second flight departed a half hour later with 2 RAAF Fairey Battles to lead them.

The first stop was at Rockhampton, 330 miles north of Brisbane, where the first P-40 was lost when Lieutenant Geis suffered electrical failure and was forced to come in without flaps or brakes. He tried to ground-loop but overshot the field and crashed into a fence.

Both flights proceeded to Townsville, where another P-40 was lost in a landing accident, and the following day the squadron flew on to Cloncurry, where the second flight was forced to remain overnight. The first flight went on to Daly Waters and on up to Darwin, arriving on the evening of January 17. The second flight came in the next day. Due to the illness of one of the pilots, the force was now down to 14 airplanes.

The 17th Squadron departed Darwin after a 3-day stay, and under the leadership of "Pappy" Gunn's Beechcraft, they successfully negotiated the 540-mile overwater flight to Koepang, Timor, without incident. Another pilot was lost to illness, so when the unit arrived at its final destination, Soerabaja, Java, on January 24, it was down to 13 airplanes and pilots.

The next few days were spent in interception practices and test flights in conjunction with the Dutch Air Defense Command. On January 26, Major Sprague led a flight of P-40s to protect a crippled Dutch submarine into port. However, the weather proved to be very bad, and the flight was recalled. It was not without mishap, as Lieutenant Neri spun in and was seriously injured.

The 17th Squadron moved to its new base at Blimbing, near Djombang, on February 1 and established itself for combat duty as best it could in the few days before the storm of battle. At 10:45 A.M. on the morning of February 3 the Japanese bombers came to Java for the first time. The P-40 pilots got their warning late, and by the time they were airborne, the bombs had fallen. One flight of 4 managed to catch the bombers about 85 miles out to sea. Lieutenant Hennon was able to make a single pass, which proved successful. The Mitsubishi Type 96 (or "Nell," as it was to become known) bomber burst into flames and crashed into the sea.

Lieutenants Coss and Roland encountered enemy fighter planes in force about 80 miles south of Soerabaja. These were a combination of Zeros and long-range fighters, and the 2 Americans attacked a 6-plane formation at about 8,000 feet. They had just opened fire on the enemy when they in turn were attacked from above. Lieutenant Roland fell to his death as a result of this attack. Lieutenant Coss was able to down one of the fighters before he had to dive away and run.

On February 5 more P-40 reinforcements arrived at Soerabaja. These 3 aircraft were the first members of the 20th Pursuit Squadron (Provisional) to complete an arduous journey that had begun at Brisbane on January 29. The unit, under the command of Captain William Lane, Jr., arrived at Darwin with 24 P-40s on the evening of January 31.

Violent storms prevented the completion of the squadron's first move northward to Koepang, but all aircraft were able to get back into Darwin safely. Late in the afternoon of February 4, fourteen P-40s were airborne on a second attempt to reach Koepang. This time their escorting B-24 was able to get them to their destination, which they reached with something like 8 gallons of fuel left in each of their tanks.

Engine trouble prevented 1 P-40 getting off the next morning, but the other 13 formed up behind the B-24 and set course for Den Pasar Airfield on the island of Bali. En route unidentified aircraft were sighted in the distance, so Captain Lane ordered his pilots to take off just as soon as they were fueled upon their arrival at Den Pasar. Only 7 of the P-40s were able to regas and take up patrol over the field before the enemy struck. Sixteen Zeros broke out of the clouds to do combat. One other P-40 managed to get into the air with partially filled tanks, but the odds were too great. At least 2 of the enemy were shot down, but 3 P-40s were lost with a single pilot, Lieutenant Landry, being killed. Two P-40s that were shot up to some extent returned to Den Pasar and landed. Captain Lane and the remaining 2 P-40s broke clear of the Zeros and managed to get through to Soerabaja.

Eventually 17 of the 24 planes that the 20th Squadron had at Darwin made it on to Java, but only 12 were fit for combat. All members of the organization were incorporated into the ranks of the 17th Pursuit Squadron.

The next few days saw the Japanese feeling out the fighter defense of Java. Enemy aircraft would be picked up by the air warning system, a flight of fighters would be scrambled, and the enemy would withdraw. The Japanese sent intruders in from all different directions. The confused air warning system was no help. The misdirection and absence of enemy aircraft caused one of the pilots to comment, "I guess we must have been chasing ourselves."

As the new arrivals came in, a new airfield was prepared for the Americans. This field at Gnoro, between Djombang and Soerabaja, was some 10 miles from Blimbing and was not discovered by the Japanese until the day before the invasion of Java.

Four flights of the P-40s were scrambled at 11 A.M. on February 4 to intercept 2 formations of Japanese bombers. By the time the Americans got to 24,000 feet they were pretty well stretched out, and only 5 of the fighters got into the bombers, which were flying in 2 flights of 9 aircraft each. Lieutenant McWherter managed to get in 4 passes on the bombers and left 1 of them with an engine smoking. Later, Dutch spotters saw a bomber go down, and this was credited to McWherter.

On February 11 the remnants of the 3rd Pursuit Squadron (Provisional), which had left Australia under the command of Captain Grant Mahony, arrived in Java. The first flight of 8 P-40s had left Darwin on the ninth, but en route to Koepang under the leadership of Lieutenant Allison Strauss encountered a violent storm. The P-40s along with 3 Douglas A-24s of the 27th Bombardment Group were being led by an LB-30, which was doing the navigating. By the time they reached Koepang the little fighter planes were just about out of fuel. One by one they went down into the storm searching for the airfield. Some made crash landing and some bailed out. All 8 P-40s were lost, along with 1 pilot.

The LB-30 returned to Darwin, while the A-24s managed to get into the field at Koepang, although they were mistaken for enemy aircraft and 2 of them were hit by ground fire.

Captain Mahony left with the second flight of 11 P-40s the next morning, and all arrived over Pasirian, a field in the southeast of Java. However, one of the planes nosed over on landing and another came in wheels up when the gear refused to come down. The surviving P-40s of the 3rd Squadron became part of the 17th Squadron. The reinforcements brought the strength of the 17th up to 47 officers, 81 enlisted men, and 30 P-40s. The devoted efforts of the ground crews managed to bring the squadron to its greatest capability of the Java campaign; 26 P-40s were in combat commission before the Japanese onslaught came.

On February 15, Singapore surrendered. Japanese invasion

fleets were already on their way to support the paratroop landing at Palembang on Sumatra, while a second force steamed off Celebes in preparations for strikes on Java. Following the warships were the transports that would bring about the full-scale invasion of the Netherlands East Indies.

Major Sprague and 8 of his pilots took off from Blimbing on the morning of the fifteenth and flew to Batavia, where they were briefed for a special mission. One of the P-40s cracked up on landing, so 8 aircraft were left for the mission, which was to bomb and strafe the airfield at Palembang.

On the morning of February 17 the little P-40s were loaded with 2 20-kilo bombs under each wing and sent on their way. As the American fighters came in from the Java Sea, they were met by 8 enemy fighters. Five of the P-40s immediately salvoed their bombs to meet the attack.

The enemy interceptors were Nakajima 97s or Nates, stubby little radial-engined craft with fixed landing gear. This opponent didn't compare to the Zero, and Sprague downed one immediately. Lieutenants McCallum and Kruzel quickly got on the tail of targets, and both of them scored as soon as they hit the trigger buttons.

Lieutenant Kiser wanted to get at the enemy, but he didn't want to let go his bombs either. He knew full well what would happen if one of the enemy should put a bullet into one of his bombs, but doggedly he hung onto them and attacked one of the Nates. A good deflection shot sent his adversary spinning to the ground. Then he peeled off and dropped his bombs on Japanese landing barges in the Moesi River.

Three of the P-40s had been able to put their bombs on the barges, and all of the flight of 8 went down to strafe the enemy before the planes pulled up and returned to Batavia. It had been a most successful mission for the little force: their bombing and strafing accomplished and 4 enemy aircraft downed.

February 18 was a day of sharp action for the men of the 17th Pursuit Squadron. Lieutenant N. H. Blanton led the squadron, composed of 4 flights, to intercept Japanese bombers at 11:15

A.M. This time the enemy timing was off, for the first flight of 9 bombers over Soerabaja was unescorted.

Blanton led the P-40s in and got 1 of the bombers immediately. As the other fighters began to attack, the Japanese formation broke up. From then on the fighters made pass after pass. Captain Grant Mahony and Lieutenants Gilmore and Irvine also claimed destruction of a bomber each.

As the remnants of the first Japanese formation scurried homeward, a second flight of 9 made its appearance over Soerabaja, but this time they had their escorts: a full dozen Zero fighters. In the wild dogfight Lieutenant Frank E. Adkins got one of the Zeros, and Lieutenant Morris C. "Jock" Caldwell turned in a stellar performance in downing 2 of the bombers.

The Mitsubishi heavy bombers came in flying a step-down formation in line, which permitted the tail gunner of each aircraft to protect the belly of the bomber above. Caldwell first attacked the top bomber in the formation and sent it down in flames. Then he dropped down and came up under the bottom bomber in the formation. It, too, plunged earthward, leaving a long streamer of black smoke.

However, the concentrated firepower of the bombers had scored many hits on the P-40, too. Caldwell found himself in his cockpit with his aircraft falling to pieces. His first effort to bail out against the slipstream was in vain, but a final and mighty push got him out, and he parachuted safely to earth.

Java was desperate for reinforcements. They needed men, materiel, and planes. In a last-ditch effort to get help to them, a convoy was put together at Darwin. Troops were loaded on 2 Australian and 2 American transports. A last-minute order was given on February 12 to have a P-40 squadron report to Darwin to escort the convoy to Koepang on the fourteenth.

The only American fighter unit available had just arrived at Port Pirie on the southern coast of central Australia when orders were sent to the commander, Major Floyd J. Pell, to head north at once. With a whole continent to cross, there was no way that the

33rd Pursuit Squadron (Provisional) could meet the deadline. However, they tried, and they did manage to arrive at the RAAF field at Darwin late on the fifteenth after the convoy had already gone.

Before the 33rd arrived at Darwin, its air defense had consisted of 2 P-40s manned by Lieutenants Robert J. Buel and Robert G. Oestreicher. The morning after the convoy had departed, it was immediately picked up by a Japanese 4-engine patrol plane. The convoy realized that it was in imminent danger and radioed for air cover. Oestreicher was on patrol, so this left Lieutenant Buel to answer the call, and this he did.

Buel arrived when the Japanese flying boat started to make bombing runs on the cruiser *Houston,* which was escorting the convoy. Apparently the craft sighted the American fighter coming in, for it dropped its bombs short of the target and fled. Buel left at about the same time, but was never seen again.

The convoy continued on toward Timor and did not come under attack until the morning of the sixteenth. Little damage was done, but the convoy was badly scattered. The ships then received orders to return to the harbor at Darwin without unloading their cargo.

The 33rd Squadron used 3 days at Darwin to get its aircraft in combat commission, and on the eighteenth the pilots were informed that they had been ordered on to Java to reinforce the 17th Squadron. They were to depart the next morning.

After a delay, Major Pell led the squadron of 10 P-40s off at 9:15 A.M. following a B-17E that had been assigned to lead them to Java. Some 20 minutes later a call was received that the weather was bad at Koepang and getting worse. In view of the fact that most of his pilots were quite inexperienced in the P-40, Major Pell made the decision to turn back to Darwin.

On arrival Pell took his flight of 5 in to land and instructed Lieutenant Oestreicher to hold his flight overhead on patrol for a couple of hours. The airborne P-40s circled the field at 15,000 feet. The patrol gradually let down and swung out over the bay. Oestreicher looked over his left shoulder to see Japanese Zeros piling down on him. Only Oestreicher was able to fight his way out of the melee. Two of the P-40s were shot down at once. Lieutenant Max R. Wiecks had to bail out, and Lieutenant William R. Walker was able to bring his craft in after being wounded, but the P-40 was then destroyed on the ground.

Major Pell and his 4 green pilots did their best to get into the fight. All came under attack from Zeros before they hardly got off the ground. Lieutenant Charles W. Hughes was shot up immediately, and Pell was no higher than 80 feet when his plane burst into flames. He bailed out, but he was too low for his parachute to open.

Lieutenant Robert F. McMahon got to 600 feet before he had to bail out, but Lieutenants Burt H. Rice and John G. Glover managed to get enough altitude to fight the enemy. Rice shook the Zeros off his tail, turned in to attack an oncoming Zero, discovered that his controls were gone, and was forced to bail out.

Lieutenant Glover caught one of the Zeros trailing Rice and shot it down. Then he broke out of his climb and dived down to protect Rice, who was being strafed in his parachute. Glover went into a tight circle around the descending Rice and no doubt saved his fellow pilot's life, while his plane was badly shot up in the process.

Glover went into a steep dive and for a few moments those on the ground felt sure that he was plunging to his death. At the last minute he pulled out and managed to crash-land his P-40. Miraculously he climbed out of the wreck, injured but intact.

Oestreicher managed to bring his plane in to land, but it was destroyed on the ground when a second attacking wave of Japanese came. All of the P-40s at Darwin were destroyed that day in addition to several bombers that were on the ground. The harbor at Darwin was completely wrecked; most of the ships in the harbor were either sunk or severely damaged.

The P-40s of the 17th at Batavia had a much better day. At noon the squadron scrambled to intercept a flight of bombers coming in with an escort of 8 Zeros. Two flights got to the Zeros before the bombers came in and destroyed 4 of them. Captains Lane and Mahony and Lieutenants Kruzel and Hague all scored that day. The other 2 flights got to the bombers and turned them back before they could even open their bomb bay doors.

The day had its tragedy for the 17th, too. Lieutenant Gilmore was shot down and burned, Lieutenant Blanton managed to crashland along the Straits of Madura, and Lieutenant Quana Fields became the first American Indian flier to be lost in the war. He managed to bail out of his crippled aircraft but was strafed in his parachute on the way down.

By the morning of February 20, the lifeline to Java had been cut. Darwin's harbor lay in ruins, and the Japanese had landed on Bali. Enemy parachutists were mopping up Penfoei Airdrome on Koepang. No more fighter reinforcements could fly to Java.

On that fateful day Major Sprague led his P-40s off on a mission to escort LB-30s, Flying Fortresses, and Douglas A-24 dive bombers attacking the invasion fleet at Bali. The little band of American fighters fought off attack after attack by Zeros to enable the bombers to reach their targets. The dive bombers attacked first and did well, scoring at least 10 hits on 4 ships in the landing force. The heavy bombers followed up and got several hits. Upon their return the bomber crews lauded the fighters highly, as they had received little interceptor opposition as a result of their escort.

Losses had been heavy for the 17th that day. Four pilots were missing; among them was the squadron commander, Major Sprague. Two of the pilots later showed up after emergency landings, but Sprague and Lieutenant Galliene were lost forever. Three Zeros destroyed was small compensation for the men of the 17th after such a loss.

The next morning a force of 18 bombers was intercepted over Soerabaja. The fighters had just started to dive on them when a bevy of Zeros swarmed down on the fighters from above. Lieutenant George W. Gynes was shot down and killed before any of the P-40s could get to him.

The third and fourth flights managed to get through to the bombers while the first 2 flights kept the Zeros busy. Lieutenant Wallace Hosky tore into the bombers continually, even though he had Zeros on his tail throughout his attacks. At least one of the bombers fell to his guns before the Zeros finally got him.

The men of the 17th were taking their toll of the Japanese day after day, but they were paying dearly for these successes, and there would be no replacements. The enemy was closing in on Java in earnest.

Captain Grant Mahony was given command of the 17th Squadron on February 23, but his tenure would be very short. Two days later he was ordered to accompany General Brereton on an inspection trip. Actually this meant leaving for India, where Mahony would continue his war against the Japanese with the new Tenth Air Force.

The twelve serviceable P-40s of the 17th rose to counter the Japanese bombers once more on the morning of the twenty-third, but the enemy had learned his lesson well. There were hordes of Zeros escorting and the American fighter forces were split in their efforts to get through to the bombers before they released their bombs.

Cy Blanton and his flight got in position to hit a formation of 9 bombers but encountered at least 15 Zeros with them. The P-40s had time to made a single diving pass and break away. Cy shot down a bomber, but the odds were too great for his flight to undertake combat with the Zeros.

The P-40 pilots seldom made claims for the bombers during the final missions on Java. The P-40s were outnumbered by the Zero escort to such an extent that they had time to make only a single pass at the bombers and then try to get away from the fighters. There was no time to look to see just what damage had been inflicted on the bomber formation or whether any of them went down. The gallant band of fighter pilots battled the odds as best they could and did their utmost to get the battered P-40s back home to fight again another day.

With the departure of Grant Mahony, command of the 17th

passed on to Lieutenant Bob McCallum. On the morning of the twenty-fifth he led his squadron for the first and final time. The bombers came in 54 strong stacked up at altitudes of from 27,000 to 30,000 feet. There was no way the worn P-40s could reach that altitude. Thirty-six Zeros dumped down on the American flights as they strained to get up to the lowermost bombers.

Eight of the P-40s went into a dive immediately to escape the Japanese fighters, but Lieutenant Kiser's flight waited and broke down on the tail of the onrushing Zeros. Lieutenants Irvin, Hennon, and Andy Reynolds all downed enemy fighters. When the other flights dived for the deck, Lieutenant McCallum broke into the Zeros in a vain attempt to break up their attack. He was quickly set upon by a swarm of the enemy, and his P-40 took hits in the engine and caught fire. McCallum managed to get out of the blazing craft and open his parachute, but was savagely strafed on his way down.

On the afternoon of February 26, the little group of American pilots, now under the command of Lieutenant Walter Coss, was joined by 6 Brewster Buffaloes and 6 Hawker Hurricanes, all flown by Dutch pilots. These planes were the remnants of the British fighter squadrons in Southeast Asia and had been handed over to the Dutch on their departure. The Dutch pilots only had 2 or 3 hours' time in the planes, but they would fly them bravely until the end.

Some of the American pilots had already departed by rail to pick up new P-40s at other points in Java. Unfortunately these aircraft would not be forthcoming. The British ship *Seawitch* would actually land 27 crafted aircraft at Tijilajap on the twenty-eighth, but there would be no time to assemble them. The U.S.S. *Langley,* which was approaching Java with 32 P-40s on her deck, would be sunk by Japanese bombers before she could arrive on the scene.

The battered B-17s were departing for Australia. The Japanese invasion fleet was approaching Java, and only the little fighter force and 3 A-24 dive bombers of the 27th Bombardment Group remained to challenge them. The P-40s escorted the A-24s on the afternoon of the twenty-seventh, and strangely no enemy fighters opposed the action. The bombers did a fine job in the face of heavy anti-aircraft fire and managed to score a direct hit on one of the transports.

On the last day of February 1942, the P-40s tried again to intercept the Japanese bombers, but their worn-out engines just wouldn't get them high enough to engage. The planes were so broken down and patched up it was pathetic. As one pilot stated, "My plane has 2 tires that have huge blisters on them. It has no brakes and no generator, and hydraulic fluid is leaking into the cockpit." Yet the men of the 17th continued to fight.

At this time the Japanese landed on Java. The initial landing was made at Rembang, some 70 miles west of Soerabaja, and the fighters were briefed for their final mission: to strike the invasion force early on the morning of March 1.

Nine P-40s took off along with the 6 Hawker Hurricanes and 4 of the Brewster Buffaloes at 0530 hours. Lieutenant George Kiser led the Americans, and the Dutch followed in 2 strings behind them. As the planes came in over the paddy fields outside Rembang they could see a long line of Japanese transports lying parallel to the coast. Anti-aircraft guns had been set up on the beach, and the attackers came under enemy fire as soon as they began their strafing run.

Lieutenant Jock Caldwell was hit immediately and crashed into the water. Lieutenant Reagan's plane was hit and caught fire. Lieutenant McWherter, who was flying Reagan's wing, motioned for him to head for the beach and bail out. Reagan acknowledged but then did something McWherter never forgot. Perhaps Reagan was severely wounded or perhaps his parachute was holed, but instead of heading for the beach he took a cigarette from his pocket, rolled back the canopy, reached forward, lighted the cigarette on the burning engine, and put the cigarette in his mouth to await the end. He flew on into the ground.

Up and down the beach the fighters flew strafing everything in their path. Several barges were sunk, anti-aircraft guns were knocked out, and many enemy troops were killed before the strike was over.

Lieutenant Frank E. Adkins was shot down and made a crash landing on the beach only 300 yards from the Japanese. As soon as his aircraft came to a halt he dove from the cockpit and flagged down a Javanese who was bicycling down the beach at high speed. Adkins jumped on the handlebars of the bicycle and yelled to the terrified Javanese, "Come on, let's go!" The two left the area at top speed. Adkins arrived at Jogjakarta in time to be evacuated.

Lieutenant R. S. Johnson got back to Blimbing, but his aircraft was covered with oil from hits he had taken in his tank and oil line. Of the surviving P-40s there were only 6 that were still flyable. These along with the surviving Dutch planes would not take to the air again.

Shortly after the pilots had landed and left their planes, 2 Zeros came in on a strafing run. When they departed there was not a flyable plane left on the field.

The air war in Java was over. The 17th Pursuit Squadron had put up a tremendous fight in the face of overwhelming odds. Its survivors departed on the last of the B-17s that were providing ferry service from Jogjakarta to Australia. With new aircraft they would take the war to the Japanese once more as leaders in the 35th and 49th fighter groups.

III

DEFENSE OF AUSTRALIA
AND NEW GUINEA

The fall of the Netherlands East Indies, coupled with the Japanese occupation of Rabaul, New Britain, in January of 1942 had brought all of northern Australia under direct threat of invasion. From the enemy's new bases in the East Indies the city of Darwin was within easy reach of his bombers. From the new base at Rabaul bombers began to attack the upper coast of eastern New Guinea and on the night of March 7–8, 1942, enemy troops went ashore at Lae and Salamaua on Huon Gulf. This put Japanese troops within 200 miles of the primary Australian outpost in New Guinea, Port Moresby. The need for American fighter units to man the northern battle line was desperate.

By mid-March of 1942 the AAF in Australia had 33 P-39s, 92 P-40s, and 52 P-400s in commission. These fighter planes were divided among 3 fighter groups:[*] the 49th, the 35th, and the 8th. The 35th had been stripped of its original pilots for the Netherlands East Indies campaign, and these men were undergoing rest and recuperation from their ordeal. The 8th Group had just arrived, disembarking at Brisbane on March 10. This left the 49th Group to fill the gap.

Lieutenant Colonel Paul B. Wurtsmith's 49th Group had ar-

* Although AAF did not officially redesignate all pursuit and interceptor units as "fighter" until May 15, 1942, most were so designated in the early spring of 1942.

rived in Australia early in February, but lacked experienced pilots. Of the complement of 102 pilots, 89 had no fighter plane time at all upon their arrival in the theater. Training in the Canberra area was begun immediately in P-40s, and by early March, Captain R. D. Van Auken led 25 pilots and planes of the 8th Fighter Squadron to Melbourne to provide combat air patrol over the city.

About the same time a flight of 7th Squadron pilots from the 49th Group was temporarily dispatched to the RAAF station at Horn Island, the advanced operational base off the northern tip of Cape York. These men, under the command of Captain Robert L. Morrissey, drew first blood for their unit on March 14, 1942, when they engaged a formation of enemy bombers escorted by fighters on their way to attack the air station at Horn Island.

Captain Morrissey got his men into the air shortly after noon and assembled them at 10,000 feet. "We had been flying around for about 5 minutes," related Morrissey, "when I saw 8 Japanese bombers at 12,000 feet 15 miles out to sea and flying back in the direction of New Guinea. In the rear of the tight formation of bombers a lone fighter, which I presumed to be Japanese, was flying back and forth off the tails of the big planes. Keeping in mind that fighters accompanied the bombers, I jockeyed our formation to attack the 8 planes. But while I was looking around to size up the situation just before the attack, 9 Japanese Zero fighters came into view, also at approximately 12,000 feet and 7,000 feet below us. I turned to attack the fighters.

"At that time I had but 3 2-ship elements in the formation. The Japanese fighters were flying in a close 'V' of 3-ship 'Vs.' I decided to attack the leading Japanese element and let my second and third elements attack the consecutive Japanese elements.

"I proceeded to the attack with my wingman, Lieutenant A. T. House. My second element hesitated momentarily because the attack signal was not received clearly, and as I passed the second Zero element they began shooting at me. Lieutenant House saw what was happening and shot 1 of the Zeros down. But at this point Lieutenant House's guns jammed, so he flew directly across another Zero fighter and deliberately dipped his wing into the Japanese fighter's cockpit. The Japanese fighter crashed, but Lieutenant House, despite the loss of approximately 3 feet of his right wing, made a safe landing.

"I shot 1 Zero in the first element, but dove out without attacking another because bullets were coming from behind me. I did not see the fighter which I shot go down but knew he had taken enough of my .50-caliber bullets to destroy him. Lieutenant House later verified this with the statement that he saw the ship dismantle in midair immediately after my pass at him.

"Lieutenant Harold J. Martin saw the 8 bombers as they came in for their initial run and dived out of our formation alone for the attack. It was Lieutenant Martin whom I had seen zigzagging behind the bombers. He attacked them immediately after they dropped their first load of bombs and drove them off the target. Lieutenant Martin was fired on by all eight of the bombers' rear gunners and states he succeeded in quieting 4 of them. He then singled out 1 bomber for an attack at close quarters. Pulling in at very close range, he unloaded the remainder of his ammunition into the bomber. Ammunition expended, he pulled away from the combat with only 4 bullet holes in his P-40. A naval report later revealed that a twin-engined bomber crashed into the sea a short distance from the scene of the raid."

One other Zero fell to the guns of Lieutenant Clarence T. Johnson. Lieutenant Clarence E. Sanford was shot up in the combat and forced down at sea about 200 miles west of his base.

Regarding his daring act of knocking down a Zero with his wingtip, Lieutenant House had this to say: "I noticed another enemy aircraft on the tail of Captain Morrissey in attack position. In my line of approach to attack this airplane I squeezed the trigger and found my guns did not fire, so I continued my course directly at the enemy aircraft, expecting to get his fuselage in the heavy part of my wing. He had started firing, but must have observed my approach and changed course. I continued to dive, and the leading edge of my right wing went through his fuselage approximately in the middle of his canopy. Following this my plane did cartwheels and other unexplainable maneuvers. I noticed in one of them that the enemy aircraft was busted up and on fire. At first I was momentarily blinded because my oxygen mask was forced over my eyes. I opened the canopy believing the ship was badly damaged and was preparing to leave the plane when I heard the engine and recovered senses. I then straightened the ship out and at 4,000 feet found that it would still fly, so I evaded enemy fighters trying to finish me off and headed south for the home base.

"I made a pass at the field with my wheels down, but when I cut the throttle back the plane rolled over. I was able to straighten it out and continued flight. On the second pass the same thing occurred. On the third attempt I came in half throttle at about 150 mph, and when my wheels were on the ground I cut the throttle and tramped on the brakes."

On March 16, the ground echelon of the 9th Fighter Squadron of the 49th Group boarded a train at Williamstown, New South Wales, while their air echelon took off for the long journey north to Darwin. Since the devastating raid on February 19, the city had become a regular target for Japanese bombers, and the RAAF had little on the base with which to defend it.

The men of the 9th were not long in seeing action, as initial interception was made on the morning of March 22. Lieutenants Clyde L. Harvey, Jr., and Stephen Poleschuk caught a Nakajima 97 reconnaissance plane over Darwin and shot it down. Apparently the enemy never knew what hit him until it was too late, for his aircraft never deviated during the diving attack of the P-40s. Both planes fired at the craft, which burst into flames. The pilot bailed out.

The Japanese bombers made their next appearance over Darwin on March 28. A flight of 4 P-40s lead by Lieutenant Mitchell Zawisza intercepted the unescorted enemy formation and shot 4 of them from the sky. The remainder were chased 80 miles out to sea before the Americans broke off and returned to base.

When the enemy bombers returned the next day they were

escorted by Zero fighters. Obviously they were aware by now of the air reinforcement of Darwin. This time the Americans didn't fare too well. One P-40 was shot down and 2 were badly damaged by the enemy escort. No claims were made by the pilots of the 9th Squadron.

Lieutenant Andrew J. Reynolds, veteran of the air war over Java with the 17th Pursuit Squadron, got the first Japanese Zero over Darwin for the 49th Group on March 29 when they escorted the bombers against the RAAF base there. Reynolds led his flight of 5 P-40s in against the enemy formation. A wild fight ensued against 10 Zeros, but Reynolds managed to down a Zero, with the Americans suffering no losses in the combat.

Lieutenant Reynolds also led a force of 14 P-40s against an attacking formation of 7 Japanese bombers escorted by 6 Zero fighters on the afternoon of April 4. This time the Americans worked the bombers over really well, for none of the bombers survived. Two of the Zeros also went down, while the 9th Squadron lost 2 of its P-40s.

"We sighted the enemy over Darwin," stated Reynolds, "7 miles south of the township. There were bombers in extended 'V'-type formation, and 3 Zeros in 'V'-type formation 500 feet above and behind as escort. We delivered a head-on diving attack. The Zeros were completely surprised and attempted to climb. I shot down 1 bomber and 1 Zero. The escort along with these bombers never took any fighting positions due to the fact that they were caught unawares."

Meanwhile, the other 2 squadrons of the 49th Group—the 7th at Bankstown and the 8th at Canberra—had been readying themselves and their aircraft for the trip to Darwin. The aircraft were flown up in detachments, and the ground echelons were flown in by a varied assortment of transport-type aircraft, the last arriving on April 19.

The highlight of the month came on April 25, when the three squadrons of the 49th took to the air together to intercept the enemy over the city. The Japanese sent down 3 flights of bombers totaling 24 aircraft and an escort of 9 Zero fighters that day. Apparently their intelligence wasn't up to date, for the 49th Group sent 50 P-40Es up to greet them. Ten of the bombers and 2 of the Zeros fell to the American onslaught.

Java veteran Lieutenant J. B. Morehead took 3 of the bombers out himself. He reported the combat as follows: "Bombers were headed out toward the sea and my flight happened to have altitude on the accompanying flight so I dived and intercepted the enemy about the tip of Melville Island. I throttled completely back on my beam approach and fired a long burst on the leader of the flight, dropping him from the flight. I did a steep turn and came up just under the right-hand echelon of ships and fired on 2 bombers of this echelon, dropping 1 to the rear, so I did a steep turn to the right and came in on his tail and sent him headlong in a dive into the sea. About this time I looked back and a Zero was on my tail, so I dove and pulled up steeply, sighting another Zero, which I met head-on and most probably damaged. About that time as I turned to go for this damaged Zero, I found another Zero on my tail, so I dived away and pulled up steeply and found about 5 Zeros a great distance at sea. I climbed, but the engine was smoking slightly and throwing oil on the windshield, so I headed for home port."

Unfortunately, Morehead's landing gear failed on his return to base, and his P-40 skidded to a stop on its belly. Luckily, he climbed from the cockpit unhurt.

The Japanese sent 18 bombers back on the morning of April 27, but this time they had 18 Zeros with them. It may be said that the tactic was successful, for the bomber losses were cut to 3 while 4 of the Zeros went down, but the Americans lost 4 P-40s that day.

Two of the 4 American pilots were lost, but Lieutenants Stephen W. Andrew and James H. Martin survived. Lieutenant Andrew took on a pair of enemy fighters and was forced to bail out after a head-on pass in which he and his opponent succeeded in shooting each other down. Lieutenant Martin was shot up in a head-on pass with a Zero and was forced to crash-land his P-40 on the beach where Lieutenant Andrew came ashore.

The downing of Lieutenant Martin had been caused when he lost his wingman on the way up. While the Americans had been quite successful against the Japanese, they still had not perfected their tactics against the Zero. This is evident at the close of Lieutenant Martin's combat report for the day: "Suggest that there be more cooperation in combat—more teamwork. Also suggest that all dogfighting with Zeros be prohibited as much as possible."

Regardless, the air raids against Darwin fell off after the bombing mission of April 27. For the entire month of May the skies remained relatively clear. However, the enemy was stepping up his operations in other areas.

Following the Japanese landings on New Guinea, the primary Australian outpost of Port Moresby had come under heavy and repeated air attack. To defend this important base the RAAF had formed and sent No. 75 Squadron equipped with American-built Curtiss "Kittyhawk" fighters (the same aircraft as the AAF P-40). The pilots of this unit did a fine job of defending Port Moresby as they took to the air to intercept the Zero-escorted bombers that attacked the vital installation day after day. No. 75 Squadron bore the defensive load from March 21, 1942, until the end of April, at which time their strength was reduced to 3 serviceable and 7 unserviceable aircraft.

Relief came in the form of the P-39 Airacobras of the 35th and 36th squadrons of the USAAF 8th Fighter Group. After their arrival in Brisbane in March of 1942 this group had begun intensive combat training. Although the young pilots were in no way ready for combat, the 2 squadrons were dispatched from Townsville, Australia, on April 28, 1942, to take over at Port Moresby.

Bad weather and primitive airfields on the way proved to be tremendous obstacles to the inexperienced pilots. Of the 41 P-39s sent, only 26—13 planes from each squadron—reached Seven-Mile Airdrome out of Port Moresby. The rest were lost in crashes along the way.

Undaunted, 13 P-39s of the 2 squadrons under the leadership of Philippine air ace Lieutenant Colonel Boyd "Buzz" Wagner, mounted their first mission against the Japanese positions at Lae and Salamaua on New Guinea on the afternoon of April 30. The aircraft climbed to 20,000 feet to clear the rugged peaks of the Owen Stanley Mountains, and upon arrival over Huon Gulf the planes dropped to treetop level and came in at Lae right on the deck. The 2 attacking flights went in strafing enemy aircraft on the ramp along the runway, shooting up shacks and supplies and setting fire to fuel dumps. Over Salamaua 15 to 20 Zeros were encountered, and a running dogfight took place all the way back to Seven-Mile Airdrome. Major George B. Green was credited with the only Zero while 4 of the P-39s were lost due to enemy action.

The following day 7 Zeros came over to greet the newcomers. After making a pass at aircraft parked on the field, the Japanese fighters were encountered by a mixed 5-plane flight from the 35th and 36th squadrons. In the sharp but brief action that took place at 8,000 feet, 2 of the Zeros were downed without the loss of an American aircraft. Lieutenant Donald C. McGee, who got one of the Zeros, had his Airacobra badly shot up but managed to make a safe landing.

The morning of May 2 saw the enemy double his fighter forces for his strafing attack, but these 15 Zeros were met by 11 P-39s of the 35th and 36th squadrons. Captain Lewis Meng took on 4 Zeros in a head-on pass and dropped 1 of them. Three other Airacobra pilots scored that day, but Captain David Campbell of the 35th was shot up badly and his aircraft was a complete writeoff.

Promptly at 9 A.M. the next day the first of the bombers came over to test the P-39s. Twelve twin-engined Mitsubishis and their Zero escort were met by 10 Airacobras at 23,000 feet. Three of the P-39s attacked the lead bomber of the formation, while a fourth went after the No. 3 aircraft on the leader's port wing. Lieutenant Charles Schwimmer took on the No. 2 aircraft on the starboard wing of the leader and sent it down in flames. Before the Zeros could get to the P-39s 3 of the bombers went down. In the heated air battle a P-39 was shot down but the pilot bailed out. None of the zeros were downed, but it was a badly depleted and damaged bomber force that left the target. A large number were streaming smoke in their wake and undoubtedly some of these didn't make it home.

Ten Airacobras of the 35th and 36th squadrons took off on the morning of May 4 to strafe the Japanese airfield at Lae. They were lost from view as they became airborne in the fog and mist that hung over the base. Steadily the aircraft climbed to attempt to get out of this weather, but it grew worse as they continued toward their target. A driving rain forced the formation to split, and this was the last time that some of the P-39s were seen. The planes that did get through to the target proceeded to strafe the field, where a bomber was destroyed and 4 were damaged. The cost to the American formation was hardly worth it, however, for 2 planes of the 35th and 2 of the 36th failed to return from the mission. Whether they became lost in bad weather or were downed over the target was never determined.

On the same morning 7 P-39s took off to intercept a formation of 9 bombers escorted by Zeros. Contact was made with the enemy after they had dropped their bombs on Seven-Mile Airdrome, and 2 of the Mitsubishi craft were shot up so badly that they were later reported to have crashed at Mount Victoria. One P-39 fell to the Zeros, and a plane was demolished in a crash landing after the combat.

The P-39 was definitely not an interceptor, nor was it a match for the Japanese Zero. Air warning usually was received too late for the slow-climbing Airacobras to intercept the bombers before they had dropped their bombs, and if Zeros were escorting, the American pilots had their hands full. All the Americans could do was make a head-on pass at the enemy and dive for the deck. The P-39 possessed good armament: a 37mm cannon and 2 .50-caliber machine guns in the nose, and 4 .30-caliber machine guns in the wings. It was a rugged aircraft and could take a lot of punishment, but it did not possess the high rate of climb or acceleration to be an interceptor, nor was its maneuverability good enough for it to be a fighter. It did prove to be a good ground-support aircraft if top cover could be provided, but nothing like this was available during the trying days in the spring of 1942. The men of the 35th and 36th fighter squadrons bravely did their very best with what they had.

Thirteen P-39s did manage to intercept 8 Zeros coming in to strafe Seven-Mile Airdrome on the afternoon of May 8. Captain George Green managed to get on the tail of a Zero before it could climb away from him, and he shot its entire tail off with his cannon.

Lieutenant John W. Jacobs, Jr., pumped some cannon shells into another Zero and had it breaking up in the air when he got another Zero on his tail. Cannon and machine-gun fire registered on his craft, seriously wounding him. Fearful that he might be gunned in his parachute if he bailed out, he struggled out to sea in his crippled aircraft. When he thought that the enemy would have left the vicinity of his base he managed to bring his plane in to a safe landing before he fainted from loss of blood.

Day after day the men of the 35th and 36th squadrons rose to provide combat air patrol over their bases and over Port Moresby. Again and again the Japanese came in ever-increasing numbers to attack. The pilots of these units were plagued not only with inferior aircraft but by primitive living conditions, poor food, and malaria. It was not unusual to have many pilots flying while suffering the throes of chills and fever.

Maintenance was carried out under the most trying conditions. Mechanics and armorers were always under danger from strafing and bombing attacks. Spare parts were almost nonexistent, and wrecks were cannibalized to keep the Airacobras going. The mere fact that the ground crews were able to keep as many of the aircraft in the air as they did is indicative of their skill, ingenuity, and devotion to duty.

Sergeant Russell C. Hutchins was typical of the hard-working mechanics who kept the Airacobras in the blue. When a force of

19 twin-engine bombers escorted by Zeros attacked Seven-Mile Airdrome on May 11, Hutchins and his crew continued to work right on through the action. Shrapnel from a fragmentation bomb struck Sergeant Hutchins, killing him instantly. He became the first enlisted casualty of the 36th Fighter Squadron.

The following day Zeros came in on the deck strafing Twelve-Mile Airdrome while Airacobras were coming in for landings. Sensing the immediate danger to the pilots as they taxied in, Corporal John E. Lang jumped into an ambulance that was sitting on the edge of the strip and rushed out to the aircraft. His quick thinking undoubtedly saved at least 2 pilots from being strafed as they got out of their planes.

By mid-May the fighter units at Port Moresby began to receive not only replacement pilots but replacement aircraft from Australia. The aircraft that were sent up were Bell P-400s, which were basically P-39s. The P-400s had originally been built for England and were taken over by the AAF after the United States entered the war. The primary difference was that instead of mounting a 37mm cannon in the nose, the P-400 mounted a 20mm cannon.

On May 18, the Japanese mounted their largest bombing mission to date against Port Moresby when 2 formations of bombers —1 of 18 and 1 of 16—escorted by 15 Zeros crossed the Owen Stanley Range. One formation of bombers headed for Seven-Mile Airdrome, and the other's target was Twelve-Mile Airdrome. Fortunately, the Airacobras had time to get into the air to intercept the bombers before they began their rain of destruction.

Three pilots of the 36th Squadron made the first attack on the enemy formation from above, at 20,000 feet. Captain Paul G. Brown hit the second and third bombers of the first formation, and as the first target took considerable hits, it burst into flames and dove earthward trailing a long stream of smoke. Captain James J. Bevlock was next to score, and his bomber target dove toward the sea like a fiery comet. Several other pilots got in good licks, but their targets were not seen to go down. The main thing was that the fighters managed to break up the attack against Seven-Mile Airdrome, and the bombs fell to the north of the target.

In this engagement Lieutenant Charles H. Chapman, Jr., was last seen diving down to attack the bomber formation. A midair collision was reported, and it was thought that Chapman crashed into one of the Mitsubishis.

Lieutenant Thomas Dabney of the 35th Squadron got one of the bombers attacking Twelve-Mile Airdrome, but it was able to drop its load on the target in this case. Two aircraft and several installations were destroyed on the ground.

During this period the first contingent of pilots from the 39th Fighter Squadron of the 35th Fighter Group began their operations with the 35th Squadron. Young Lieutenant Thomas J. Lynch of the 39th Squadron, who was to become one of the top fighter aces of the Fifth Air Force, got into his first combat during the interception missions over Port Moresby.

Lynch got in on a sharp air battle on May 26, when a mixed force of 7 aircraft from the 35th and 39th squadrons joined forces with a flight from the 36th Squadron to escort C-47s carrying supplies and men to Wau. Just southwest of Mount Lawson 16 Zeros made their appearance, and the fight was on. Lieutenant Lynch made head-on attacks on 2 Zeros. His first opponent burst into flames and dived into the ground. Good hits were scored on the second fighter, but it was not seen to crash.

Lieutenant Clifton Troxell of the 35th Squadron dove down on another Zero, got good strikes with his cannon, and downed the Zero. Troxell's squadronmates, Lieutenants Eugene A. Wahl and Frank E. Adkins, also scored, giving the Americans a total of 4 Japanese fighters for the day. One P-39 was lost, but the transports completed their mission unmolested.

The weary and bedraggled pilots of the 35th and 36th squadrons took on the Japanese until the very end of their initial combat tour in New Guinea. Relief was on the way up, but the enemy continued to visit Port Moresby day after day. The 35th got another

3 Zeros on May 28, when 20 Zeros came down to strafe the air-fields. Six P-39s and P-400s caught 6 Zeros over Seven-Mile Air-drome and dove down on them from above. Lieutenant J. W. Egan all but blew the tail off one, and Lieutenant Irving Erickson saw his target roll over and dive straight down with smoke streaming from it before he had to shake a Zero off his tail. Lieutenant Edwin Connell got another of the enemy fighters before he had to dive away to safety. Two Airacobras were lost, but both pilots returned to base the same day.

On June 1, the 35th and 36th squadrons finished up their com-bat tours, but not without a battle. Eighteen enemy bombers es-corted by 12 Zeros were intercepted by 24 P-39s and P-400s. Lieutenant William G. Bennett got in the first shots, attacking a bomber in a steep, diving turn. His cannon shots entered the center of the bomber, probably killing or wounding the crew. Another cannonburst struck the port engine, setting it on fire. The bomber rolled over on its back and dove earthward.

No other bombers were confirmed as shot down, but the diving attacks of the Airacobras effectively broke up the formation of Mitsubishis, and many of them left the target streaming smoke. Three of the Airacobras fell before the concentrated firepower of the bombers, with only a single pilot being recovered.

Since their arrival in late April, the defenders of the Port Moresby area had downed 45 enemy aircraft. Twenty-six Aira-cobras had been shot down, but 13 of the pilots had been recov-ered. Later in the war this would not be considered an exceptional record, but in early 1942, when inexperienced American pilots were being thrown into combat under the most trying conditions in inferior aircraft, it was exceptional. The dogged tenacity of these pilots had prevented the most important outpost and airfields that the Allies possessed in New Guinea from being bombed com-pletely off the map.

On June 2, 1942, the remaining units of the 39th, along with the 40th Squadron of the 35th Fighter Group, took over the defense of Port Moresby. These newcomers still faced the task of providing interception in inferior Bell P-400s.

Far to the east a major sea battle was shaping up. This action would not only have a great effect on future operations in the Southwest Pacific, but its outcome was one of the primary turning points in the Pacific war. The bulk of the Japanese fleet under the personal direction of Admiral Yamamoto was steaming for the island of Midway. This action was initiated not only to establish a new Japanese base far to the east in the Pacific, but also to draw the remnants of the United States fleet out to do battle. The Americans accepted the challenge and sent the carriers *Yorktown, Enterprise,* and *Hornet* racing up from the Southwest Pacific to intercept.

The preliminaries of the battle took place on June 3, 1942, when AAF B-17s attacked the task force in which the troop transports were interspersed. Unfortunately, the bombs dropped did little to impede this force.

The main battle took place the following day. Early on the morning of the fourth, AAF, Navy, and Marine Corps bombers went out to attack units of the Japanese fleet. Once more the efforts of the land-based aircraft were in vain, for neither the high-level bombers nor the torpedo bombers were able to get any hits. Incoming Japanese planes bombed Midway and severely damaged installations there while their Zero escorts all but wiped out the obsolete Marine Corps Brewster Buffalo fighters.

However, the dive bombers from the U.S. carriers were methodically destroying the Japanese carriers. The *Soryu* was heavily damaged and later sunk by an American submarine. The *Kaga,* too, was sunk, and the escaping *Hiryu* was caught by dive bombers from the *Enterprise* and *Hornet* late in the afternoon and damaged so badly that it sunk the next day. The fourth Japanese carrier, the *Akaga,* had left the battle area gravely damaged and burning, and it went down on June 5.

The U.S. carrier *Yorktown* was badly damaged by Japanese

bombers and was left dead in the water. The *Yorktown* was still afloat on June 6 and tow lines were attached, and the ship began its journey toward Pearl Harbor. Late that afternoon a Japanese submarine slipped by the escort and managed to put torpedos in the big ship and one of its destroyer escorts. The destroyer went down immediately, but the *Yorktown* lingered on until the next morning.

The planes of the U.S. fleet struck their final blow on June 6 when they bombed and sunk the cruiser *Mikuma*. The Japanese had lost 4 fleet carriers, a heavy cruiser, nearly 300 airplanes, and 3,500 men. Their loss was a crushing blow from which the Japanese never recovered.

The 49th Group at Darwin had experienced little aerial activity during the month of May 1942. The Japanese broke the lull when they came down on 4 consecutive days, beginning June 13. At 11:20 A.M. that day 36 P-40s of the 49th Group were scrambled to intercept a flight of 27 bombers escorted by 10 to 12 Zeros. In their attempt to break through the escorting fighters to get to the bombers, 3 of the P-40s were shot down.

The next day approximately 25 Zeros came into the Darwin area by themselves. This marked the first time that a fighter force had approached the area without escorting bombers. The P-40s gave battle, and 4 of the Zeros were downed for the loss of a single American aircraft.

At 11:30 A.M. on the fifteenth, the Japanese arrived once more, with a force of 28 bombers and a cover of Zero fighters. On this mission they attacked the downtown and dock areas of Darwin. Twenty-eight P-40s made the interception. As the P-40s made contact with the bombers, the Zeros gave violent opposition. None of the bombers was downed, but the Americans did manage to break up the formation and cause the bombers to miss their targets. In the air fighting with the enemy 6 of the Zeros were downed. Two P-40s were lost in the combat, but both pilots were recovered.

The usual formation of 27 bombers escorted by some 15 Zeros returned the next day, and this time they managed to hit 2 of the oil tanks on Darwin's docks. Lieutenant Andrew J. Reynolds got one of the bombers in a very determined attack. "I intercepted the bombers and Zeros 30 miles west of Darwin over Point Charles. The enemy aircraft were at approximately 23,000 feet. Leading the flight, I dove on the bombers, setting 1 on fire at first and later setting fire to a No. 3 man in the enemy formation. I put bullets in all 9 bombers. In going by the bombers and Zeros a stray bullet hit my cowling, damaging oil and Prestone coolers."

Reynolds managed to made a wheels-up landing in a small field west of Darwin.

Three of the Zeros were downed, but so were 3 P-40s. Two of the P-40 pilots were recovered. The 49th did an excellent job of defending the target areas for 4 consecutive days, and while the Japanese realized they could still get through to Darwin, they had to pay a price each time.

The enemy was not engaged again in numbers until July 20, 1942, when the bombers appeared with their escort shortly after noon. This time the P-40s had an altitude advantage and attacked out of the sun with very good results. Six of the Zeros and 3 bombers were confirmed as destroyed, with many more being damaged.

The 49th would only encounter the enemy over Darwin one more time before they were relieved from their defensive assignment—and their last interception was definitely their best. The P-40s were alerted in plenty of time to get to altitude, and 3 separate attacks were made on the enemy formation before it reached its target, which was the Australian medium bombers base south of the city.

One flight from the 8th Squadron led by Captain George E. Kiser made a diving head-on attack 25 miles off the coast, and 4 of the bombers received heavy fire. Three were smoking and dropping from the formation as the flight continued in its dive.

Four pilots from the 7th Squadron made the next attack, which took the enemy completely by surprise. Lieutenant Gene Drake shot down a bomber and a Zero, while 2 other members of the flight got a Zero apiece.

From the coast on in to the target area the Japanese were kept under constant attack as the 49ers used excellent tactics to break up the bomber formation and pick off its escort. The final count for the day was 7 bombers and 8 Zeros destroyed, 5 bombers and a Zero probably destroyed, and a Zero damaged.

The finale had been a well-deserved triumph for the P-40 pilots. A few days later the 49ers were informed that they were being withdrawn from Darwin for a new assignment.

IV

GUADALCANAL

Early in the war the United States had realized that the lifeline to Australia must be preserved. In the spring of 1942 Army and Air Force units had been sent to man installations in the island groups of Fiji, New Hebrides, and New Caledonia. In the initial shipment had been the 67th Fighter Squadron, which had been bolstered by an additional 15 pilots from Australia. In less than a month after their arrival at Nouméa, New Caledonia, in March of 1942, the majority of the squadron's 45 P-400s and 2 P-39s had been unloaded from their crates and been assembled. Training was conducted from muddy airstrips on the island, and some pilots managed to get away to the island of Efate for gunnery training under the tutelage of Marine Corps pilots.

In Washington high-level planners were making moves to cut the southward movement of the Japanese. On May 4, 1942, the enemy had established a base at Tulagi on Florida Island in the Solomons chain. In early June Japanese troops went ashore just across the channel from Tulagi and began construction of an airfield on the island of Guadalcanal. A base on this island supported by other installations such as Bougainville in the northern Solomons put the Japanese in a position to strike southward from Guadalcanal against the New Hebrides or New Caledonia. The die was cast: The enemy must be stopped on Guadalcanal before he could complete his air bases there.

The 1st Marine Division, based in New Zealand, was alerted

for the invasion of Guadalcanal. While this operation would primarily be a Marine Corps and Navy operation, units of the AAF would play a primary role in it. B-17s of the 11th and 19th bomb groups flying from Efate and Australia began long-range operations against the enemy bases in the latter part of July in a softening-up process.

On the morning of August 7, 1942, Marines hit the beach at Guadalcanal. The enemy did not choose to fight on the beachhead but took off to the hills, leaving large quantities of materiel and supplies. Navy aircraft from the carriers covered the invasion area, and enemy air attackers were driven off in sharp action.

Immediately after the landing, Marine Corps engineers and Navy Seabees began preparing the landing strip that the Japanese had started. Late on the afternoon of August 20, the first 2 Marine Corps squadrons landed on the newly named Henderson Field. These units were VMF-223, equipped with 19F4F Wildcat fighters; and VMSB-232, flying 12 SBD Dauntless dive bombers. Two days later they were reinforced by 5 P-400s of the 67th Fighter Squadron. These aircraft, under the command of Captain Dale D. Brannon, flew up from New Caledonia through Efate and Espiritu. An additional 9 P-400s arrived on August 27. This first AAF unit on Guadalcanal was put under the operational control of the Marine Air Group and joined them in the defense of the island. The Marines were reinforced on the thirtieth by VMF-224 and VMSB-231.

From the beginning, the 67th operated under a great handicap. The Bell P-400s, as had been proven in New Guinea, were no match for the Japanese Zero. No supply of high-pressure oxygen bottles were available for their system, so the men of the 67th could perform low-altitude operations only. As a consequence, the P-400s had to leave all interception missions to the Marine Corps.

After four days of counterair action against the enemy, the 67th was reduced from the original 14 planes to only 3. General Vandergrift, commander of the 1st Marine Division, recognized that the P-400 was being called upon for duty far beyond its capability and informed General Delos Emmons, commander of the Hawaiian Department, that "P-400s will not be employed further except in extreme emergencies; they are entirely unsuitable for Guadalcanal operations."

When replacement aircraft came up they were still P-400s. There was nothing else to send.

In addition, the situation on the island became an extreme emergency shortly as the Marines were hard pressed to hold onto their positions. Beginning on September 2, the 67th began bombing and strafing enemy troop concentrations, landing barges, gun emplacements, and supply dumps. These attacks were generally small, utilizing not more than 5 aircraft, but they proved to be very effective in supporting the Marines on the ground.

So long as conditions of the field permitted, the P-400s of the 67th were in the air after enemy ground targets. The condition of Henderson Field as a result of bombing attacks, mud, and harassment from an enemy heavy gun in the hills known as "Pistol Pete" prevented the AAF from sending medium or heavy bombers up to operate in support of the Marine forces. Both Marine Corps and AAF pilots were operating under extremely difficult conditions. Food was very scarce and poor. Supplies and reinforcements could only be brought in under the threat of Japanese air attack. The field was bombed by day and shelled by enemy surface vessels by night, affording no rest to anyone on the island. Jungle heat and insects brought on malaria and dysentery, which sapped the strength of the fighting men. Only through sheer guts were the pilots able to rise day after day to meet the enemy threat.

The Japanese launched a drive on September 12 to retake the island. Some 6,000 ground troops began a concerted offensive against Marine installations under the cover of bomber attack by day and shelling from the cruiser forces by night. On September 13 the Japanese directed a mass attack against a ridge that lay to the south of Henderson Field. Throughout the night the enemy pressed his attack against the Marine battalion defending the ridge, and by dawn had secured the crest and was moving down the south side of the ridge. The 67th had only 5 aircraft in commission, but at 8:30 A.M. the next day these P-400s, under the leadership of Captain John A. Thompson, swept along the ridge, where they strafed the Japanese columns unmercifully. After this attack the Marines hit the enemy with a counterattack and all but wiped out his ranks. Over 600 enemy soldiers were left dead, many of them attributed to the excellent strafing of the pilots of the 67th.

The enemy continued to land reinforcements, and the desperate battle for Guadalcanal continued. Each night the "Express," composed of enemy battleships, cruisers, and destroyers, returned to the channel between Tulagi and Guadalcanal to extensively shell the American positions. All the Americans could do was take to their foxholes, cursing and praying that they would make it through the night.

A particularly heavy shelling took place on the night of October 13, and the next morning enemy bombers took up where the surface vessels left off. When the heavy bombers departed, dive bombers came in to attack the airfield. Then, to make matters worse, the "Pistol Pete" gun went into operation. It was only through the valiant efforts of the Seabees that the airstrip was kept operable.

Between bursts, 4 P-400s of the 67th were hung with 100-pound bombs while the pilots waited in nearby foxholes. One at a time the pilots dashed to their aircraft between explosions and roared off the runway. Futilely the P-400s searched up and down for the Japanese guns but were unable to spot them. When their fuel was low they dropped their bombs on suspected enemy positions and came back in to land.

The Japanese planes and guns kept on shelling and bombing Henderson Field throughout the day, and by midafternoon the field was inoperable. A Marine colonel visited the pilots of the 67th and told them, "We don't know whether we'll be able to hold the field or not. There's a Japanese task force of destroyers, cruisers, and troop transports headed our way. We have enough gasoline left for one mission against them. Load your airplanes with bombs and go out with the dive bombers and hit them. After the gas is gone we'll have to let the ground troops take over. Then your officers and men will attach yourselves to some infantry outfit. Good luck and good-bye."

Some 2,000 yards distant and parallel with Henderson Field was a grass strip that the Seabees had laid out back in September. The men of the 67th utilized this strip not for 1 last mission but for 3 on that fateful afternoon of October 14. At 11:45 A.M. 4 recently arrived P-39s loaded with a 300-pound bomb each and 3 old P-400s loaded with a 100-pound bomb each took off with 4 Marine Corps SBDs to attack the Japanese task force off Santa Isabel Island. Six transports were strung out in line astern escorted by cruisers and destroyers on each flank. The enemy vessels went into violent evasive maneuvers, and intense anti-aircraft fire filled the air. Try as they may, the little bank of American aircraft were unable to score any hits on the enemy ships.

Upon their return, the aircraft were equipped with bombs again, and a second futile mission was flown. When the planes returned, the pilots remembered that there were still 2 B-17s at Henderson Field that had been abandoned by the 11th Bombardment Group. Several times during the campaign the Flying Fortresses had staged through Guadalcanal for missions against the enemy, and these 2 B-17s had been badly damaged in a Japanese attack while they were on the ground.

Fuel was siphoned from the bombers, and this provided enough gasoline to mount a third mission. This time the Marine dive bombers managed to get 2 hits on enemy transports, but the 67th lost an aircraft to anti-aircraft fire. Another Airacobra was lost in landing when the pilot ran off the runway and hit a pile of steel matting.

As enemy shells rained down on the defenders again that night, 5 Japanese transports anchored offshore only 10 miles from Henderson Field and unloaded troops and supplies. Come morning this would be a prime target for bombing and strafing, but the little group of American airmen possessed no fuel.

However, fuel was on the way. Twin-engine C-47s from Espiritu, each laden with 12 drums of fuel, began to arrive by mid-morning of the fifteenth. The transports came in just long enough to unload the cargo and get right out. "Pistol Pete" saw to it that they didn't tarry. At the same time Marines were scouring the beachhead for fuel that had been cached shortly after the invasion. By the end of the day more than 400 drums had been located.

Immediately upon the delivery of fuel the pilots and ground crewmen of the air squadrons went to work. Many pilots belted their ammunition as the crewmen loaded bombs and poured gasoline into the empty tanks of the aircraft. As quickly as they could become airborne, the AAF fighters plus Navy and Marine Corps dive bombers went after the enemy reinforcements. All the rest of the day the pilots of the 67th dive-bombed and strafed the enemy ships and men along the island shore. Anti-aircraft fire was intense and Zeros came down to contest their operations, but the P-39s and P-400s accomplished a tremendous job. One pilot got a probable hit, 2 others scored hits that damaged 2 transports, and a fourth got a direct hit on a transport that caught fire, exploded, and sank. One Zero was shot down, but the 67th lost an Airacobra in the day's operations.

On October 16, the 67th made 7 separate attacks on the Kokumbona area, bombing, strafing and harassing the Japanese relentlessly. Continuous operations had worn the P-39s and P-400s of the squadron completely out. On 1 of the missions 4 of the surviving P-400s were sent out. The first aircraft carried a bomb, but only 1 of its machine guns would fire; the second aircraft had a bomb but no machine guns in working order; the third and fourth planes had machine guns in working order but carried no bombs. If the aircraft were limited in the amount of damage they could inflict, at least they could keep the enemy troops dispersed and moving.

Marine Corps fighters were doing a terrific job against the Japanese aerial opposition during these trying days. While the AAF P-39s and P-400s went up to cover the field at low altitude, the Grumman Wildcats would break up the Japanese bomber formations and pick off the escorting Zeros. However, the enemy ground forces still were the main threat to the survival of the airfield.

On October 23 the first great assault came. Four times the Japanese infantry, supported by 10 tanks, threw themselves against the 1st and 2nd batallions of the 5th Marines, who were dug in along the Matanikau River to the west of Henderson Field. Four times the enemy was stopped.

On the night of October 24, Japanese troops attacked Marine Corps forces along Lunga Ridge, south of the fighter strip. All through the night the enemy infantry made *banzai* charges against the hard-pressed 1st Battalion, 7th Marines, under the command of Lieutenant Colonel L. B. "Chesty" Puller. A few of the enemy infiltrated the lines and were so optimistic that word was radioed to the Japanese fleet that the airfield had been taken.

When word was received that the airfield had been taken, units of the Japanese fleet arrived offshore off Guadalcanal bringing in reinforcements. Over Henderson Field 5 Zeros arrived early on the morning of the twenty-fifth and began to circle the airstrip, making no effort to strafe it. Soon 7 more Zeros and a bomber joined them. Apparently they were awaiting a signal to land. Marine Corps fighter pilots scrambled in their Wildcats and shot down some of them and dispersed the rest.

Once the Japanese realized that their troops were not in possession of the airfield, an intense shelling from surface vessels began. For most of the day personnel around the field had to keep to their foxholes while the rain of steel descended.

During the afternoon Douglas SBD dive bombers and P-39s flew 4 missions against the 2 cruisers and 2 destroyers lying offshore. On 1 of the missions Lieutenants Dinn, Purnell, and Jacobsen in P-39s caught the ships northeast of Florida Island and barely missed them with 500-pound bombs. Later in the day the same pilots, with Captain John Mitchell, were back in the area. This time Lieutenant Jacobsen put his bombs squarely on the cruiser *Yura*. The ship was damaged so badly that it was later sunk by its escorts.

On October 26 the United States Navy met the Japanese Imperial Fleet in the Battle of Santa Cruz northeast of Guadalcanal. Two Japanese carriers, the *Zuiho* and the *Shokaku,* were hit and damaged by Navy dive bombers, but the U.S.S. *Hornet* was sunk and the U.S.S. *Enterprise* was damaged. The Japanese had come out on the long end of the sea battle, but their over-all aim had been defeated. Henderson Field still remained in the hands of the Americans.

In early October the first echelon of the newly formed 339th Fighter Squadron had come up to join the 67th Fighter Squadron, and a number of its pilots flew their P-39s along with the 67th on their missions. By late October the 339th was operating on its own and assisted the Airacobras of the 67th in their strafing and bombing attacks.

The AAF had several fighter units training at Espiritu Santo in the New Hebrides, and these pilots and planes were used to relieve and reinforce the 67th of Guadalcanal. Most of the AAF bombardment units, too, were either at Espiritu Santo or in New Caledonia. To attack the Japanese forces it was usually necessary for the bombers to fly to Henderson Field during a lull in the shelling, refuel, and take off to seek their targets.

While the AAF had been rotating pilots into the 67th Fighter Squadron, the Marine Corps had been rotating entire units. VMF-121 and VMF-212 arrived in October to relieve VMF-223 and VMF-224. The Marine Corps dive bombing squadrons along with Navy fighter, dive bomber, and torpedo squadrons that had been based temporarily at Henderson Field would be relieved shortly thereafter.

Operational command of the aircraft on Guadalcanal still remained with the Marine Corps air wing commander, Brigadier General Roy S. Geiger. In November, Geiger would be relieved by Brigadier General Louis E. Woods, who came to Guadalcanal as his chief of staff.

On the morning of October 28, the P-39s were loaded with 500-pound bombs and along with a group of SBDs and Marine fighters flew a mission against Rekata Bay, a Japanese seaplane base on Santa Isabel. After dropping their bombs the P-39s dived to strafe 8 seaplanes on the water. All 8 were destroyed, but Lieutenant Wallace S. Dinn was hit by anti-aircraft fire and had to bail out.

Dinn landed on the island of Santa Isabel, which was some 160 miles from home base. There he met 4 local inhabitants, one of whom could speak English, and started the long water journey home in their boat. While passing one small island the English-speaking person told Dinn that there was a Japanese pilot downed in the vicinity. Dinn decided to capture him, and with the aid of his new-found friends did so. Two days later the Japanese pilot managed to overturn the boat near shore and escaped in the general melee. Later he was recaptured and had his ration cut to one banana and a little sugar cane each day for the remainder of the trip. Lieutenant Dinn arrived at Henderson Field on November 4 with his prisoner in tow.

AAF and Marine aircraft continued to harass the Japanese on the ground and at sea. As the enemy continued to attempt to reinforce his ground forces, the U.S. aircraft struck again and again. It seemed that the Japanese would never give up, and continued to send transports loaded with troops. At the same time the Americans were doing their utmost to reinforce their forces.

Japanese dive bombers escorted by Zeros attacked 3 cargo vessels off Lunga on November 11 but were intercepted by Marine Grumman Wildcats. One American vessel was damaged, while the enemy lost a bomber and 3 of his fighters. However, this encounter cost the Marines 6 Wildcats and 4 of the pilots.

The next day the Japanese returned to attack 4 American transports moored off Kukum. As the enemy dive bombers approached, Marine Captain Joe Foss positioned his Grumman fighters at

29,000 feet in the clouds while 8 P-39s of the 67th Squadron circled down below. As the Japanese bombers came in low behind Florida Island, the Americans dove to the attack. One after the other the Val torpedo bombers were cut down, and when the fight was over some 20 of them had been downed by the Americans, along with 5 or 6 of their escorts. Three of the Wildcats and an Airacobra were lost in the combat. The P-39s had managed to down a Zero and a bomber, but by breaking up the formation they had set up many of the enemy craft for the Marine pilots. When the Airacobras returned to base Captain Foss told them, "You fellows can play ball on our team any day."

On November 12, 11 Japanese transports loaded with 13,500 troops left the Shortland area supported by a heavy force of cruisers and two battleships. If this force broke through, the battleships alone were capable of demolishing Henderson Field. All possible aircraft reinforcements were rushed to the island. Among the arrivals were 12 P-38s under the command of Major Dale Brannon, who in August had brought the first P-39s up to Guadalcanal. This second air echelon of the 339th Fighter Squadron would initiate the twin-boomed fighter to Pacific combat.

That night in one of the wildest battles in naval history, the Japanese heavy vessels were intercepted by American cruiser forces under the command of Rear Admiral Daniel J. Callaghan. In their battle off Savo Sound, the ships blasted each other at point-blank range. The conflict cost the Americans 3 cruisers, but a Japanese battleship was severely damaged. The shelling of Guadalcanal did not take place that night.

The next day all available aircraft from the island took to the air. Bolstered by aircraft from the U.S.S. *Enterprise* in addition to Martin B-26s and B-17s from Espiritu, the American aircraft attacked the enemy transports unmercifully. Seven of the 11 were sunk. The crippled battleship *Hiei* was put under constant attack, but it managed to get in range of Henderson Field and subjected it to heavy shelling before it went down on November 14.

On the night of the fourteenth the surviving Japanese battleship *Kirishima* was met by the U.S. battleships *South Dakota* and *Washington*. In the ensuing fight the *Kirishima* was sunk. The action broke the back of the attempts to land large numbers of Japanese troops on Guadalcanal or to demolish Henderson Field using warships.

A sign of the times was clearly indicated on November 18 when a force of 11 B-17s of the 11th Bombardment Group and 4 Martin B-26s of the 38th Bombardment Group staged out of Guadalcanal to attack targets at Buin. Also for the first time there was fighter escort all the way—8 Lockheed P-38s of the 339th Squadron. There was a mixup in arranging proper coverage, for the fighters had been instructed to fly 4,000 feet above the bombers, but the bombers went in at 12,000 feet, putting the P-38s at only 16,000 feet. However, the twin-tail fighters put on a good show against the 39 intercepting Zeros. Three of the Zeros were shot down, and the Americans came home with no losses.

The war on Guadalcanal had taken a change. Now it was the Americans who would remain on the offensive, not only on the ground but also in the air. For the AAF fighter forces it was a change also. There had been no glory for the P-39 and P-400 pilots of the 67th and 339th fighter squadrons, but they had done a wonderful job with what they had. With the arrival of the Lockheed P-38s, the AAF fighter pilots could not only meet the Japanese Zero on even terms, but they could also carry the bombers to his airfields, where the enemy fighter was on the defensive. The days of Zero dominance in the Pacific were over.

V

THE CENTRAL SOLOMONS

The hard-pressed P-38s of the 339th Fighter Squadron and the P-39s of the 67th Fighter Squadron on Guadalcanal were reinforced during November 1942 by a portion of the air echelons of the P-39-equipped 68th and later the 70th fighter squadrons. All four of the aforementioned squadrons had become a part of the 347th Fighter Group, which was activated and headquartered in New Caledonia in October.

The P-38s of the 339th were primarily used for patrol over the island during November and December, while the P-39s continued their strafing and dive-bombing missions supporting the ground troops.

The P-38s of the 339th turned in 2 notable escort missions during the month of December. On the tenth of the month 8 Lightnings escorted the B-17s of the 11th Bombardment Group striking Tonolei Harbor, Bougainville. On this mission the Zeros came up in force, and 5 of the enemy were destroyed. All the P-38s returned safely, although 1 limped home on a single engine.

When the 339th escorted the B-17s back to the same target on December 20, the Zeros were sitting upstairs waiting for them. In the dogfight that took place, 2 Zeros were destroyed. However, the Lightning pilots found that they were in for an extremely hard time when they had to fight the Japanese Zero from an initial altitude disadvantage. No P-38s were lost, but several of them returned pretty well shot up.

The P-39s did yeoman duty during the month going after the enemy and his supplies. Early in the month a formation of Airacobras sighted several groups of 100 to 200 oil drums lashed together to support wooden boxes that were slowly drifting ashore off Tassafaronga. Apparently these supplies had been left by either enemy barges or submarines to drift ashore. The P-39s had target practice for 2 days as they repeatedly bombed and strafed the oil drum rafts.

The Japanese were also busy building airfields. When the first indications were received that an airstrip was being built at Munda Point on New Georgia, it immediately came under air attack. On December 6, P-39s strafed the area from an altitude of only 50 feet. Trucks, steam rollers, carts, and other materiels were destroyed.

Despite repeated attacks by Allied bombers and fighters, the airstrip on Munda was operating by December 9. This strategically located strip was only 196 miles from Henderson Field, and when it was developed, its fighters could cover the movement of all Allied surface craft down to the lower Solomons and be in a position to intercept any missions being flown against Japanese shipping attempting to come down the sealane from Buin, Bougainville, to Guadalcanal, or "the Slot," as it was more popularly known.

Munda was put under day-and-night attack. The B-17s flying from Henderson Field sometimes remained over Munda for 3 or 4 hours on a night mission, causing constant harassment of enemy troops. One of the more successful missions against the base was flown on December 24, when 9 P-39s and 4 Marine Corps F4Fs escorted 9 Douglas SBD dive bombers in an early-morning strike. There they caught 24 Zeros attempting to take off. All of the enemy fighters were either destroyed on the ground or in the air, and none of the American aircraft was damaged.

To reduce the Japanese forces still on Guadalcanal, the Americal Division, together with some units of the 2nd Marine Division, was to move along the north coast of the island while the U. S.

Army 25th Division was to carry out an enveloping movement to the south and west of the Japanese forces.

When the ground assault started against enemy positions on Mount Austen on December 17, the P-39s were right in the middle of it. The Airacobras and Marine Corps Wildcats escorted the Douglas SBDs to the target areas, and after these preliminaries the P-39s went back and were loaded with 500-pound bombs for their own bombing mission. As the enemy was pushed into this pocket on the northwest corner of the island, the Airacobras hit him day after day, strafing and bombing incessantly.

In mid-January 1943, the Thirteenth Air Force was officially born. All Army Air Force units in the South Pacific were placed under the command of General Nathan Twining. Commander of the new 13th Fighter Command was Colonel Dean C. Strother. Operationally this new setup had little effect on the fighter squadrons on Guadalcanal, for they continued to fly their missions under the operational control of Marine Brigadier General Francis Mulcahy, who had relieved General Louis Woods in late December. In mid-February all aircraft on the island would come under Rear Admiral Charles P. Mason in Air Command, Solomons, or COMAIRSOLS. This mixed force of interservice aircraft would operate most efficiently and effectively throughout the central Solomons campaign in the months to come.

The Airacobras continued to go after the enemy tooth and nail. On January 13 they went after enemy troops on the beach at Kokumbona, and later in the day they hit Visale. The following day they flew all day long using improvised gasoline bombs, and on the sixteenth they attacked enemy positions on Mount Austen with depth charges.

By January 23 the Japanese had lost their nearest good landing beach west of the airstrips on Kokumbona. At about this same time the enemy lost his artillery positions that had dominated Henderson Field plus his supply routes to the south and to the east.

Allied troops were in position to begin the final offensive ground phases of the struggle for Guadalcanal.

In January of 1943 the 18th Fighter Group's 44th Squadron's P-40s arrived from Efate, to be followed in early February by the 12th Squadron in P-39s. These units joined the mixed force of P-39s, P-38s, and Marine Corps F4Fs. The cooperation and coordination with which this mixed force operated is exemplified by a fighter interception that was flown on January 27.

Eight to 10 Mitsubishi bombers with a heavy fighter cover were reported on their way south to attack installations on Guadalcanal. A dozen Marine Corps F4Fs scrambled at 9:50 A.M. and were immediately followed into the air by 6 P-38s. Ten P-40s were airborne at 10:15 A.M.

Unfortunately, the bombers were not intercepted, for they chose to come in right on the deck under the radar screen. The P-38s sighted some 20 to 30 Zeros 10,000 feet below them after they had climbed to 30,000 feet. The enemy fighters were fairly close together and were in loose string formation doing loops and rolls.

The Lightnings made diving attacks on the Zero formation, and in the course of these combats Captain John Mitchell became the first ace of the 339th Squadron. One of the Zeros came in from the right on a firing pass at Mitchell, who turned into the enemy craft, fired a good burst into the cockpit, and sent the plane spinning down. It leveled off momentarily at 3,000 feet but then rolled over and fell into the trees near Cape Esperance.

While the 10 P-40s were climbing, they were jumped from above by Zeros. The P-38s and 4 of the Wildcats joined in a massive dogfight that scattered all over the sky.

Several of the Zeros got right down over the water, and when the P-38s would dive on them the Japanese pilots would turn sharply and the Lightnings would have to pull up. This put the P-38 pilot in a precarious position. One Lightning pilot was lost in this manner when he pulled up from a pass. He had been unable to drop one of his fuel tanks, and the enemy pilot hit it, sending the P-38 down in flames.

Captain Mitchell observed this combat and pulled in right on the tail of the Zero that had downed the P-38. One good burst sent the enemy plane down in flames.

Two of the P-40s had been shot down as they climbed up to join the combat, and a third was so badly damaged that it had to dive away from the combat and streak for home. One of the P-40s entering combat was piloted by Lieutenant Robert Westbrook of the 44th Squadron, who would become the top ace of the Thirteenth Air Force. Westbrook got a Zero on his tail and took some hits before he managed to elude the enemy by diving and going around the field. As he came up he sighted 3 Zeros and turned into one. He raked it with machine-gun fire, and it crashed in flames.

Nine of the Zeros were destroyed: 4 by P-40s, 3 by P-38s, and 2 by F4Fs. American losses were 2 P-40s and 2 P-38s. Had the P-40s had sufficient time to get to altitude, American losses would certainly have been less.

For months the night nuisance raids by Japanese bombers had been the cause of much irritation and loss of sleep to the troops on Guadalcanal. A number of the P-38 pilots of the 339th Squadron had volunteered to take off in an attempt to get at the night raiders, but permission had been denied.

The offer of the P-38 pilots was finally accepted, and before dawn on January 29, Captain John Mitchell was airborne to make the first contact. Mitchell caught a twin-engine bomber after it had dropped its bombs, and he pulled right in on its tail. A long burst slowed the craft down and a short burst was fired as he closed in. The bomber burst into flames and dived into the sea. The men on the ground had witnessed the combat, and when the enemy aircraft fell earthward streaming its long cometlike tail of flames on the night sky, they cheered loud and long.

February saw the end of enemy resistance of Guadalcanal, and the fighters turned their attention to offensive work. The P-38s' role was to provide high cover for the heavy bombers attacking the targets to the north, particularly shipping in the harbors of southern Bougainville, the Shortland Islands, and New Georgia.

The Lightnings got off to a good start on February 2 when 4 P-38s were providing high cover for B-17s bombing shipping in Shortland Harbor. Through the use of mutual support tactics, the Lightnings accounted for 3 Zeros without a loss. Captain John W. Mitchell, Lieutenant Besby Holmes, and Lieutenant Jim Shubin all scored.

On Valentine's Day, 10 P-38s and 12 new Marine Corps F4U Corsair fighters of VMF-124 escorted 9 PB4Y bombers attacking shipping in the Shortland area. Approximately 10 minutes from the target area enemy fighters were observed taking off from Kahili, and as the formation approached the target, some 30 fighters were met. All were at between 20,000 and 30,000 feet, and they came in from all sides with guns blazing.

Three P-38s stayed with the bombers throughout and made only feinting attacks at the fighters. The bombers made successful runs on enemy shipping and scored several direct hits on their targets. Only a single bomber was lost to enemy aircraft.

In the violent air battle between the fighter contingents 3 of the enemy were destroyed by the P-38s and 2 by the F4Us, but 4 Lightnings and 2 Corsairs were lost. The successful bombing mission had proved most costly to the American fighters.

There was very little contact with enemy aircraft during the month of March 1943. The Allies occupied the Russell Islands, and the move through the northern Solomons was begun. The P-39s, P-40s, and the P-38s still continued to make routine patrols over the Russells, and local patrols over Guadalcanal and many escort missions were flown with photo aircraft farther north.

March also saw the beginning of operations for the 6th Night Fighter Squadron. Six P-70s had arrived at Henderson Field on the last day of February without fanfare, and the men had gone to work immediately to construct the ground radar station whence the fighters would be vectored to their night targets. The P-70 was basically a Douglas A-20 attack bomber with 4 20mm cannon and an airborne radar set in the nose. By the middle of the month their ground station was complete, and the black-painted aircraft moved from Henderson up to Carney Field, near Koli Point, where they commenced operations.

On March 29 pilots of the 70th Fighter Squadron, flying P-38s, attacked a Japanese destroyer south of Poporang Island. Captain Tom Lanphier was first on the strafing run, and his fire took out most of the anti-aircraft guns on the ship. Lieutenant Rex Barber knocked off a half foot of his left wing on the destroyer's funnel as he tore down the aerial and the mast during his strafing run. The destroyer was left dead in the water with several fires burning and heavy smoke coming up from the afterhatch.

April 1943 was not only a great month for COMAIRSOLS, but one of its events had a momentous effect on the entire Pacific war. In the Solomons, Allied men, planes, and supplies were arriving in quantity. The Japanese realized that it was only a matter of time before the Allies launched another invasion, and the Japanese were determined to strike supply installations and Allied shipping in force as quickly as possible.

On the first day of the month coast watchers reported 2 large waves of Zeke and Hamp fighters forming up to head south for Guadalcanal. Forty-two fighters scrambled and flew north to meet them. There ensued an air battle that lasted for 3 hours as formation after formation rose from opposing bases. At the end of the melee some 20 Japanese fighters had been downed at the cost of 6 Allied planes.

Following this defeat the enemy reverted to his sporadic night bombing for the biggest part of the next week. Then on April 7 he returned to the offensive on a grand scale. Just before noon coast watchers reported 67 Val dive bombers escorted by no less than 110 Zeros en route to Guadalcanal.

Rising to the occasion were 76 Army, Navy, and Marine Corps fighters. While the American fighters engaged the horde of

Zeros, the dive bombers did manage to get some of the shipping in Tulagi Harbor and off Guadalcanal. A tanker, a New Zealand corvette, and the American destroyer *Aaron Ward* were sunk that day.

The fighter pilots downed 12 of the dive bombers and 27 Zeros. In an outstanding performance, Lieutenant James E. Swett, a young Marine Corps pilot flying an F4F Wildcat, braved friendly anti-aircraft fire to down 3 Vals in their dives, then chased 4 more of them across Florida Island and downed all of them—7 victories in 15 minutes.

Also aloft that day were P-38s of the AAF's 339th Fighter Squadron. Tom Lanphier, Rex Barber, Joe Moore, and Jim Mc-Lanahan dove down on a formation of 11 Zeros from an altitude of 30,000 feet, and working in pairs, they cut the enemy to pieces. Lanphier got 3 of the Zeros, Barber got 2, and Moore and McLanahan got a Zero apiece.

Allied losses that day were 7 planes, but only a single pilot was lost.

Early in April 1943, United States intelligence, which had broken the Japanese code, intercepted a message stating that Admiral Isoroku Yamamoto, chief of Japanese naval forces, would be making an inspection tour of advanced bases, including Buin on Bougainville.

When it was ascertained that the admiral was scheduled to arrive at 9:35 A.M. on April 18, word was immediately sent to Admiral William Halsey. On April 17 Admiral Halsey informed COMAIRSOLS that they were to schedule a mission to intercept and shoot down the plane carrying Yamamoto. This mission was to be carried out at all costs.

Due to the extreme range from Guadalcanal to Buin, it was obvious that the only aircraft that could make the trip would be P-38s. Even for them to have enough fuel to assure that the job was accomplished it would be necessary to fly drop tanks in for their aircraft. Veteran fighter pilot Major John Mitchell was selected to lead the mission. Sixteen P-38s would take part: Twelve aircraft would fly top cover, and 4 Lightnings would form the attack section that would make the actual kill. Captain Tom Lanphier and Lieutenants Rex Barber, Joe Moore, and Jim McLanahan were selected to go in to get Yamamoto.

The Lightnings would be going against the Japanese formation in the immediate vicinity of the big enemy airdrome at Kahili, and intense opposition could be expected. To lessen the chances of detection and interception en route, a long, low-level circuitous route of 435 miles was planned. If the admiral lived up to his usual passion for punctuality, the P-38s would make the interception some 35 miles up the coast from Kahili. This would give them the opportunity to shoot the aircraft down before the enemy at Kahili could be alerted.

Early in the morning of April 18 the P-38 pilots taxied out for takeoff. One by one they became airborne, but as his Lightning raced down the runway, Lieutenant Jim McLanahan had a tire blow out. Desperately he fought to regain control of the aircraft, but it veered off the strip. As the P-38s formed up Lieutenant Joe Moore's aircraft developed engine trouble and he was forced to return to base. The attack formation was down to 2 planes. Lieutenants Besby T. Holmes and Raymond K. Hine slipped in to take their places.

After 2 hours and 9 minutes in the air, the P-38s approached the coast of Bougainville at the designated time of 9:35 A.M. As they reached this point the enemy was sighted.

The Lightnings were at 30 feet, heading in toward the coast and ready to begin their climb to altitude. The enemy was sighted in a "V" about 3 miles distant proceeding down the coastline toward Kahili. Two Betty bombers were together, flying at 4,500 feet with 2 sections of 3 Zeros each some 1,500 feet above them and slightly to the rear. As the enemy force, apparently unaware of opposition, pursued their course, Major Mitchell led his covering group in their climb for altitude. When his flight reached 15,000 feet they leveled off and stood their protective vigil.

Lanphier led his force parallel to the course of the enemy, gradually edging toward them and climbing until Lanphier's force reached a level with the bombers about 2 miles away. Lanphier and Barber dropped their belly tanks and swung in to the attack. Lieutenant Holmes had difficulty getting rid of his tank, so Lieutenant Hine remained with him until he could do so.

Lanphier and Barber were within a mile of the enemy when they were observed. The bombers nosed down as the first flight of 3 Zeros dropped their tanks and peeled off to intercept Lanphier. When he saw that he could not get to the bombers without engaging the fighters, Lanphier turned into them head-on, exploded the first, and fired at the others as they passed. By this time he was at 6,000 feet, so he nosed over and went down to the treetops to make his pass at one of the bombers.

Barber had gone in with Lanphier on the initial attack, but in lining up on a Betty he had closed too rapidly and overshot. Barber quickly reefed his aircraft around and made a second pass at the bomber, scoring good hits.

Lanphier made his pass on the bomber broadside, saw a wing fly off, and the enemy aircraft crashed into the jungle. By this time both P-38s had Zeros on their tails and were taking violent evasive action.

Holmes finally had been able to drop his tank, and along with Lieutenant Hine came in to engage the Zeros. Holmes and Hine both got in shots at various Zeros without conclusive results. When the flight was on its way out, Holmes noticed a bomber near Moila Point flying low over the water. He and his wingman, Lieutenant Hine, both made passes on the twin-engine craft, but Lieutenant Barber dove in on it, pulled right in on its tail, and sent it crashing into the sea.

Zeros now came in on the tails of the outbound P-38s. Holmes whipped up and around and shot down a Zero. Barber engaged Zeros that attempted to block his way out and exploded another of the enemy fighters. During this time Hine's left engine started to smoke, and he was last seen losing altitude south of the Shortland Islands. It is believed that Hine also accounted for a Zero during the air battle.

Both Lanphier and Barber made passes at the Japanese Betty bomber that was carrying Admiral Yamamoto, and both are positive that they downed the aircraft that went down into the jungle. Regardless of who put the telling shots into the aircraft, the chief of the Japanese naval forces had met his death.

The second bomber that was definitely downed by Lieutenant Rex Barber carried Vice Admiral Matome Ugaki, chief of staff of the Japanese Combined Fleet. Miraculously, Ugaki and 2 others survived the crash.

The jubilant P-38 pilots returned to their base without mishap, although Lieutenant Holmes did run low on fuel and was forced to make an emergency landing in the Russell Islands before completing his journey home. One of the most successful missions of the war in the Pacific had been carried out to perfection.

The pilots of the 6th Night Fighter Squadron were still seeking their first victory over "Washing Machine Charlie." They had forced him to change his tactics, and instead of harassing the island for hours each night, he would occasionally sneak in just before dawn or just after dusk. The night fighter pilots were hampered by the 90mm anti-aircraft guns on the island, which insisted on firing at anything that got in the searchlights, including the P-70s.

The night fighters finally scored on the evening of April 19 when Lieutenant Bennett and Corporal Ed Tomlinson shot down a Betty bomber right over the island. With an audience down below that cheered wildly, the P-70 flew through the 90mm anti-aircraft fire to get on the tail of the enemy. Tracers flashed in the night sky, and the Betty exploded. All the audience clapped and cheered the performance.

Marine and Navy TBFs and AAF heavy bombers continued to apply pressure on Japanese bases on Bougainville, particularly the airfields at Buin and Kahili. To counter these efforts, the Japanese continued to send fighters down to Guadalcanal in growing numbers. The largest air battle fought during the month of May occurred on the thirteenth, when 2 dozen enemy fighters were met by a cosmopolitan force of AAF P-38s, P-40s, and P-39s; Marine Corps F4Us; Navy F4Fs; and New Zealand P-40s. This force downed 16 of the Japanese craft and sent the remainder scurrying for home. Such losses would normally seem exorbitant to any force, but the Japanese seemed ready and willing to accept them to keep the pressure applied on the Allied buildup to the south.

By the end of May the new Allied strips on the Russells were ready, which permitted more fighter attacks on the enemy airfields. Marine Corps Dauntless dive bombers were also equipped with drop tanks that permitted them to harass the Japanese at Buin from Solomon bases. Both of these factors caused great concern to the enemy, and the base of Rabaul was reinforced until its airfields held a massive force of some 225 aircraft. Enemy shipping filled Rabaul Harbor, and the entire area became a beehive of activity.

On June 7 a week of concerted aerial assault by enemy fighters from Rabaul began. Some 40 to 50 Zeros were sent down the Slot, where they were intercepted by numerous Allied fighters. Among those involved were 12 P-40s of the 44th Fighter Squadron.

One of the more outstanding feats of the day was turned in by Lieutenant Henry E. Matson of the 44th. His first 2 passes at the enemy were without result, but on his third attack he exploded a Zero. Another Zero came at him with guns blazing, but Matson flamed him with a single burst.

However, the P-40 pilot was in too close, and as he pulled up his propeller chewed through the wing of the burning Zero. "There was a marked rise in temperature in my cockpit," Matson related. Loosening his safety belt, he went over the side and pulled his ripcord. As he floated down from 18,000 feet, he examined himself and found that he had been severely burned about the head, neck, and hands. Three Zeros came in to gun him down in his parachute, but through the use of "various gestures of friendship and victory," to quote Matson, he seemingly convinced them that he was Japanese. Regardless, the Zeros looked him over and left him to descend safely into the water. Once in the drink he got into his rubber liferaft and waited 2 hours for his rescue.

Allied fighters downed 23 Zeros that day for the loss of 9 of their own. Fortunately, every Allied pilot that was downed that day was recovered.

The Japanese fighters returned to Rabaul, licked their wounds, and returned on June 16 with their greatest force to date. Allied aircraft received ample warning from the coast watchers, and the biggest air battle of the Solomons campaign was on.

Between 12:30 and 12:45 P.M. 2 large formations of Japanese aircraft, one of 38 and another with about 80 planes, appeared on the radar screen converging on the Russell Islands and headed toward Guadalcanal. Allied fighters began to take to the air by 1:15 P.M., and all were airborne by 1:45 P.M.

Initial contact was made by 12 P-38s from the 339th Fighter Squadron. Leading one of the flights of 4 was Lieutenant Murray J. Shubin, who would have his greatest day of combat on this memorable occasion.

"I led a flight of 4, including myself, Lieutenant Harris, Lieutenant Rake, and Lieutenant Van Bibber," stated Shubin's combat report. "We spotted àn enemy formation of about 50 planes, 15 miles from the western end of Guadalcanal and headed toward the south coast of the island. They were at approximately 23,000 feet and we were at 27,000. We made an initial attack breaking into the rear cover of 10 to 15 Zeros. We opened fire, pulled up, and began a long period of combat.

"Following my initial burst and a long burst into a Zero peeling up, I saw 5 or 6 planes going down, 4 of which were flamers, of which 2 were mine. My wingman, Lieutenant Rake, was hit and returned to base. I continued combat with 4 or 5 of them, gradually working toward the Experance-Savo area some 40 miles away. After 5 to 10 minutes of combat Lieutenant Harris returned to base out of ammunition, accompanied by his wingman, Lieutenant Van Bibber.

"In the ensuing 40 minutes I was in constant contact with 5 Zeros, who seemed determined as hell to get me. . . . Taking advantage of the speed and climb of the P-38, I made passes at their tail-end Charlie, getting a good burst into the area behind the cockpit. This Zero then turned on its back, hung for a moment, and did the first half of a split 'S.' No. 1 probable.

"Following the long burst into this Zero, I continued in a steep spiral dive to the right, getting a full deflection shot at the last Zero in a string of 4, who were making a tight climbing chandelle to get behind and under me. Eventually, the airplane slowed up remarkably. Evidently my lead was too great. He started to climb with his buddies, but evidently had no power, and changing his mind, he whipped into a steep vertical turn and peeled off going down—apparently under control except of his engine. That was No. 2 probable.

"By this time the other 3 were well on my tail and firing like hell. My speed was about 350 mph from the spiral dive. I pulled out and up to the left into the sun in a fast gentle climbing turn. Having a 1,000-foot advantage, I dived slightly at 1 of the Zeros trying to turn into him to get a head-on burst. I fired but missed, going over him. I tried to get a burst at the last in the string, but he peeled off. I fired but couldn't even get a lead on him. I climbed again toward the sun; the 3 of them had gotten together and were maneuvering for altitude as I was. This occurred 3 times. Each time when I got above and to the rear, I made a pass on the rearmost Zero. Twice I did this, and each time when I got within a good range the last Zero saw me in time and split essed before I could get a lead on him. More misses. In the meantime No. 1 and No. 2 Zeros naturally turned into me, took a burst, and dove. Again I climbed and maneuvered into position. This time I resolved not to get too much altitude and made a rear quarter pass with reduced speed and shallow dive so I could really nose over and get a good lead on the Zero as he split essed. I did this and he took too long staying on his back because I really shoved my nose down and got a good lead and reduced it, slashing back toward him and right across his belly and fuselage angularly with the tracers. (My cannon was gone by this time.) He was smoking and still on his back as I passed over him. I never saw him again. That was No. 3 probable.

The other 2 had advantageously worked around to my tail with a little altitude, too. And they were really firing—seemed like tracers all around me. Uncomfortable as hell, I dove until I outran them. I pulled out and climbed in the direction of Savo Island. The 2 had climbed, after I had gotten away and in the direction of Tulagi, where they orbited. I climbed some more and then started a pass toward their orbit. I fired at long distance and with lots of lead at the rearmost, who was about 100 yards from the first. The tracers went overhead and he saw me in plenty of time to split ess safely and go down—evidently home.

"By this time the No. 1 man was left, and he was on the diametric opposite of the orbit in a right-hand turn. He was turning into me, and I had a continued long burst, gradually bringing it into him into a frontal attack. But even though it seemed my tracers raked across his engine, no damage was apparent. I immediately pulled up and racked around, almost blacking out. The Zero continued on a straight line. I went in pursuit, finally getting within gun range a few miles east of Savo. There were P-40s and a P-38 milling around below. I joined on the Zero and started firing from the rear above. My tracers were behind, but as I got closer I led more, and there were hits in back of the pilot on top of the fuselage and in front of the tail. Strangely enough he continued straight for a while and then started a steep forward dive. I watched, shoving my nose as far forward as possible. He was still diving straight as I passed over. I pulled out, leveled up, and turned to catch sight, but could see nothing. My altitude was 11,-000 then. That was No. 4 probable."

Captain F. P. Mueller, G Company, 35th Infantry, witnessed the Esperance-Savo part of the combat and definitely established the fact that Lieutenant Shubin shot down 3 of his 4 Zero probables, giving the P-38 pilot a bag of 5 Zeros for the day.

After the initial interception by the P-38s, some 21 P-40s took off in relays and continued the air battle. One of the more terse and concise descriptions of an encounter was given by Captain W. P. Norris.

"Contact at 9,000 feet over Henderson Field. Dive bombers started to dive. Shot at 'em all way, got smoker (black). Shortly after Lieutenant Jennings got dive bomber I got another good shot into another dive bomber which went into water. Rolled over and shot him in. Was shot at when he broke off, 150 feet off water. Hit with 20mm shell. Shot off part of left aileron and elevator. Shot in both legs and left arm and hand. Landing gear wouldn't work, made belly landing on Fighter Strip No. 2."

Two flights of P-39s got into the air in the vicinity of Henderson Field, and undoubtedly their action against the Val dive bombers that had managed to get by the P-38s and P-40s saved the shipping off Guadalcanal from taking more damage than it did. The hard-pressed old Airacobras took on the Zekes and Vals at low altitude and turned in a magnificent job by downing 6 of the fighters and 5 of the dive bombers.

The P-38s were credited with 11 Zekes, and the P-40s claimed a total of 10 Zekes and 10 Vals. Navy F4Fs destroyed another 30 aircraft, and Marine Corps F4Us got 5. Allied losses were 6 aircraft, of which only 1 belonged to the AAF.

Considerable damage was inflicted on ground installations on Guadalcanal, and 3 American ships in the harbor took hits, but without the tremendous victory of the fighter pilots it could have been a real catastrophe.

Allied ground forces had built up to the point where they were ready to make new conquests in the Solomons. The first phase of the move north was the invasion of Rendova Island. Allied bombers struck targets in the area repeatedly in the few days preceding the landings, and on the morning of June 30, 1943, 32 fighters went up to protect the shipping. Initial opposition came early, but once more the enemy paid dearly. Sixteen of the thirty-odd Zeros were downed. Early that afternoon an enemy force of dive and torpedo bombers escorted by fighters came out, but Marine Corps and Navy Wildcats cut the formation to pieces.

The next morning the fighters were off to protect shipping between Rendova Harbor and Munda Point. Eight P-40Fs of the 18th Fighter Group; 8 P-40s from No. 14 Squadron, Royal New Zealand Air Force; and 8 Navy F4Fs met an enemy flight of some 30 Zekes, Hamps, and Vals just off the west coast of Rendova at 21,000 feet.

Flying one of the 18th Group P-40s in the conflict was Lieutenant M. W. Francis, who would have the fight of his life and a most harrowing experience that July day. Lieutenant Francis, along with Lieutenant C. E. Newlander, dove on a formation of Vals and exploded one of them immediately. Rolling out of his attack, Lieutenant Francis got on the tail of a Hamp fighter and blew it up. Francis pulled up from his attack to join Lieutenant Newlander and spotted another of the dive bombers preparing to make an attack. A long burst into the wing root set the aircraft on fire, but at this time the Val came under attack from a Navy Wildcat, which flamed the left wing.

Lieutenant Francis then pulled in over Lieutenant Newlander, who had lost his elevator and rudder when a Zeke had shot him up while he was concentrating on downing another enemy fighter. Francis followed Newlander down, continuously fighting enemy fighters off until he was only 500 feet off the water. As he was rolling out from one of the attacks a warning came over his radio that he had a Zeke on his tail. Lieutenant Francis immediately broke right and went into a snap roll, which caused the Japanese pilot to overshoot. Lieutenant Francis caught him with a good burst just as the enemy turned to get back to him, and the enemy plane crashed into the water.

The P-40 pilot then resumed cover of Lieutenant Newlander and chased away 3 more enemy fighters but then was suddenly hit from behind. A bullet hit the armor back on the left side of his head—the splinters bruising him and blackening his eyes. At this moment the ammunition box in the right wing exploded, disabling the aircraft. At 600 feet Lieutenant Francis bailed out.

As he came down in his chute he sighted Lieutenant Newlander in a slow dive heading for Rendova Harbor with a Zeke on his tail. Then enemy fighters came at Francis, making 2 strafing passes on him just as he hit the water. Quickly Lieutenant Francis got out of his chute harness and swam away from the floating canopy.

Three hours later a Navy PBY came over and dropped a float but continued on. Shortly afterward the PBY returned, and after 2 attempts managed to get down in a very rough sea. Lieutenant Francis was hauled aboard and a search was made for Lieutenant Newlander, but he could not be located.

Lieutenant E. M. Wheadon of the 18th Group got onto the tail of a string of 9 Val dive bombers. Picking the No. 3 plane in line, he fired and burst and flamed it. Making a continuous turn right, Lieutenant Wheadon blew up another just off the water. Pulling up to the left, he circled and then joined with another P-40 and an F4F, which were after the dive bombers. One dive bomber pulled up at a 45-degree angle in front of Lieutenant Wheadon, who put a long burst into it. Turning right, he sighted another Val turning away with the F4F firing at it from out of range. Wheadon raked the craft from stem to stern and it went into the water.

A call from his flight leader sent Wheadon climbing for altitude to join in a dogfight with a bevy of Zeroes. Latching onto the tail of one of the enemy fighters, he pushed the gun tit and shot him down.

The better-than-hour-long combat had cost the enemy 13 fighters and 12 of his dive bombers. Three AAF P-40s went down, but only Newlander was lost.

The excellent air support that the fighters gave the landing parties made it possible for all landings on New Georgia to be carried off without a hitch. Several landings were made on the southern tip of the island, and on July 4 troops crossed over from Rendova to land on the beach at Zanana to begin the drive to take the airdrome at Munda. The following day U. S. Marines went ashore at Rice Anchorage on the north coast of the island to prevent enemy forces from coming down from Kolombangara.

The fight through the impenetrable jungles of northern New Georgia toward the airfield at Munda was a long and tedious task. The enemy had constructed an excellent defense system complete with log dugouts and pillboxes. His troops were in excellent physical condition, were well equipped, and all were ready to die rather than yield. The biggest foe, however, was the jungle. The density of plant growth and entanglements made it impossible for the fighter pilots to support the operations.

The bombers were the only aircraft that were able to effectively carry out operations against enemy installations, and this they did with considerable effectiveness. Escort was provided by the fighters of COMAIRSOLS, and they continued to prove very efficient.

The tactics of the P-40s flying escort for the bombers on these missions is vividly described by 2 pilots of the 44th Fighter Squadron. "It must be remembered that our job was not to shoot down Zeros," stated Lieutenant John E. Wood. "It was to protect the bombers, whatever it was we were escorting. On such missions it is a hard rule that we must hold our formation and not let the enemy suck you out for a fight. Ours was a defensive job, and what we got we got in holding to those tactics—to get the mission through."

"And it's hell to have to sit there, holding that formation when surrounded by Zeros pecking away at you," Captain D. F. Tarbet added. "You get scared, as scared as hell. Your mouth gets dry and you suck your oxygen as if it's the only thing to hold on to. You want to dive out and get away, but you know you can't. Even after you get safely back home you are still scared from the reaction. After one encounter, I couldn't sleep very well for 2 nights. Every time I closed my eyes I saw Zeros flocking around me."

To compound the problems of the pilots, the Japanese continued to send night raiders down to Guadalcanal to keep the men up all night and disrupt things in general. The P-70s continued to attempt interception, but for the greater part of the time they were unsuccessful. P-38s seemed to meet with a bit more success.

On July 17, 1943, Lieutenant James A. Harrell III took off at 9:32 P.M. and circled the orbit light for about 45 minutes. At approximately 10:15 P.M. a Japanese Betty bomber was sighted about 2,000 feet below. A small light, apparently from the enemy bomber, was visible, and Lieutenant Harrell brought his P-38 down into firing position. He pressed the gun button and put a short burst into the Betty, which immediately went into a steep dive and disappeared into the darkness.

A few minutes later he sighted another Betty at 22,000 feet going toward Fighter Field No. 2. The searchlights on the ground illuminated the enemy plane, and Lieutenant Harrell slowly closed on the tail of the aircraft. The first shot from his machine guns missed, but the second burst caused large pieces to fly off the Betty, and heavy smoke began to emit from its right engine. Lieutenant Harrell, momentarily blinded by the muzzle blast from his own guns, pulled up and the enemy plane vanished.

The men on the ground noted a streamer of fire and heard a small explosion when the Betty was hit, and it was assumed that this nocturnal raider didn't make it back home from his nuisance mission.

By July 25 the final push for the Munda airfield by American ground forces was on. Light, medium, and heavy bombers pounded the area incessantly. Infantrymen fought their way yard by yard against a fanatical enemy and finally broke the last resistance on the afternoon of August 4. Their remaining opposition on the island was not sufficient to prevent Navy Seabees from working on the airstrip at Munda. On the afternoon of August 14, 2 P-40s of the 44th Fighter Squadron landed at Munda to remain overnight, but it would be October before work was complete. However, this gave the fighter planes an emergency strip to come into as the air offensive pressed on against the enemy to the north.

While the base at Munda was undergoing reconstruction, the decision was made by Admiral William Halsey and General Millard Harmon, commanding general, South Pacific, to bypass the Japanese base at Vila on Kolombangara and to invade the island of Vella Lavella instead. On August 15 ground troops landed on the island. The incomplete base at Munda proved to be invaluable as an advanced strip for the fighter planes that provided air cover for the invasion. The Japanese continued to oppose the Americans in the skies over Munda as well as over Vella Lavella, but the fighter pilots were not to be denied. The P-38s, P-40s, and F4Us ripped the enemy's formations to pieces. At sea all attempts to reinforce the Japanese garrison on the island met with disaster. The aerial supremacy of the Americans made it impossible for heavy ships to come down from Rabaul with reinforcements, and the Japanese were forced to attempt transporting troops down in barges that could hide along the shoreline of the islands during the day. The veteran P-39 pilots found that their heavy nose cannon was an excellent weapon in the antibarge campaign. The P-39 and F4U Corsair pilots made the enemy pay dearly as they caught his barges by day and methodically shot them up.

The bypass of Kolombangara paid off handsomely, for the Japanese began to evacuate their troops from the island once Vella Lavella was invaded. Slowly and surely the enemy was being pushed north, leaving him only a single major base in the Solomons: Kahili, on the island of Bougainville.

In a classic example of the close cooperation among the fighter pilots of COMAIRSOLS, Major Paul S. Bechtel, an AAF pilot, scored his fifth victory and became an ace flying a Marine Corps F4U Corsair. On September 2, Major Bechtel, who was assigned to a staff position with COMAIRSOLS, along with Marine Corps Major Donald K. Yost, took off in F4Us and tagged onto the tail end of a squadron of Corsairs that were escorting a formation of B-24s attacking the Kihili airstrip on Bougainville.

Yost and Bechtel were flying off to the right side of the bomber formation as they made their run over the target when Bechtel sighted a Zero coming up low and fast from behind. The enemy fighter was alone and apparently intended to pick off Major Yost before he was discovered. Bechtel rolled over and fired a long burst ahead of the Zero in an attempt to frighten him off. The results were much better than expected. Two big pieces came off the Zero's tail, and the Zero rolled over and went down to crash in the bay.

On return to base Bechtel reported the combat, but Yost was not aware that he had even been under attack. However, several people had seen a plane crash into the bay as the formations were leaving the target, so the victory was confirmed. Undoubtedly, Major Bechtel is the only AAF pilot of World War II to become an ace flying a Marine Corps aircraft.

September was a month of increased bomber raids on the base at Kahili, barge busting in the central Solomons, and solidifying the advance base at Munda. Lieutenant Mack V. Bunderson was one of 11 P-39 pilots of the 347th Group escorting 27 B-24s over New Georgia on September 3, when the bombers came under attack from enemy fighters. Bunderson made a couple of passes to drive them off and found himself alone. A damaged B-24 called for help, so the P-39 pilot immediately set out to assist. Bunderson put a burst into a Zero that was after the bomber and then found himself under attack from 5 more Zeros. The enemy fighters damaged his controls; put a bullet through his left wrist, which paralyzed his arm; and put a piece of shrapnel in his left eye. Bunderson managed to break clear of the Zeros and head for home. Several times he nearly fainted, and he was almost blind. His compass was shot out, so he flew completely by the sun. He hoped to make it in to Munda, but he blacked out, and when he regained consciousness he had passed the island. Through nothing less than a miracle he managed to make a wheels-up landing on the strip at Segi.

Such was a prime example of the tenacity and determination of the pilots who had won aerial supremacy over the Solomons and who had done so much to make the conquest of the islands possible.

VI

THE PAPUAN CAMPAIGN

Preparations for the Guadalcanal campaign cut deeply into the flow of men and planes to Australia and New Guinea. The Japanese continued to press their New Guinea ground offensive in the summer of 1942 in the direction of Port Moresby, while Australian infantrymen fought a desperate holding action. Not only were Allied ground forces restricted by shortages of personnel and equipment, but Allied airpower was also forced into a holding and defensive role. It was the mission of the American fighter units to defend Port Moresby as best they could and to participate in limited escort and ground-support duties.

As the Guadalcanal campaign progressed, the role of the Allied ground forces and air units became more and more important, for the approaches to Australia had to be held or the costly campaign in the Solomons would have gone for naught.

The tour of duty of the 39th and 40th squadrons of the 35th Fighter Group at Port Moresby in June and July of 1942 was not to be marked with a great deal of combat. Their P-400s got off to an early start when the 39th Squadron tangled with a bevy of Zeros over Morabe, New Guinea, on June 9. Five of the enemy craft were downed in the combat.

After that day there were few encounters with the Japanese in the air. The primary missions of the P-400s during June and July were to bomb and strafe enemy installations up and down the

Papuan peninsula. Port Moresby still was being bombed, but not nearly in the numbers or the intensity as it had been during the earlier months. The Port Moresby area was a beehive of activity during June and July, however. New airfields were being built, and all installations were being rapidly improved.

The Japanese did mount a large mission on July 11. With ample warning and by using diving tactics to best advantage, the pilots of the 40th Squadron managed to bring down 4 of the bombers and a Zero.

July was to bring to New Guinea the opening of the Papuan campaign. Early in the month an Allied reconnaissance party began the long trek over the Owen Stanley Mountains with the intention of surveying an airfield site near the town of Buna on the northern coast of Papua. For the Allies to start an advance in the Bismarck Archipelago it was essential that air bases be constructed in northern New Guinea. To enable bombers to raid Rabaul and other targets in the area it was necessary for them to leave their bases in northern Australia and fly to Port Moresby to refuel and stage out of the airfields there. Putting up missions in this manner was entirely too hard on crews and aircraft, and Allied commanders sent this expedition as an advance party for new airfield construction.

Unfortunately, the Allies were beaten to the punch. On July 21, Japanese forces landed just north of Buna. All Allied air reinforcements were put into the air to attack the beachhead. The 39th and 40th squadrons of the 35th Group were ready to return to Australia for rest, but they were pressed into service along with their replacements, the 41st Squadron of the 35th Group and the 80th Squadron of the 8th Fighter Group. All squadrons were equipped with P-39s and P-400s. Flying Fortresses, North American B-25s, and Martin B-26s came up from Australia to stage through Port Moresby for their missions.

The pilots of the 41st and 80th squadrons had just arrived when they received the report of the Japanese force being sighted off Cape Ward Hunt traveling south. American bombers attempted an attack on the convoy that afternoon, but due to poor weather their attacks were ineffective.

Early the next morning missions were launched against the enemy landing parties. Aircraft from all 4 fighter squadrons took off from Seven-Mile and Fourteen-Mile Airdromes to provide cover for B-25s and B-26s on their bomb runs. The medium bombers destroyed a number of the enemy barges and killed many troops. Then the fighter planes went down and strafed the area. On their departure the American pilots observed 2 enemy ships on fire and a transport sinking.

Bad weather prevented attacks on the following day, and on the twenty-fourth the Japanese came down in spotty weather to bomb airfields at Port Moresby. Before the fighters could get to altitude the Japanese bombers had dropped their loads and departed.

On July 29, both the 80th and the 41st squadrons were called upon to provide escort for 7 A-24s of the Port Moresby-based 8th Bombardment Squadron on a bombing mission against 2 transports and 4 destroyers in Buna Bay. On arrival over the target, a thick overcast at 9,000 feet was encountered. The fighters followed the dive bombers through the overcast and then met Zeros coming up. Lieutenants Dix and Sponenberg of the 80th Squadron got hits on a Zero, which was last seen going down. As the fighters mixed it up they lost sight of the A-24s as they continued on course for their targets. One P-400 sighted an A-24 with a Zero on its tail, but as he dove at the enemy aircraft, both planes disappeared into the overcast. All of the P-400s made it back, but only a single A-24 returned.

After the Japanese landed, their troops quickly pushed inland toward Kokoda, where the sole opposition was an Australian militia unit. The Australians were forced to give ground, and the little villages of Deniki and Isuraba, which controlled the entrance to "the Gap," or pass, that led through the Owen Stanley Mountains on the route to Port Moresby were threatened.

The P-400s were pressed into strafing service against the on-rushing Japanese troops and as escorts to the C-47s that were supplying the ground forces. During this period the air raids on Port Moresby slowed, and enemy opposition in the air was limited.

The enemy did mount a heavy raid on Port Moresby on the morning of August 17, and 3 bombers and 7 transports were destroyed on the ground at Seven-Mile Airdrome. Some of the American fighters managed to get in the air, but they were too late to intercept the enemy bombers.

During the third week in August the Allies moved in a force of American and Australian engineers and infantry to construct airfields near Milne Bay on the southeastern tip of New Guinea. This strategic area guarded the sea approaches from the Solomon Sea to New Guinea; the mistake of getting to Buna too late was not to be repeated.

As quickly as an airstrip could be completed, 2 RAAF P-40 squadrons and a few Lockheed Hudson bombers moved into the installation. It was none too soon, for on August 26, a force of about 2,000 enemy troops was landed on the northern shore of Milne Bay. To take some of the pressure off the Australian fighter squadrons, the 80th and the 41st squadrons pressed attacks upon the Japanese airfield at Buna.

The 80th Squadron got its first taste of victory in the air during a strafing mission against the enemy airfield at Buna Mission on the morning of August 26, 1942. Ten P-400s under the leadership of Captain Greasley were airborne at 6 A.M. Greasley developed electrical trouble immediately and had to return to base. Three more Airacobras were forced to abort the mission before the target was reached, and as the remaining 6 aircraft slipped down over the mountains, they were being led by Lieutenant William A. Brown.

This time the Americans had the advantage. They caught 10 Zeros in the process of taking off. One after the other the attackers caught the enemy fighters as they became airborne and shot them from the air. Lieutenant Brown got 2 of them, as did Lieutenant

Daniel T. Roberts. Singles were scored by Lieutenants George Halveston and Gerald T. Rogers.

Lieutenant Roberts, a former divinity student who was to become one of the foremost aces in the Southwest Pacific, uttered his closest approach to profanity on his return. His crew chief asked him how the mission had gone. "I got 2 of the devils," Roberts replied.

The 41st Squadron repeated the action the next day, and once more the Japanese were caught from above. Five Zeros fell to the guns of the P-400s.

By August 29 the Japanese drive on the airfield at Milne Bay had been broken. In the sharp action nearly half of the enemy force had been killed, and the remainder of these forces were evacuated by Japanese warships. This brief action marked the first real victory over the enemy in New Guinea.

However, along the Kokoda track the Japanese were still pushing toward their objective of attacking Port Moresby. Despite poor food, dysentery, and lack of sleep, the ground crews of the American fighter squadrons went about their tasks in an admirable manner. Parts were still very hard to come by, and often replacements had to be "borrowed" from another plane until the next supplies came in from Australia. As the enemy troops came within 30 miles of the airfields there was double duty for the men. A camp defense was put into effect, with machine gun positions at strategic points and personnel assigned to operate them. Guard posts on the flight line were doubled, and at night passwords were used and rigidly adhered to.

September 3 saw an administrative change of great significance take place in the Southwest Pacific. The administrative difficulties that had existed under the organization of the Allied air forces were eliminated by the organization of American units into the Fifth Air Force with bomber, fighter, air base commands, and all headquarters under American officers. The new air force was commanded by General George C. Kenney, who had taken over command of the Allied air forces on August 2. The new 5th Fighter Command was headed by Colonel Paul B. Wurtsmith, who had led the 49th Fighter Group during the defense of Darwin.

At the time of its inception, the Fifth Air Force was badly understrength and utilizing many aircraft that were worn out from earlier campaigns. The 19th Bombardment Group and the 63rd Squadron of the 43rd Bombardment Group possessed some 70 B-17s, of which perhaps 30 could be made operational at any one time. The 22nd Bombardment Group was flying 40 B-26s that had been in action ever since their arrival in Australia in early 1942. Only 10 of the 45 B-25s of the 38th Bombardment Group and the 3rd Bombardment Group were in commission. The remainder of the 5th Bomber Command was composed of approximately 20 A-20s belonging to the 3rd Bombardment Group.

The 5th Fighter Command was composed of 250 fighter planes, of which 100 were inept Bell P-400s, while the remaining strength of the 18th, 35th, and 49th fighter groups was made up of Bell P-39s and Curtiss P-40s.

Early September also saw the American 32nd Infantry Division moved into New Guinea to help stem the drive on Port Moresby. The 41st and 80th squadrons flew many escort missions in this reinforcing phase as well as escorting the bombers staging out of the Port Moresby bases.

Lieutenant Gerald Rogers, who had failed to return from the strafing mission to Buna on August 26, returned to the 80th Squadron on September 13. After destroying a Zero, he had dived on another that had just landed, but the aircraft made it into the revetment area before he could bring his guns to bear. While strafing the field a Zero got on his tail, and Rogers attempted to escape southward flying right on the deck. The Zero pumped several bursts into Rogers' plane, which caught fire. Rogers cut his speed while skimming right over the water and went in.

Although he had suffered shrapnel wounds from enemy action

and several deep cuts from the crash, Rogers managed to get out of his aircraft and swim to shore. There he was picked up by friendly local inhabitants and taken to a mission, where he was nursed back to health. The locals then got him to a grass strip, where he was picked up by an Australian pilot and brought back to Allied control.

By September 17 the Japanese had driven to Imita Range, which was only 20 miles from Port Moresby. Allied air reinforcements began to arrive in the form of P-40s of the 49th Group's 7th Squadron. This Darwin combat-experienced unit went into action on the nineteenth, when 8 of their aircraft escorted a flight of Australian Beaufighters on a strafing mission to Buna. Four of the P-40s set 4 or 5 Japanese barges and a gasoline dump on fire.

Allied bombers and fighters kept constant pressure on the Japanese troops while infantry reinforcements were rushed to the scene. Three fresh Australian battalions went into the line to face the Japanese in the ridges above Port Moresby, and units of the American 32nd Division were brought into Seven-Mile Airdrome by AAF troop carrier C-47s. The Japanese push along the Kokoda track had been stopped.

Ten P-40s of the 7th Fighter Squadron took off on the afternoon of September 21 on their initial dive-bombing strike against the enemy in the Kokoda-Buna area. The target was an important river bridge that the enemy utilized in getting supplies to their troops at the front. No direct hits were scored with the 500-pound demolition bombs, but strikes were close enough to cause the bridge to sag and partially disconnect an end of it.

The next day a dozen P-40s went back and hit the Wairope bridge with 300-pound bombs. Further damage was inflicted on the bridge and supply warehouses, and buildings were bombed and strafed. For good measure the 7th pilots strafed gun emplacements at Buna Airdrome and motor launches in the bay. All of the P-40s made it home safely, although they had come under heavy machine-gun fire from the ground.

During the latter part of September the Japanese sent a number of nuisance raids out against Port Moresby, but most of these were largely ineffectual, and no interceptions were made by the American fighters.

By October 1 the AAF fighter forces had been bolstered by the return of the 39th and 40th squadrons of the 35th Fighter Group. The highlight of their return was the fact that the 39th had completed transition to Lockheed P-38 Lightning fighters. The appearance of the twin-boomed fighters had a tremendous effect on the morale of all AAF personnel at Port Moresby, for now they had an aircraft that could intercept the Japanese raiders at will.

One battalion of the American 32nd Infantry Division that had taken part in the fight at Kokoda pushed off into the jungle and over the mountains on a parallel course south of the Kokoda track against the Japanese on October 5, but the over-all plan was to land the balance of the division by airlift in the vicinity of Wanigela, some 65 miles down the coast from Buna. From that point the American infantry would push up the coast against Buna while the Americans and Australians on the Kokoda front pushed the enemy back toward Buna from the west.

All during the month of October the AAF fighters flew missions escorting the C-47s dropping supplies to the ground troops on the Kokoda front and strafing the enemy's supply lines to his rear. The hectic battle taking place on Guadalcanal had all but cleared the New Guinea skies of enemy air opposition, so the bombers and fighters of the Fifth Air Force were able to hammer at the Japanese incessantly.

To protect the eastern flank in New Guinea the 35th and 36th squadrons of the 8th Fighter Group had been sent to Milne Bay in mid-September. They were joined by the 80th Squadron by early November 1942. By this time the 8th Fighter Group was largely equipped with new P-39Ds, which were an improvement over the bedraggled P-400s.

Also on the move were the 8th and 9th squadrons of the 49th Fighter Group. A wing of RAF and RAAF Spitfires moved into the Darwin area in October, and the men of the 8th and 9th squadrons were given a short breather before moving on to the Port Moresby area late that month.

On November 1, the P-40s of the 8th Fighter Squadron escorted 14 A-20s of the 3rd Bombardment Group to Lae Airdrome for a bombing and strafing attack. Eight to 10 Zeros came up to oppose the mission. Some 10 miles from the target the enemy fighters dived down on the P-40s, and Lieutenant Glenn Wohlford was hit immediately and was last seen in a dive with white smoke trailing from his aircraft and with 2 Zeros on his tail.

Lieutenant Richard Dennis, a flight leader, fired bursts at several of the Zeros and finally pulled up to get a good burst directly into the engine of one of the enemy fighters. Parts of the cowling and engine were torn loose, and the Zero went into a final dive. Lieutenant William C. Day, Jr., managed to send another of the Zeros down in flames.

By November 3 the Australian ground forces had completely occupied Kokoda and its airstrip on the east side of the Owen Stanley Mountains. The immediate danger to the Allied bases at Port Moresby was over. A great deal of credit must be given to the fighter pilots of the Fifth Air Force who had escorted the bombers attacking the Japanese supply lines and who through their own strafing attacks had contributed much to the destruction of the enemy.

By early November engineers had managed to complete a number of landing strips south of Buna. As quickly as the strips were completed, C-47s utilized them immediately to move in Allied ground troops. One excellent site that was found by the engineers was Dobodura, a site within 15 miles of Buna. By November 21 a small strip was complete on this site. Dobodura would become one of the major air bases in New Guinea in the days to come.

In one of the largest military airlifts at that stage of the war,

Fifth Air Force troop-carrier C-47s transported the largest part of the American 32nd Infantry Division into the new airfields south of Buna for the new offensive. On November 19 the attack was launched. It was up to the fighter pilots to not only provide cover for the troop transports, which had to furnish a great portion of the supplies for the offensive, but they also had to provide air cover for shipping that was landing the balance of the supplies on the coast.

As Allied ground troops began to move up the coast toward Buna, enemy air opposition began to make itself known once more. Pilots of the 7th Squadron were escorting A-20s to the airfield at Lae when they sighted 6 Zeros outbound for Buna with 2 bombs under each wing.

"We sighted 6 Zeros coming toward us at the same altitude," Lieutenant Paul J. Slocum reported. "They were all nearly on line. Captain Martin's flight circled to the right, my flight met them head-on. Captain Martin's flight attacked from the rear. After the initial attack it became one huge dogfight. I circled and dropped my belly tank and pulled up and fired at a Zero. He rolled and started to spin; I fell out and lost sight of them. I flew out about a mile, climbed above the others, and headed back toward the fight. I started after one Zero but pulled up after another, which had just attacked a P-40. My attack was from the rear, and I fired from about 200 feet. My shots struck the wing and in the fuselage just behind the cockpit. The plane immediately burst into flames."

Lieutenant Irving Voorhees took another of the Zeros out on a head-on pass, and several of the enemy fighters were damaged in the fight. Two of the P-40s went down in the action.

The 49th Group scored 3 more times on November 26 when Zeros pounced upon a C-47 in the vicinity of Buna. The pilots of the 8th Squadron dove to the attack, and Lieutenant William B. Harris flamed a Zero in a head-on pass. Lieutenant Warren A. Blakely had downed a Zero when he saw Lieutenant Harris under attack from the rear. At this time, Lieutenant Harris was firing on another Zero that was on Lieutenant Earl Kingsley's tail. Around and around they went in a big Lufbery circle. Lieutenant Harris managed to down the Zero on Lieutenant Kingsley's tail for his second victory of the day before the combat was broken off.

Sixteen P-40s of the 7th Squadron were patrolling over Buna shortly before noon on November 30 when a dozen Zeros appeared out of the clouds and dove on them. Lieutenant Donald H. Lee got on the tail of an enemy fighter, which immediately pulled up in a stall turn and came back at him head-on. One burst from Lieutenant Lee's guns set the Zero on fire. Lieutenant Lee then saw 2 Zeros on the tail of a P-40 but was unable to get to the enemy before the American was shot down.

Lieutenant Sheldon Brinson attacked 2 Zeros at once and shot one down in flames, but then he made the near-fatal mistake of watching his opponent go down. The second Zero got on his tail, and Brinson was forced to dive for cloud cover.

Four other Zeros fell before the onslaught on the P-40s, but 2 of the Americans failed to return from the mission.

Later in the day 12 P-40s of the 8th Squadron dropped 20 300-pound antipersonnel bombs on enemy installations before the P-40s were attacked by 10 Zeros. Lieutenant Robert A. Moose saw a Zero being chased by 2 P-40s and joined in. When the Zero did a vertical reversement it exposed its belly to him and received 3 long bursts for its error. The wing of the enemy aircraft was almost severed near the fuselage, and the plane went down in flames.

Lieutenant Harold Learned met a diving Zero head-on, and his machine gun fire set the plane to blazing in the nose and belly. The enemy fighter went down past him without firing a shot.

One of the P-40s was hit in the fuselage, but the pilot managed to bail out and later make his way back to base.

In late November the 35th and 36th squadrons of the 8th Fighter Group were dispatched to Fourteen-Mile Airdrome at Port Moresby from their bases at Milne Bay to assist in the operational air cover over Buna.

AAF bombers and fighters constantly flew missions in the Buna area in early December 1942 to prevent enemy troop and supply buildups and to intercept Japanese attempts to reinforce their forces from the sea.

Shortly before noon on December 7, a flight of 4 P-39s led by Lieutenant George S. Welch encountered 9 Val-type dive bombers and an equal number of Zeros, which were attacking the Buna ground station. Welch spotted a Zero pulling up from a strafing pass and dove on him from 4,000 feet. On his first pass Welch failed to score hits, but after coming out of his dive he followed the Zero toward Kokoda. As the enemy fighter changed course for Buna, Welch chased him for 10 miles, finally getting within firing range east of the Buna strip. A 5-second burst resulted in hits entering the engine and cockpit of the Zero. The enemy fighter burst into flames and fell into the sea in a steep glide.

Seconds later, Welch latched onto a Val at 5,000 feet and attacked from the rear. His first burst struck the bomber in the section between the pilot and the gunner, causing the plane to explode and crash into the sea.

Before turning for home, Welch went after a second Val and closed in to within 100 feet before he opened fire. A 3-second burst from all his guns caught the Val at the wing roots and center section of the fuselage. The bomber crashed into the sea. This destruction gave Welch 3 victories for the day. This action occurred exactly a year from the day that he had gained his initial victories over Pearl Harbor, when 4 Japanese dive bombers succumbed to his fire.

That afternoon the Japanese returned with heavy bombers. Four P-40s of the 7th Fighter Squadron were on patrol when they sighted 18 twin-engine Mitsubishi bombers escorted by approximately 12 Zero fighters. Lieutenant John J. Hood reported, "As I started my pass I noticed the Zeros about 2,000 feet above the bombers. I believe we surprised them because there was no fire at Lieutenant Nichols, who made a head-on attack, as did all of us. As Lieutenant Nichols passed across the top I noticed one of the bombers smoking. Lieutenant LaCroix was next to attack, but the only thing that I observed of his pass was the violent spin he went into immediately behind the bombers. I thought at first he had been hit. On my attack I opened up with my guns out of range and observed my tracers falling short. I then raised my sights and alternated or swept my guns from his right engine to the cockpit, holding a very long burst and raking back and forth from engine to cockpit. As I came close and passed over him I noticed him falling back and out of formation but observed no smoke. I immediately nosed over and went down to about 3,000 feet where, upon looking, I noticed 2 big clouds of smoke rising from the water just offshore."

Lieutenant Robert H. Vaught made his dive into the face of intense fire from the bombers with 2 Zeros diving on him as well. He dove and came up under the bombers, firing bursts into 2 of them. They dropped out of formation and went down in flames. Six of the twin-engine bombers fell to the P-40s, while no losses were suffered by the attackers. Lieutenant LaCroix had recovered from his spin and made it home.

On December 15 the Japanese got their last reinforcements into Buna. A convoy of warships was spotted during the afternoon, but bad weather prevented the heavy bombers from making effective attacks on the vessels. Troops were landed that night, and all through the next day Allied aircraft flew against supply dumps and troops on shore. All available fighters were put into the air, escorting bombers in addition to doing some bombing of their own.

As American and Australian troops pushed toward Buna, enemy resistance became more and more fierce. The Japanese were well dug in, and many missions were flown against their installations. A-20s, B-25s, and B-26s dropped ton upon ton of bombs on the enemy targets as the fighters flew continuous patrols overhead to prevent enemy fighters from getting through to the bombers.

The day after Christmas the pilots of the 9th Fighter Squadron broke up a Japanese formation that was directing its strafing attack on Dobodura. High scorer for the day was Lieutenant John D. Landers, who downed 2 Zeros before he was shot up and forced to bail out himself. In all, 7 Zeros were downed for the loss of Lieutenant Lander's P-40.

The following day the P-38s of the 39th Squadron saw their first big action and had one of their best days of World War II. Three flights of the unit dived on a Japanese formation of more than 20 fighters and seven dive bombers in the vicinity of Cape Endaiadere. Captain Thomas J. Lynch became the first ace of the squadron when he destroyed 2 Oscar-type fighters; and another young pilot of whom much would be heard downed a Zeke fighter and a Val dive bomber. His name was Lieutenant Richard I. Bong.

However, with the sweet came the bitter, when 2 P-40s of the 9th Fighter Squadron came under attack by the P-38s in a case of mistaken identity and just managed to escape. All told, the 39th Squadron was credited with 9 fighters and 2 dive bombers in the action.

The score of the 39th Squadron increased steadily over the next few days as they flew escort for bombers that were attacking Japanese targets at Lae and Gasmata. Ten Zeros were destroyed on the mission against the airdrome at Lae on December 31, and another 9 were destroyed near Gasmata on January 6, 1943, when the P-38s escorted the bombers to hit the convoy bringing enemy reinforcements to Lae.

P-40s of the 49th Group went out after the convoy on January 7. Two flights from the 7th Squadron contacted the ships 20 miles east of Salamaua in a convoy that consisted of several transports, 3 destroyers, and a cruiser. Lieutenant A. T. House and Lieutenant C. S. Burtnette picked the rear transport, while 5 other P-40s dive-bombed the first transport. Lieutenant House's 2 300-pound bombs exploded right under the stern of the ship. Lieutenant Burtnette did not observe his bomb strikes but saw smoke rising from the stern when he looked back. The transport went down by the stern and sank.

Lieutenant Franklin A. Nichols' bombs exploded at the starboard side of the first transport, damaging it severely. After bombing, the P-40s flew down in the face of intense anti-aircraft fire and strafed the crowded decks of the transports.

When the convoy made it into harbor at Lae, 16 P-40s of the 8th Squadron were sent to strafe it. This formation was intercepted by 20 Japanese fighters, 13 of which were shot down by the P-40s.

Lieutenant Ernest A. Harris reported the combat as follows: "I was leading a flight of 4 airplanes. Before reaching the target we were attacked by Zeros. My flight split up and engaged the enemy. I continued on and strafed one transport. I observed pieces flying from the deck of the ship but was unable to observe other damage. I pulled up into the fight and attacked a Zero that was on the tail of a P-40. I closed in on him, shooting, and saw him burst into flames. I pulled up and made a pass at the second Zero and put 3 long bursts into him and observed the bullets striking the plane and pieces disintegrating from it. The plane rolled over out of control and into a layer of clouds. I immediately pulled up and made a pass at a third Zero. I pressed the attack to a very close range and fired 2 bursts into him and saw my bullets striking him at the cockpit. The Zero began spiraling down, seemingly out of control into the clouds. I dove, circling the clouds and getting under them. I observed the plane burning on the water and two other large circular wakes where planes had hit the water. These were all in the vicinity of where planes I had attacked had gone through clouds."

While this was taking place the P-38s of the 39th Squadron were having another big day by downing 7 enemy fighters over Huon Gulf.

On January 8, 1943, the P-38s of the 39th went to Lae Harbor, attacking shipping. The enemy reacted violently to the bombing attacks and sent up a horde of fighters. In the combat that took place throughout the day, the 39th downed 16 enemy fighters. Lieutenant Richard I. Bong was among those scoring, bagging his fifth enemy plane, making him an ace.

Allied ground forces at this time were engaged in vicious

close-in combat with the enemy at Buna. On January 12 the Japanese made a final effort, but their attack was contained. The counterattack by the Allies began the impetus that would all but destroy all organized Japanese resistance in Papua by January 22, 1943.

The Papuan campaign had seen the Fifth Air Force fighters come into their own offensively. The P-40s and P-39s had done yeoman duty as bomber escorts, dive bombers, and strafers, while the initiation of the P-38 in combat over New Guinea had been nothing short of sensational. With experience, confidence, and new airplanes, the 5th Fighter Command had taken its first big step forward.

VII

HOLDING THE LINE—NEW GUINEA

While the primary force of Allied ground troops in New Guinea had directed its attention to the task of ousting the Japanese from the Papuan peninsula, a small force of Australian infantrymen had been very busy inland.

This small group, known as Kanga Force, had moved north-eastward through the mountains and jungles to establish an air-base at Wau, some 30 miles southwest of Salamaua. This move threatened the next objective of the Allies, which was the Japanese base at Lae on Huon Gulf. The threat was compounded when Buna fell, and Allied troops made ready to continue their push on up the coast of New Guinea. It became essential that the enemy make every effort to reinforce his troops through the base at Lae. His first offensive effort in this situation was made against the Australian base at Wau.

While Japanese troops and ships were being assembled at Rabaul, the Allies continued to rush troops and equipment into the base at Wau by air. It was on February 6 that P-39s from the 35th Fighter Group, escorting a flight of C-47s, encountered an enemy force of Zekes and Sally bombers on their way to attack the airfield. The C-47s streaked for home while the fighters engaged. In the initial encounter the Airacobras downed 11 of the enemy fighters and a bomber.

Simultaneously fighters from the 7th Fighter Squadron roared down on another formation of 12 Lily bombers and a like number of Zekes and Hamps in the process of bombing the airfield at Wau. The P-40s tore into the bombers, broke up their formation, and accounted for 2 Lilys and 5 of the fighters. P-38s from the 9th Fighter Squadron arrived on the scene as the enemy was fleeing, and the P-38s knocked down another of the fighters.

This was to prove the last air action for the remainder of the month for the fighters of the 5th Fighter Command, which gave them sufficient time to get their aircraft in commission and to bring up reinforcements. A number of shiny new P-38s were brought up for the 9th Fighter Squadron, and on February 9 they were officially deemed a twin-engine fighter squadron.

One very unusual occurrence during the month was the presence of a P-40 with no identification numbers on it that was reported at times buzzing the strips in the Port Moresby area. All units were checked and all P-40s accounted for, so it was determined that the enemy was using a P-40, presumably captured in the Philippines, for reconnaissance purposes. On February 27 the aircraft was sighted in the Kokoda area, and attempts from other American aircraft to reach it by radio proved unsuccessful. Although the P-40 bore no unit markings, it did have the usual stars on the wings and fuselage and had "Mary" painted on the nose. American fighter pilots were alerted for its presence, but an interception was never made.

On the evening of February 28, 1943, a convoy of 8 Japanese transports escorted by 8 destroyers left the harbor at Rabaul laden with 6,900 troops destined for Lae. The convoy was first sighted on March 1 by a Fifth Air Force reconnaissance aircraft, but contact was lost due to the storm front that the enemy was using for cover.

The convoy was sighted the next morning, and a dozen B-17s and 17 B-24s took off as quickly as possible to attack. The Battle of the Bismarck Sea was on! Sixteen P-38s of the 39th Fighter Squadron took off to escort the B-24s, but due to stormy weather they experienced great difficulty trying to keep in sight of the bombers. The fighters never sighted the convoy, but between breaks in the clouds during the day the bombers were able to drop their loads with good results. One transport was sunk and 2 were damaged. The P-38s did sight a flight of 3 Oscar-type fighter planes on their way back to Port Moresby and downed 2 of them.

Early on the morning of March 3 16 P-38s of the 39th Squadron and 16 P-38s of the 9th Squadron were in the air to escort General Kenney's 1–2 punch to the convoy. First a formation of B-17s came in to attack from medium altitude, and then B-25s, A-20s, and Australian Beaufighters came in at mast height to create havoc.

One of the more effective weapons that caught the enemy completely by surprise were the B-25s. The twin-engine Mitchell bombers had everything pulled out of the nose, and in their place 8 .50-caliber machine guns were mounted. This installation gave the pilot of the B-25 a tremendous strafing potential. These same aircraft carried 500-pound bombs that were armed with 5-second delay fuses, permitting the planes to come down just off the water and attack without exposing themselves to the effect of the blast. Utilizing this "skip bombing" tactic, the aircraft could approach the enemy vessel at masthead height, drop its bombs, and be on its way before the bombs exploded. By detonating in the water alongside the ship, the mining effect of the bomb caused great damage.

When the mixed formation of P-38s from the 39th and 9th fighter squadrons was some 25 to 30 miles from the convoy they sighted approximately 25 Zekes, Hamps, and Oscars between them and the target. The fighters swiftly pulled to the forefront and hit the enemy before he could bring his force to bear on the bombers. As the bombers began to make their runs on the convoy, another 15 enemy fighters put in an appearance at 3,000 feet right over the ships. In an effort to keep them from attacking the bombers, part of the P-38s went down and engaged this formation, while the rest stayed with the bombers until they left the target.

The Japanese ship commanders chose to ignore the attack from medium altitude by the B-17s, but when the low-flying B-25s came in the ships went into evasive action against possible torpedo attack by presenting their bows or sterns to the aircraft. This is just what the B-25 pilots wanted. The Mitchells went down with nose guns blazing, sweeping enemy troops off the decks with withering machine-gun fire before dropping their bombs. One after the other they swept in and stopped the transports and destroyers in their tracks. Then in came the A-20s and RAAF Beaufighters to sweep the crippled ships with their guns.

That afternoon the bombers went back to finish off the enemy convoy. The sea was covered with sinking ships, liferafts, and enemy survivors bobbing up in the water. Once more P-38s provided top cover while the bombers proceeded with their grisly task. Survivors were strafed repeatedly, and the surviving ships took more hits from the bombers.

At the end of the day all of the ships save 4 of the destroyers were sunk or crippled. In one of the greatest classic victories of airpower over seapower, an entire convoy had been smashed for the loss of a single B-17 and 3 of the P-38s.

The P-40s of the 7th and 8th squadrons of the 49th Group couldn't get in on the action against the convoy due to the bad weather and the limited range of their aircraft, but they had a tremendous day in the vicinity of Lae against barges from the convoy. The pilots of the 8th Squadron were greeted by a formation of enemy fighters in the area, 6 of which they promptly downed.

The 7th Squadron bombed and strafed the airfield at Lae and then picked on an enemy barge loaded with troops headed for the beach. Lieutenant A. T. House went down to strafe the barge, and 7 enemy fighters got on his tail. Major William P. Martin saw Lieutenant House's predicament and drove 3 of them away. Lieutenant House glanced over his shoulder, saw what was going on, and turned back into the enemy. In the ensuing fight Lieutenant House downed 2 of his attackers.

Navy PT boats attacked the surviving ships of the Lae-bound convoy on the night of March 3–4 and succeeded in sinking a crippled transport and finishing off many of the surviving troops in the water. The next morning AAF B-17s and B-25s went out and sank 2 crippled destroyers.

P-38s of the 5th Fighter Command escorted A-20s and RAAF Beaufighters bombing and strafing the airfields at Lae and then proceeded to the airfield at Finschhafen, where 10 to 15 enemy fighters rose to challenge them. Six of the enemy were downed, and all Allied fighters and bombers returned unscathed.

The failure of the convoy to get reinforcements through to Lae incensed the Japanese and frightened them. They realized that the disaster that had befallen the convoy would make it possible for Allied forces to move on up the eastern coast of New Guinea against their depleted forces. Such action was just what General Douglas MacArthur had in mind, and plans were already in the mill for landings to be made at Dona and Morobe, some 75 miles from Salamaua.

A series of Japanese missions against Allied air bases in New Guinea began on March 9, 1943, when the field at Wau was hit with little effect. The raid 2 days later met with much better results, when bombers with heavy fighter escort attacked the 49th Fighter Group base at Dobodura. Two enlisted men were killed on the ground, several were wounded, and 3 aircraft were destroyed on the ground.

Two flights of the 8th Squadron and 3 flights from the 9th Squadron went up to intercept the enemy. One flight from the 8th was on combat air patrol when the enemy approached, and it joined the other fighters to give the Japanese a warm welcome.

Lieutenant Richard I. Bong, the young ace whose star was fast rising, was one of those who made the interception that day, but this combat almost had a tragic ending for him. In his own words, "I took off just ahead of the falling bombs and climbed up to 24,000 feet. We intercepted the bombers on their way home. I made a 20-degree pass from ahead and above and put a good burst in the last bomber. There were no observed results. Nine fighters dove on me, and I had to dive to 475 mph indicated to get away. I tried to go back for another pass at the bombers but was intercepted by Zeros and chased down to water level.

"We were headed toward Gasmata. I flew straight until I could see only 1 Zero behind me. I made a 180-degree turn and put a long burst into the Zero head-on. Instead of only 1 Zero, there were 9 or more, and I turned 5 degrees left and put a short burst into another Zero head-on. Both of these had their belly tanks on. Turned 10 degrees right and put a long burst into another Zero from 20 degrees' deflection, then I turned 20 degrees left to observe the results.

"The first 2 Zeros were burning all around the cockpit, and the third one was trailing a long column of smoke. Three Zeros splitessed down on me and shot up my left engine and wing while I was running for home. I feathered the left engine and landed at home field safely."

The enemy didn't return in force until March 28, when a large plot was picked up on radar, and 16 P-40s of the 8th Squadron and 15 P-38s of the 9th Squadron went up to meet the bombers and fighters over Oro Bay. The Japanese paid with 11 fighters and 2 dive bombers, but they managed to demolish a new wharf and sink 2 small ships. One P-40 failed to return.

During this period Allied ground forces had been moving up the coast of New Guinea. On March 31 troops landed at the mouth of the Waria River and at Dona. On April 3 other elements of the 162nd Combat Team of the U. S. 41st Infantry Division went ashore at Morobe Harbor. The infantrymen moved inland swiftly and ascertained that the enemy was not present within 10 miles northwest of Morobe. This not only provided Allied aircraft with another emergency landing strip at Dona, but put American troops within 75 miles of Salamaua.

Intelligence sources reported that the Japanese were once more building up their air strength in the area, although most of their aerial operations were being utilized in air attacks in the Solomons at this time. However, the enemy returned to Oro Bay on April

11 with a formation of 15 Val dive bombers heavily escorted by fighters.

Among those intercepting that day were P-38s of the 80th Fighter Squadron, which had just returned to Port Moresby with their new twin-engine aircraft. Leading the flight of 4 was veteran Captain Danny Roberts. Eighteen to 20 dive bombers were sighted, and as they made a wide circle and went into a string formation and headed for shipping off Oro Bay, Roberts thought, "This is our meat." Down they went after them.

"My first burst at about 17,000 feet caught a bomber, which lost pieces as my wingman and I passed very close on our way over," stated Roberts. "No. 3 man in the flight, Lieutenant Mathers, pulled out to the side and headed for one plane. The second half of the formation seemed to split wide open and they made no attack; however the first half had apparently scored a hit on one of the ships, as it was smoking badly. At this point 3 enemy planes flew under me, and a sharp turn downward set me in a position for a good burst, which was fired at about 5,500 feet. A part of his right wing was lost and he immediately made a violent turn, apparently out of control, and headed for the sea, smoking as he went. The first plane was seen to strike the sea, and my No. 3 man passed under me with dive bombers in front of him and fighters on his tail. A dive toward the water to help him was in order, but he had destroyed the plane in front of him. It burst into flame and hit the water burning, and he 'sold out' for land, running from the enemy."

The 49th Group was up and proceeded to rip the enemy formations. Eleven fighters and 3 of the Val dive bombers fell before their guns. One of the more determined pilots was Lieutenant Theron Price. His flight saw some 10 to 15 Zeros at about 15,000 feet over Oro Bay and attacked. As they approached the enemy aircraft, a Zero dived on 2 of the P-38s. Price was out of range but fired to scare the enemy away. It worked, and as the Zero pulled up, Price fired again without effect. Price then pulled up and fired at the other Zero. As he held his trigger button down and closed, the enemy went up in flames.

Price looked to his rear just in time to see 3 other Zeros on his tail with the guns of 1 twinkling at him. Several shots ripped into his Lightning and 1 exploded in the cockpit. Pieces of shrapnel hit his face and left arm. Wounded, Price dove down through the clouds, leaving the enemy behind him.

As he pulled out at 7,000 feet he saw a Zero go into the bay; the plane was later confirmed as the 1 he had hit. He then tacked onto another P-38, which assisted him back to base.

Impervious of his losses, the enemy continued to throw his aerial forces against Allied targets in New Guinea. Port Moresby was attacked for the 106th time on April 12 when the Japanese sent over an aerial armada of 45 bombers escorted by 60 fighters.

The P-38s of the 39th Fighter Squadron took on the bombers head-on, and in their first 2 passes managed to disorganize the formation. Then P-39s of the 40th and 41st squadrons got in a wild dogfight with the fighters. The 9th Squadron of the 49th Group also hit the bombers over the target, and finally the P-40s of the 8th Squadron caught the bombers on their way home over Cape Ward Hunt. In all, a total of 17 bombers and 10 fighters were downed by the defenders.

The top scorer for the day was Lieutenant Grover E. Fanning of the 9th Fighter Squadron, who got a bomber and then had to play tag with a Japanese fighter before he got him and the bomber that he was trying to protect.

"I saw 2 formations of 18 bombers with lots of Oscars above the formations," Fanning related in his report. "We made our pass and came back from the other side for another one. This was a close pass, and I shot into the right engine of 1 Betty bomber, and as it dove away in a left turn it was smoking. I peeled away to the right and Lieutenant Alger to the left because the fighters were coming down on us. After outrunning the fighters I turned back toward the bombers and saw 1 going down in flames. I came back at the bomber formation from the right. I made a quarter head-on pass and attacked the front of 1 bomber formation. One bomber dove out of formation.

"Again I had to dive away from fighters. They were coming down mostly in threes. I came back at the bomber that had dived out of formation and made a diving pass as an Oscar was covering it. The bomber began to smoke. I believe I got the tail gunner because I passed right behind the tail and there was no fire this time. I chased the bomber back over the mountains, heading approximately 15 degrees. I caught up with the 2 after passing over the range. I had trouble getting in a position for a pass because of the Oscar. Finally he got close to the bomber, and I made a quarter tail pass. The Oscar moved to a position over the nose of the bomber. When I started firing, the bomber started a diving left turn. The Oscar went straight up, whipped over, and went straight down. I managed to avoid going under him.

"I fired a good burst into the bomber as it started to dive away again. The bomber burst into flames along the right side of the fuselage at the wing roots. The Oscar was ahead of the bomber and above. He went up again, and I caught him at the top of his stall. I fired, apparently right into the nose and cockpit of the plane. The Oscar fell off out of control and started smoking from both sides. It went into the low overcast, out of control, diving too low to the ground to pull out."

The Japanese came back using a storm front as cover to attack Milne Bay on the fourteenth. This mission was largely ineffective due to clouds. Interception was made by 2 flights of P-38s from the 9th Fighter Squadron, and 2 were downed for the loss of a single Lightning, which crashed upon its landing attempt.

Following this raid the fighter pilots enjoyed a month of respite. Combat air patrols were maintained, but the enemy did not put in an appearance. This gave the hard-pressed maintenance men of the 5th Fighter Command a chance to repair and overhaul their aircraft, which had performed so well. Try as he might, General Kenney had been unable to bring in new aircraft for his units in anything like the desired quantity. The European and especially the Mediterranean theaters held priority over the battered forces of the Pacific in all respects at that time.

The 49th Fighter Group at Dobodura took the opportunity to improve its camp conditions, but rain and wind storms caused it more trouble than the bombing raids of the Japanese. Dry rot, mold, and insects continued to take their toll, although improvement in sanitary conditions did cut the malaria rate down from the extreme. At long last the 49th said good-bye to its first group of personnel to leave for the United States after a year of combat. Theirs had been a job well done.

On the night of May 13 the Japanese paid a visit to the men of the 49th at Dobodura. Five enemy bombers made a pass over the field and dropped their bombs, but on the whole the mission was quite ineffective, as most of the explosives came down in fields a mile or more from the base. Two Japanese bombers dropped their loads on Port Moresby without effect.

However, the enemy came back in force the following day. Twenty bombers and 25 fighters made up the striking force that arrived over Oro Bay that afternoon. The 49th Group was up in force, with all 3 squadrons represented.

Lieutenant Lawrence N. Succop was an element leader in 1 P-40 flight of the 7th Squadron. Succop took his element in to attack the bombers, gave 1 a burst, and pulled up over the formation. One bomber left the formation, so Succop closed in on its tail and opened fire. Apparently the tail gunner was killed, as his fire was not returned. Another burst knocked parts off the tail, and as Succop's slugs hit forward to the aircraft's left engine, it burst into flames. Succop nearly overran the aircraft and was forced to break violently to keep from hitting the bomber. Just as he broke underneath the enemy aircraft, it exploded, completely enveloping the P-40 in oil. Using his wingman as a guide, Succop returned to base.

Ten of the enemy bombers and 9 fighters were downed for the loss of a single P-38, and its pilot who was last seen swimming in shark-infested waters.

The fighters did not see action again until May 21, when the P-38s of the 80th Fighter Squadron took off to act as top cover for C-47s en route to Wau. Immediately after takeoff the 12 Lightnings were ordered to intercept enemy aircraft over Salamaua. One P-38 was forced to abort the mission, but the remaining 11 were flying below a broken overcast at 23,000 feet when 20 Hamps, Zekes, and Oscars were sighted slightly above and to the left of the formation. Belly tanks were dropped and the attack was made by turning into the enemy.

The Japanese fighters were in no definite formation but in groups of 3 at various altitudes. This made it impossible for the Lightnings to maintain formation, so attacks were made by elements. Captain Ed Cragg made the first pass on a Hamp-type aircraft, and his first burst took more than half the fighter's wing off. It went down in an uncontrollable spin.

During a pass at another Hamp, Captain Cragg came within 20 feet of the enemy and saw his tracers enter the cockpit. In this head-on encounter, Captain Cragg received slugs in the nose and wings of his own aircraft. This caused the left engine to go out and caused him to break off his attack on the Hamp. At the time he was hit a Zeke was attacking Captain Cragg from the rear, so Cragg dived toward Wau without attempting to feather the prop. The Zeke, unaware that he was chasing a crippled plane, finally gave up the chase. Cragg then feathered the prop and made a landing at Seven-Mile Airdrome.

Lieutenant Cy Homer almost met with disaster in a head-on pass at a formation of 3 Zekes. Homer saw his bullets tear into the leader's aircraft, but had to dump the yoke over sharply to barely pass below the onrushing Zeke. Undoubtedly, the leader had tried to ram him.

Six of the Japanese fighters were downed by the men of the 80th in that fight, and all P-38s returned safely.

Allied strategy for the summer of 1943 in the South and Southwest Pacific set forth several targets. One of these was Rendova in the central Solomons, while in the New Guinea sector the moves called for the invasion of Woodlark and Kiriwina islands, near the south coast of New Guinea and of Nassau Bay, some 50 miles up the New Guinea coast from Morobe Harbor. This would set Allied forces in position for the invasion of Lae, as it had been decided that the enemy base at Salamaua would be bypassed.

Australian troops inland in New Guinea would move toward the coast from Wau, and an airfield at Bena Bena some 100 miles northwest of Lae would be built up and serve as a supply base and troop embarkation point for the Australians, as Wau had been in the past.

The fighters continued to fly escort for the bombers and transports as buildups for the coming moves were assembled. On June 21 the P-38s of the 80th Fighter Squadron had been flying top cover for B-25s for a supply drop at Guadagasal Ridge when they were called for an interception over Lae and Salamaua. On arrival the Lightning pilots spotted several flights of enemy aircraft in the area.

Interception was made over Salamaua against some determined opposition. Captain George S. Welch dropped tanks and got a shot at a Zeke but had to break off when he discovered that his fuel was not transferring properly.

He proceeded to Lae, where he sighted 8 Zekes doing aerobatics over the field at 10,000 feet. Immediately he dove on them and set a Zeke on fire from a head-on pass. Welch then pulled up through a cloud formation and on breaking out sighted another Zeke only 100 feet ahead. Apparently he wasn't sighted, for as the enemy craft crossed his nose from 90 degrees he raked the plane from stem to stern. One wing fell off and it tumbled to the ground.

The formation of 11 P-38s downed 13 of the enemy fighters in the brief encounter.

Ground forces went ashore on Kiriwina and Woodlark on June 30 without enemy opposition. Engineers were landed a few days later, and airstrip construction got under way. The landing on Nassau Bay had been made on June 26 against enemy opposition, but Allied air cover was held up for several days immediately thereafter by bad weather. However, by June 30 the Fifth Air Force Command was able to send bombers and fighters out to their support.

The fight over Nassau Bay came as more or less of an accident on July 3 when P-40s of the 7th Fighter Squadron were returning from escorting C-47s on a supply drop to Mubo. On return an enemy formation of 6 to 8 bombers escorted by fighters was sighted bombing the coast between Salamaua and Nassau Bay. Four of the fighters and 1 of the bombers were shot down by the P-40 pilots, who were able to celebrate their "Fourth of July" a day early.

The P-39s of the 36th Fighter Squadron tangled with a bevy of Zekes and Oscars in the vicinity of Nassau Bay and Salamaua on July 11 and downed 6 of them. The veteran Airacobra pilots continued to show the enemy that at the proper altitude and using the proper tactics they were more than a match for him.

While the Japanese continued to press their attacks against the Salamaua area of New Guinea, Fifth Air Force bombers continued to concentrate their operations against Japanese bases at Lae. American ground troops pushing in from the coast linked up with Australians in the vicinity of Mubo by the thirteenth of July, and by the twentieth of July American troops were within 5 miles of Salamaua.

The 39th and 80th fighter squadrons escorted B-25s on a strike against the enemy base at Bogadjim on the morning of July 21, and on their return both squadrons were heavily engaged by enemy fighters. In a wild and woolly air battle that covered a wide area, 22 enemy fighters were shot down. One unusual occurrence was the first appearance over New Guinea of the new inline engine Tony fighter. Initial speculation on the part of the pilots created a rumor that the Japanese were flying Messerschmitt 109 fighters imported from Germany. Of course, this proved to be completely false.

The high scorer for the day was a member of the 80th Squadron, who was to become one of the leading aces of the Fifth Air

1. Typical of the obsolete equipment with which the Philippine Air Force was equipped was the Martin B-10 bomber shown here in U.S. Air Corps markings. (USAF)

2. A P-40 in the new wartime markings of the AAF at the start of hostilities in the Philippines. The red circle in the center of the insignia caused confusion with the red circle of the Japanese insignia. (USAF)

3. The 34th Pursuit Squadron was equipped with Seversky P-35s, which were obsolete and in dire need of engine and machine-gun replacements. (USAF)

4. The Japanese Zero caught the American pilots by surprise with its excellent maneuverability and rate of climb. (USAF)

5. The 19th Bomb Group was equipped with the Boeing B-17D. This model of the Flying Fortress possessed neither the power turrets nor the tail guns of the later models. (The Boeing Company)

6. The pride of the old Army Air Corps had been the Boeing P-26A "Peashooter" during the mid-1930s. By 1941 it was grossly obsolete for use by the Philippine Air Force. (USAF)

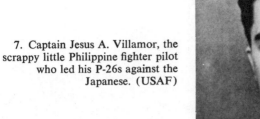

7. Captain Jesus A. Villamor, the scrappy little Philippine fighter pilot who led his P-26s against the Japanese. (USAF)

8. Lieutenant Boyd D. "Buzz" Wagner, first AAF ace of World War II, carried the air war to the enemy with great tenacity. (USAF)

9. Captain Villamor was forced to utilize a Curtiss O-1 (similar to one illustrated here) for observation in the final days before the fall of the Philippines.

10. An export version of the Curtiss Hawk 75 fighter. This aircraft type formed the nucleus of the obsolete Dutch fighter force in Java. (via Christie)

11. The Mitsubishi G3M "Nell" bomber had been used over China before the United States ever became involved in the war. The "Nell" saw much service early in the war but was so outclassed by Allied fighters that by 1943 it had been relegated to support duties. (Koku Fan)

12. The Nakajima Type 97 "Nate" fighters were no match for the P-40s over Java. (Aireview)

13. Lieutenant Andy Reynolds scored his early air victories in the skies over Java and went on to become one of the first aces of the Fifth Air Force. (USAF)

14. The Brewster "Buffalo," shown here in Royal Air Force markings, saw service against the Japanese in Southeast Asia and with the Dutch on Java, but was no match for the Japanese Zero. (National Archives)

15. The AAF's attempt to utilize the Douglas A-24 early in the war met with little success. As the Navy SBD, the aircraft became famous. (USAF)

16. Lieutenant William A. Levitan of the 9th Fighter Squadron at Darwin, Australia, in 1942. This was one of the first of many "jungle strips" for the 49th Group. (Watkins)

17. Boeing B-17s fly over Henderson Field on their way to attack Japanese targets while Marine Corps Grumman F4F fighters are readied for another mission. (USMC)

18. The P-39 was a real workhorse in the Solomon Islands campaign. Its cannon and machine guns in the nose made it a excellent strafing platform. (USAF)

19. The majority of the air-to-air fighting over the Solomons in the battle for Guadalcanal was carried out by the Marine Corps F4F Wildcats shown here at Henderson Field. (USMC)

20. The AAF on Guadalcanal got a real shot in the arm with the arrival of the 339th Fighter Squadron with its P-38s. (USAF)

21. The arrival of Boeing B-17s equipped with power turrets and the new tail gun installation, as illustrated here, vastly improved the Fortresses' defense against the Japanese Zeros. (USAF)

22. Pioneer night fighter is this P-70 of the 6th Night Fighter Squadron. The converted Douglas A-20 equipped with early radar had little success at night interception.

23. Captain Thomas G. Lanphier is decorated for his role in the Yamamoto mission. (USAF)

24. Lieutenant Murray J. Shubin with *Oriole*, the P-38 in which he shot down 5 Japanese Zeros over Guadalcanal. (USAF)

25. A P-38 coming in after a mission to land on a coral airstrip. Aviation engineers and Navy Seabees worked wonders in producing runways from the native coral in the Pacific. (USAF)

26. A Bell P-39Q taxies out for a mission. Note the .50-caliber machine gun mounted under each wing on this version of the Airacobra. (USAF)

27. *Princess Pat II* was a P-40 of the Thirteenth Air Force flying from Munda Field on New Georgia Island. (USAF)

28. The shark's teeth paint job on this 8th Fighter Group P-39 presented a much greater menace on the ground than this aircraft presented in the air. (80th Fighter Squadron Association)

29. Captain John Landers of the 49th Fighter Group and his P-40 at Port Moresby. (McDowell)

30. The last of the Curtiss P-40s to see action was the P-40N shown here, still with the familiar white tail. (Wox)

31. The 8-gun installation in the nose of the B-25 bombers made its debut in the Battle of the Bismarck Sea. (USAF)

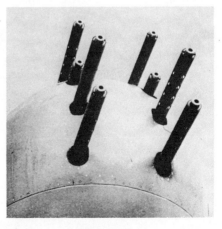

32. A B-25 Mitchell pulls up after scoring a bomb hit on a Japanese cargo vessel. (USAF)

33. Douglas A-20s taxi out for takeoff from New Guinea base. These aircraft were very good at low-level bombing and strafing. (Tansing)

34. The quiet-spoken ministerial student, Major Danny Roberts, who became one of the top aces of the Fifth Air Force. (80th Fighter Squadron Association)

35. P-38 with shark's teeth in a jungle setting. Note the steel mat hardstand. (80th Fighter Squadron Association)

36. Pumping fuel into the drop tanks of a P-38 from 55-gallon drums. The ground crews in the Southwest Pacific were often without the luxury of a gasoline truck. (USAF)

37. The Nakamima Ki. 43 or "Oscar" fighter saw much service over New Guinea with the Japanese Army Air Force. (64th Association via Izawa)

Force, Lieutenant Jay T. Robbins. In an exceptional exhibition of shooting, Lieutenant Robbins downed 3 Zekes and got another probable.

The 39th Squadron tangled with the Tonys again 2 days later in the Lae area and downed at least 5 of them. The same day the 80th Squadron encountered 20 Zekes and Tonys when they provided top cover to heavy bombers on a mission to Bogadjim. The bombers had just completed their run when the Japanese fighters were sighted flying north at 14,000 feet.

The P-38s had an altitude advantage, so they made the most of it. Major Ed Cragg closed in on a Tony at a speed of 500 mph and set it on fire with a short burst. He then latched onto the tail of a Zeke, which disintegrated after a large explosion, and pieces of the plane glanced off Cragg's P-38.

At this time Major Cragg sighted a P-38 with its left engine on fire. The Lightning was climbing for altitude, and Major Cragg and Lieutenant Ladd remained with him for protection against enemy fighters still in the area. However, the P-38 could not maintain altitude and gradually descended in a turn toward a small river 10 miles west of the mouth of the Nuru River. At this point the Lightning crashed and exploded on impact.

Three flights of P-38s from the 9th Fighter Squadron were on patrol over Lae on the afternoon of July 26, 1943, and after encountering no opposition over the area they went down over Markham Valley just back of Lae flying at 16,000 feet.

On the way, enemy aircraft were called out at the 12 o'clock position. There were 20 fighters: 10 Tonys and 10 Zeros. Lieutenant Dick Bong took a quick shot at a Tony, missed, dove out, and then shot at a Zeke head-on, and it burst into flames.

Bong then positioned himself above and behind a Tony and gave him a squirt of lead which knocked pieces off the fuselage. A long burst set another Tony on fire. Then a Zeke came in head-on. Bong gave him a long burst, which knocked off the Zeke's canopy and shot its engine to pieces.

Four victories had been scored by the ace.

Captain James A. Watkins really found the new Tonys to his liking and downed 4 of them in the combat.

Bong and Watkins were back in action two days later, when they helped provide escort for B-25s on a mission to Rein Bay, New Guinea. The action is described by Captain Watkins: "We were at 6,000 feet when we sighted 12 to 18 enemy fighters 3,000 feet above us off Cape Raoult at 0815 hours. We dropped belly tanks, and the flight turned 90 degrees into the attack. I fired at the attacking leader and missed. I climbed to 8,000 feet out to sea and made a head-on pass at 1 of 2 Oscars attacking Lieutenant Bong. This plane burst into flames about 75 to 100 yards in front of me.

"I turned to find Lieutenant Bong and made a head-on attack on 1 of 3 Oscars coming down on me. This plane burst into flames and pieces barely missed me as he passed under. The other 2 didn't bother me.

"I went back toward the fight in a steep dive. At 4,000 feet I leveled out to meet a head-on attack of 2 Oscars. Neither one would meet me. The lead ship of the attackers pulled straight up into a stall at about 6,000 feet. I fired a long, 2- or 3-second burst into him while he was handing on his prop and he went straight into the sea, exploding as he hit. I got in several more short bursts at others but was chased off."

Lieutenant Bong went into a dive and got away from his attackers. After making several unsuccessful passes at other enemy fighters, he spotted one of the B-25s under attack from 2 Oscars. Diving down, he put a long burst into one, which slid off on a wing and crashed into Rein Bay. He was then attacked by 2 Oscars from the rear but he pushed throttles to the firewall and outran them.

On August 2 16 P-38s of the 9th Squadron, while on an escort mission with B-25s to Bogadjim and Heldsback Harbor, were intercepted by 12 Oscars flying in a loose formation. The P-38s were at various altitudes, so some dove and some rose to meet the enemy.

Captain Watkins made a head-on pass at a lone Oscar, which

was trying to climb out of the fight. Pieces flew off the Oscar's canopy and wing, and it went straight into the water.

Another head-on pass at an Oscar that was trying to make a pass at the bombers started it smoking, and it crashed into the water.

Captain Watkins then dove down just level with the water to chase another Oscar. A long burst in the rear was continued as the enemy attempted a turn to the right. When the Oscar reached about 300 feet, it fell off and hit the water and cartwheeled end over end.

Watkins had scored 10 times in a week, bringing his score to 11 victories. This was only 5 behind Lieutenant Dick Bong, who had gone on leave the day before and missed the action of August 2.

For many months the veteran pilots of the 49th, 8th, and 35th fighter groups had held the line in New Guinea as well as provided escort for all the bomber and transport missions in the theater. At long last reinforcements had arrived, and they would soon be supplemented as the ground forces in New Guinea readied themselves for the push onto Lae and Finschhafen.

VIII

LAE AND FINSCHHAFEN

On June 17, 1943, Major George W. Prentice, a veteran pilot of the New Guinea actions, took command of the original cadre of the new 475th Fighter Group at Amberly Field outside Brisbane, Australia. This Fifth Air Force organization, composed of the 431st, 432nd, and 433rd fighter squadrons, would be the only AAF fighter group in the Pacific to be formed completely outside the United States.

Major Prentice, along with his veteran staff and squadron commanders, put the newly arrived pilots from the United States into an intensive training program as quickly as possible. The group was fully equipped with new P-38s, which proved to add greatly to the morale of the men. Both new and old hands went all out to ready themselves for the combat road that lay ahead.

Also arriving in Australia in June of 1943 to reinforce the Fifth Air Force was the 348th Fighter Group, under the command of Lieutenant Colonel Neel E. Kearby. This P-47 Thunderbolt unit had originally been destined for the European Theater, but at the last minute it had been diverted to the Southwest Pacific.

Some of the ground echelon were sent on to Port Moresby to prepare for the arrival of the air echelon. As swiftly as their P-47s could be unloaded and assembled, the pilots began to put the aircraft through test flights. On July 12, the first of the 348th's squadrons flew up to Port Moresby, and by the twentieth of the month all 3 squadrons—the 340th, 341st, and 342nd—were on their initial combat base.

In preparation for the offensive against Lae and Salamaua, a new airfield was built at Tsili Tsili on the Watut River some 50 miles to the west of Lae. Aviation engineers with their dirt-moving equipment were flown in by C-47s, and construction began on 2 runways. By the end of July 1943, an Australian infantry battalion to guard the approaches to the new base was in position, and anti-aircraft defenses were set up.

Through extensive use of camouflage and devious routing of the C-47s it was possible to keep the existence of the airfield from the Japanese until August 15. A formation of transports bringing up the ground echelon of the first fighter squadron to be based at Tsili Tsili was just arriving when a formation of 12 Japanese Lily bombers escorted by fighters roared in through the mountain passes.

Luckily, only a single C-47 was lost to the enemy before escorting P-39s from the 40th and 41st fighter squadrons tore into the enemy. Four P-39s went down, but not before 11 of the bombers and 3 of the Oscar escorts had been downed.

The following day the Japanese returned to Tsili Tsili but were intercepted by P-38s from the 431st Squadron of the 475th Group and P-47s from the 348th Group. Oscars and Zekes dropped down on the P-38s from above, but the Lightning pilots dove away, and using mutual support tactics, came back up in pairs and shot 10 fighters and 2 bombers from the sky with no losses of their own.

The P-47 pilots scored their initial victories also by shooting down 2 of the fighter planes.

During the period in which the airfield was being constructed at Tsili Tsili, the enemy airfield at Wewak, with its satellite bases at But, Dagua, and Boram, were largely ignored by the AAF bombers. During this time the Japanese continuously built up their air strength at these bases. By mid-August the American base at Tsili Tsili was able to take care of fighter aircraft in such numbers that the bombers could hit Wewak in strength and be under a large escorting umbrella all the way.

A night bombardment mission on August 16 did some damage in the Wewak area, but the next day 6 squadrons of P-38s took 5 squadrons of B-25s to the area. Strangely, there was no fighter interception, and the B-25s did a magnificent job strafing the rows of enemy aircraft while they were simultaneously releasing 23-pound parafrag bombs. Well over 100 enemy planes were either destroyed or damaged in the devastating attack.

On the eighteenth, Wewak was the target once more, and B-24s and B-25s of the 5th Bomber Command were up in force escorted by the P-38s. Weather proved to be a problem for the heavies, but the B-25s went in on the deck strafing and dropping their parafrags with excellent results. Savage fighter attacks opposed the mission, and the pilots of the 475th Fighter Group found themselves in the middle of a big fight.

In his first big air battle that morning was a tenacious young fighter pilot whose name would be known far and wide over the Pacific Theater before the end of the war. Lieutenant Thomas B. McGuire, Jr., gave the Japanese his first taste of what they could expect from him that day.

"As part of escort for B-25s, I was leading the last flight of our squadron over Wewak as close cover. Our flight consisted of 3 ships, one man having had to return to base.

"At 8,000 feet and at 0945 hours, Zeros started attacking us. One made a pass from 45 degrees at my flight, and I turned the flight into him. Then as he went by I turned again and fired 2 long bursts. I saw him burst into flames and head down. Lieutenant Sieber, my No. 3 man, saw him crash.

"Lieutenant Lent, my No. 2 man, called in there was a Zero on his tail. I turned to the left and got several shots at the Zero, chasing it toward Dagua Field. I saw hits around the cockpit, Lieutenant Lent saw him burning and crash.

"My No. 3 man had lost the formation at that time. We made a head-on pass at a Zeke, which held a collision course. As I went under the Zeke, his left wing scraped my left wing. I had shot a couple of good bursts but observed no results. Lieutenant Lent and I closed up and chased a Zeke down to 1,000 feet above the water near Dagua Airdrome. After several shots I started back upstairs. Lieutenant Lent says he saw Lieutenant Lutton (who had joined us) shoot it down into the water in flames.

"Light and heavy flak was intense over most of the Wewak area. I saw another Zero going down in flames at the same time, chased by Lieutenant Czarnecki. We made a pass at a Zeke, which pulled up, and Lieutenant Lent shot pieces off of it—it then exploded.

"We started for home escorting 3 B-25s. About 10 minutes out of Wewak a Tony attacked the bombers. In the start of his pass we headed him off, and I got 2 or 3 good bursts at him. The Tony started down smoking, and the B-25s saw him crash. The Tony was camouflaged bright green, yellow, and brown. He appeared very fast."

Fifteen enemy fighters were polished off by the 475th pilots for the loss of 2 of their own.

The P-38 pilots got a day off on the nineteenth, but the following day they escorted the bombers back to Wewak and ran into a whole bevy of Zeke and Tony fighters. Captain George Welch of the 80th Fighter Squadron made short work of 3 of the Tonys as they came in to attack the B-24s, one of which was rammed by an enemy fighter. Welch downed his Tonys one after the other, and all the Tonys crashed right around Wewak.

Welch then had a Tony dive on him from above and behind at about 22,000 feet. The enemy pilot latched onto the tail of the Lightning, and Welch tried to lose him by outrunning him, but the Tony held on. By climbing at 250 mph, Welch was able to lose him.

August 21 found the B-25s returning to Wewak and its satellite bases to finish up their job. In sheer desperation, the Japanese threw everything they had at them. The escorting P-38s were engaged in a massive air battle. Thirty-five fighters were shot down by the Lightning pilots in the aerial encounter.

F/O Edwin L. DeGraffenreid engaged the enemy for the first time that day and met with great success. Quickly he flamed 2 enemy fighters and then shot the wing off a third. When he broke off the combat he found himself all alone, so he set sail for home. A Zeke came down on him from above and scored hits on the tail, canopy, and engine of the P-38 before DeGraffenreid was able to find safety in a cloud. Limping along, he managed to make it back to Port Moresby, where he crash-landed on the beach.

By the end of August the enemy airfields in the Wewak area were in shambles. The planes that had not been destroyed on the ground had been shot down from the sky. The decimation of the Japanese air forces in the area set up the stage for the next move by Allied ground forces.

Allied forces were assembled late in August for the seaborne amphibious assault on Lae and for the airdrop at Nadzab. To protect the beachhead from enemy air bombardment, the U.S. destroyer *Reid* took up station some 45 miles southeast of Finschhafen as a radar warning station. Fifth Air Force bombers and fighters continued to apply pressure on the Japanese air bases at Wewak, Madang, and Cape Gloucester on the island of New Britain.

As the amphibious force assembled off Buna, the fighters of the 5th Fighter Command continued to take the war to the enemy in the air. On September 2, fighters of the 80th and 39th fighter squadrons went with the B-25s to Wewak to further deplete forces there. As the P-38s of the 80th Squadron came in over the target, they received a call from the P-38s of the 39th Squadron that they were in a battle with enemy fighters.

Captain George Welch led his Lightnings down to the attack and immediately made a pass on a Zeke without results. A stern attack on 2 Zekes flying in a close formation resulted in hits on both of them. The Zeke on his right rolled off, and when the Zeke on the left also rolled in that direction, the 2 collided and went down together.

A 90-degree deflection shot sent another Zeke spinning down in flames. For good measure Welch latched onto a Dinah twin-engine bomber on its way home, put a long burst into the cockpit and watched it roll off and crash into the side of a mountain.

While these units were engaged over Wewak, P-38s of the 49th Fighter Group were taking bombers to Cape Gloucester on the western tip of the island of New Britain. The B-17s had difficulty in dropping their bombs and were intercepted by twin-engine Kawasaki Ki-45 "Nick" fighters.

Captain Gerald R. Johnson turned to attack one of the fighters that was finishing a pass at one of the Flying Forts and sent the fighter down streaming smoke. He then teamed up with Lieutenant Theron D. Price to get after another of the twin-engine craft. Price hit it from astern and then Johnson pulled in to point-blank range, fired, and had to pull up to keep from overrunning the aircraft. Another burst from Lieutenant Price at 1,000 feet over the water put the enemy fighter in the trees just off the beach.

On the morning of September 4 the largest Allied amphibious force yet assembled in the Southwest Pacific moved in off Lae. After a bombardment by 5 U.S. destroyers, the infantrymen, both American and Australian, hit the beach at approximately 6:30 A.M. The landing area was well covered overhead by the fighter planes of the 5th Fighter Command.

A few enemy bombers attempted to get through to the task force and transports shortly after the initial landing but were chased off by the aerial umbrella that constantly orbited over the beaches. While landing craft shuttled back and forth carrying men and supplies, another force of 5th Fighter Command aircraft escorted medium bombers to attack the Japanese base at Cape Gloucester. The Mitchell bombers swept in first, and their attack was followed a few minutes later by Martin B-26s. Numerous fires were started, but the Japanese put no opposition in the air over the target. On the route home the B-25s went down and strafed the airfield at Finschhafen.

The destroyer *Reid,* which was acting as radar warning station off Finschhafen, alerted the combat air patrols early in the afternoon of a large formation of enemy aircraft coming in from the north. When the Japanese formation arrived the P-38s were there to greet it.

Lieutenant Jay T. Robbins had shot the wing off a Zeke when another 20 enemy fighters dived on him in 2s, 3s, and 4s. A frantic call of warning and for assistance went unheard by his fellow pilots due to radio failure.

"One Zeke came past me," stated Robbins, "and as I turned into him I had a good deflection shot as he went straight up. I let him have a very short burst right under the belly. He immediately blew up and went into flames.

"I did a wing-over to the right, and one of the other Zekes was slightly below, and I fell off on his tail. Other Zekes were in perfect formation. The enemy made a quick turn and I had a large deflection shot. The deflection shot was perfect. I got beautiful hits all over his plane. Entire right wing tip flew off and numerous hits in the cockpit. He went into a spin and into the sea.

"Enemy flight above then sent down 4. I was calling everyone for help, as they were gradually driving me down and out to sea. As I turned into this flight I got another perfect belly shot. I got good hits and he fell off on 1 wing. With a good slow deflection shot I put hits into him and his left wing and rudder came off in large chunks. I fired another 10-to-12-second burst before he started going straight down. I followed until I knew I'd have to pull out or dive in myself. He must have been less than 700 feet and going straight down. I did pull out above water and started a slow climb toward home.

"I was jumped again at 6,000 feet or thereabouts and made a pass at a Hamp. I noticed hits but couldn't see results. At this time I was 60 to 70 miles out to sea northeast of Salamaua. Last 2 passes I had made I fired only 6 or 8 rounds. I got hits on the next pass and saw pieces flying off a Zeke but had to dive away so saw no results. I was out of ammunition and was diving and running. Two Tonys and 1 Zeke were behind me and slightly above. I was headed toward Dobodura. I had been running with engines all over for over 45 minutes. They were shooting to my left and slightly above. I got a few holes in wing and tail. I leveled out at 200 feet and finally left Tonys. They would fire and I'd dip lower. I fired all my cannon and all my .50s. I started to pull up and bail out then I noticed I was gaining."

Robbins was credited with 4 Zekes destroyed and two probables in this combat.

The Japanese had hits on 2 Navy LSTs, but they paid heavily, with loss of 15 of their fighters and 4 of their bombers. The enemy put in no further aerial appearances that day.

The following day the second phase of the 2-pronged drive against the Japanese in the Lae area was launched. American paratroopers and Australian supporting forces jumped from C-47s onto the kunai grass plains of Nadzab. Some 1,600 men were dropped in a beautifully executed and unopposed landing. B-17s joined in with the transports in the drop of supplies to the men on the ground. By noon all of the transports were back safely at Port Moresby. The enemy made no attempt to tangle with the fighter escort that hovered high above the drop area. By late that afternoon the grass had been burned for the initial strip, and the next day the first transports began to arrive.

Within a week 2 runways had been built at Nadzab, and by the fourteenth of the month the base could boast 2 6,000-foot runways capable of handling 36 C-47s simultaneously.

The ground troops made good progress in their drive on Lae and Salamaua. American and Australian troops were in possession of the airfield at Salamaua by September 11, and Australian forces moved in to take over Lae on September 16.

Enemy air opposition during this time was quite sporadic. There were some attempts to get to shipping in Morobe Harbor, but this largely met with no success. The P-38s of the 475th

Fighter Group and from the 80th Fighter Squadron met a formation of bombers and fighters over the harbor on the morning of September 13 and downed 9 of the fighters and 2 of the bombers before the enemy could escape.

The rapid conquest of Lae and Salamaua set the stage for another jump forward. The date of the invasion of Finschhafen was moved up to September 22. Heavy and medium bombers with heavy escort once more set out to neutralize Japanese air bases at Wewak, Cape Gloucester, and Gasmata.

P-38s of the 80th Squadron took the heavies to Wewak on September 15 and were intercepted by 30 to 40 enemy fighter planes. The combat was joined at 12,000 feet over the bay near Boram Airstrip. The Lightnings downed 7 of the fighters for the loss of a single plane of their own. The pilot of the missing aircraft bailed out and returned to base after an exhaustive 11-day hike in the jungle.

While the invasion force assembled off the coast of Lae, the fighters maintained constant vigil. Sixteen P-40s of the 8th Fighter Squadron were returning to their base at Dobodura when 12 Betty bombers accompanied by fighters were sighted in the Huon Gulf area.

Lieutenant John D. Hanson fought his way through the escort to close on the formation of Betty bombers in the waning light of late dusk. Lieutenant Roger Grant took a hit from the tail gunner of one of the bombers as he and Hanson closed on them, and he was forced to break off the combat. Hanson made several beam attacks from side to side, concentrating on the bomber on the left side of the formation until it went down streaming smoke and flames. Hanson continued to make beam attacks until he put a long burst into the cockpit of a second Betty, which went into a shallow dive and never pulled out.

Hanson pulled up, looked around, and spotted a single fighter some 1,000 feet above, which he assumed to be Lieutenant Grant. On pulling alongside he found it to be a Zeke. Immediately he peeled off and dove down into the twilight.

The skies were filled with aircraft before dawn on the morning of September 22. Bombers headed out to hit airfields at Cape Gloucester and to bomb and strafe enemy installations at Finschhafen before the troops landed. At 4:45 A.M. the invasion craft followed the naval and aerial bombardment to the beachhead. Within 7 hours some 5,300 troops and hundreds of tons of supplies had been landed.

The invasion convoy moved out and started back for Buna shortly before noon. Up until this time there had been no aerial interference by the Japanese, and all had gone off without a hitch. The U. S. Destroyer *Reid*, which was continuing its role as air warning station, reported a large formation of incoming enemy aircraft just after noon. The Japanese could not have picked a more inopportune time for themselves nor a more opportune time for the combat air patrol.

Three fighter squadrons were in the air over the invasion beaches waiting for their relief when the call came in that the enemy was on the way. These units still had sufficient fuel to stay for another hour or so, and they were joined shortly by 2 more squadrons, making 5 fighter outfits in the area when the Japanese arrived.

The *Reid* plotted the enemy formation all the way in for the fighter pilots. The 432nd Fighter Squadron had 4 flights circling at 10,000 to 12,000 feet until the fighter control ship called, "Bandits in sight from 6,000 feet on down."

The P-38s dove to 5,000 feet, where they saw 8 to 10 Betty bombers with 4 Zekes covering very close. The task of the enemy was to bomb shipping from about 100 feet off the water. Up above them, an additional 25 to 30 enemy fighters were diving and swarming. The bombers disappeared into a cloud layer at 2,000 feet. Two flights of P-38s hit the Zekes, and the others continued on down and hit the bombers. Three of the Bettys jettisoned their bombs, while the rest continued to attack the shipping, hitting a large barge, which was seen to list. The Lightnings of the 432nd dove through anti-aircraft fire from the ships to down the Japanese aircraft one after the other. In the furious fight that lasted 45 minutes, the 432nd accounted for 18 enemy aircraft. Lieutenant Vivian A. Cloud was forced to bail out after accounting for one of the enemy, but he was picked up by one of the ships in the harbor. Another of the P-38s failed to return, and the pilot was not seen again.

Shortly after the P-38s made the initial contact, the P-40s of the 35th Fighter Squadron got into the act. In his first combat, Lieutenant Dick West accounted for 2 Hamps, while his mates accounted for 5 more enemy aircraft. Lieutenant John T. Brown, Jr., got on the tail of a Zeke and stayed with it until it crashed into the water while trying to take evasive action.

In a little less than an hour the combat air patrol had accounted for 10 or more bombers and 29 fighters. Anti-aircraft fire from the American destroyers got another 9 torpedo bombers. Three American fighters went down, but only a single pilot was lost.

By September 23 the main landing force had captured one of the Finschhafen airstrips, and an air liaison party had a radio setup. However, the enemy was well entrenched, and going was slow for the ground troops the first few days.

On September 26 a fighter sweep preceded an attack by B-24s and later B-25s on Wewak. The 80th Fighter Squadron sent a force of 16 P-38s up ahead of the bombers, and finding no opposition, they orbited at 16,000 feet for rendezvous. As the P-38s approached the strip at Wewak, 2 or 3 enemy fighters were sighted very low off the water. Immediately after this sighting, 10 Tonys were sighted at 15,000 feet. The P-38s dropped their belly tanks and gave combat. Most of the enemy fighters were more inclined to either half roll or go straight down rather than attempt head-on passes. No doubt these pilots had learned something of the tremendous firepower that emanated from the nose of the Lightnings. The mutual support tactics of the American pilots worked well, and 3 of the Tonys were downed in the process.

As an experiment, P-40s of the 35th Fighter Squadron were sent to escort B-24s to Wewak on the twenty-seventh. From

Port Moresby to Wewak was such a great distance that the P-40s had to be refueled at Tsili Tsili. From there they went to Bena Bena to stage for the mission. Sixteen P-40s completed the trip and managed to down 3 Tonys in the action. The P-40s were getting long legs!

P-38s went back to Wewak on the twenty-eighth as escort to a force of 40 B-24s. The heavies had just come off the bomb run when the enemy put in his appearance. Lieutenant Tommy McGuire was a member of the 431st Squadron that tangled with him. As he made his first pass on a Zeke at 18,000 feet, McGuire was forced to dive out as 2 Zekes jumped him and his wingman. The 2 became separated at this time.

In the course of another pass McGuire sighted a P-38 with a Zeke on his tail, which he drove away. As the Zeke pulled up to the left of McGuire, McGuire pounced on his tail, gave him a couple of good bursts, and sent him down in flames.

Turning back and climbing, McGuire sighted another Zeke attempting to attack a flight of P-38s. The enemy pilot sighted McGuire and attempted to rack his craft around for a head-on pass but failed. A deflection shot at very close range by McGuire started the Zeke smoking, and as the Zeke passed underneath the left wing of the P-38 the propeller began to windmill and the plane burst into flames.

McGuire headed for another Zeke, but when he commenced to clear his own tail McGuire found that he had a visitor. Quickly McGuire shoved the yoke forward and went into a steep dive, but not before the Japanese pilot had shot out his left engine. Down and down McGuire went, building up speed until he finally left the enemy craft behind. A few seconds later McGuire pulled out, feathered his prop, and headed for the advance strip at Tsili Tsili.

Veteran Australian troops fought their way into the town of Finschhafen on October 2, only 10 days after their landing. Although this placed Allied troops on the north side of Huon Gulf, it still didn't mean the end of the campaign. The enemy pulled into the jungle and readied himself for the next step by the Allies.

The Japanese airfields at Wewak had been neutralized for the landings, but the enemy still had men and planes to feed into the battle. However, many of the better pilots of the Japanese Army Air Force were being lost, and these would prove to be impossible to replace. The enemy was beginning to have to go to other theaters of operation to pull veteran units into the Battle of New Guinea. The aerial supremacy that the Fifth Air Force had gained was beginning to pay off.

Work on the airbases at Lae, Nadzab, Finschhafen, and a new site to the north known as Gusap went on steadily. As quickly as the fighter units could be moved to these fields the sooner operations could begin to eliminate Wewak and neutralize the enemy bastion of Rabaul on New Britain.

IX

BOUGAINVILLE AND THE REDUCTION OF RABAUL

By mid-October 1943 the stage was set for the invasion of Bougainville. This island is the largest in the Solomons chain and at that time possessed several Japanese airfields, harbor installations, and was manned by over 20,000 enemy troops. To enable U. S. Marines to land on the island by the first of November it was necessary for General Kenney to direct the operations of the Fifth Air Force bombers and fighters against the enemy bastion of Rabaul on New Britain while the planes of COMAIRSOLS sought to neutralize the Japanese air bases on Bougainville itself.

To enable the P-38s from Fighter Strip II on Guadalcanal to escort the bombers striking the enemy airfield of Kahili on Bougainville it was necessary to send ground crews of the 339th Squadron up to Munda. These men did a fantastic job of keeping the Lightnings going during their tour. Quite often the P-38s would not land until dusk. Nevertheless the planes had to be serviced, the guns cleaned and armed that night to prepare them for another mission the next morning. Quite often the men worked far into the night making the most of inadequate lighting, using gasoline drums for maintenance stands, and improvising for repair parts that were not available.

The P-38s of the 339th made their first contact for the month of October when they escorted B-24s over Kahili on the fourth. Japanese Zekes came up to challenge, and the "Sun Setter" Squadron once more proved the proficiency of its pilots in mutual support tactics. Lieutenant Pedro developed engine trouble over the target, and 3 Zekes jumped him immediately. His wingman, Lieutenant McCloud, kept them off his tail despite their constant attacks to shoot him down. Lieutenant Bill Harris downed one of the Zekes, which made his fifth victory, and his squadronmates got another 3. All of the Lightnings managed to get back to Munda.

On the morning of October 10 the P-38s again escorted the bombers to Kahili. On this mission the Lightning pilots had their hands full trying to get the Zekes off the B-24s. Lieutenant Jim Shubin got 2 of the Zekes and Lieutenant Bill Harris of the 339th and Major R. B. Westbrook of the 44th Squadron teamed up and disposed of a Zeke apiece.

That afternoon while covering a PBY Dumbo seeking survivors of a B-24 from the morning mission, the Lightnings were jumped by about 15 Zekes, who surprised them with an attack out of the sun. The P-38s immediately went into scissor tactics for mutual protection. The Japanese made no coordinated attacks, but chose to come at the Lightnings singly. As a result 5 of the Zekes were definitely shot down and another 5 went into the record books as probables. There were no American losses, although 1 plane was written off when its engine failed and it crashed coming in to Munda.

Before the fighters and bombers of the Fifth Air Force began their concentrated efforts against Rabaul, it was necessary to continue strikes of the Wewak area to insure its neutralization. It was on such a fighter sweep to the area on October 11 that Colonel Neel E. Kearby, commander of the 348th Fighter Group, got into a scrap that earned him the Congressional Medal of Honor.

In his own words, "I was leading a flight of 4 P-47s over Wewak. We took off from Tsili Tsili at 0915 and arrived over Wewak at 1030 at 28,000 feet. The weather was excellent, with a few scattered clouds between 2,000 and 8,000 feet. We saw a number of aircraft parked on Boram strip, and 1 aircraft taxiing on the runway. He did not take off. The fuel in our belly tanks had been consumed, so we dropped them to increase our speed and conserve fuel. At 1115 1 Zeke was sighted at 9 o'clock below at 20,000 feet. I came in on him from 7 o'clock above and opened fire at 1,500 feet. He took no evasive action, caught fire, and dived into the sea.

"We climbed back to 26,000 feet and at about 1125 saw about 36 fighters, Tonys, Hamps, and Zekes, and 12 bombers approaching from the southeast along the coast. The fighters were at about 10,000 to 15,000 feet and the bombers at about 5,000 feet. We came in from above. I opened fire on a Zeke at 1,500 feet and closed as he burst into flames. No evasive action was taken.

"I turned slightly and opened fire at 1,500 feet from 7 o'clock on a Hamp, which burst into flames taking no evasive action. I looked up and another Hamp was turning slightly to the left. I closed to 1,500 feet and opened fire from slightly above and from about 1 o'clock. He burst into flames after he had passed beyond my sights in the turn. I was indicating over 400 miles per hour during this period.

"By this time the Japanese realized we were there so I pulled up sharply to about 20,000 feet and saw Captain [William D.] Dunham. I joined him and we started home. Immediately at 2 o'clock below at about 10,000 feet I saw Captain [John T.] Moore in a P-47 with one Tony about 3,000 feet to the rear and another Tony about 3,000 feet behind the first one. Captain Moore was headed for home. I turned and came in at 400 miles per hour on the tail of the rear Tony opening fire at 1,500 feet. He took no evasive action and burst into flames. I closed for the other Tony, which was on Captain Moore's tail, but he must have seen me as he turned and dove down in front of me. I opened fire from about 2,000 feet closing in and saw tracers going into him and pieces of his wing and fuselage flying off. I did not see him catch fire nor did I see him crash, as I did not have time to watch him. Captain Moore saw this Tony burst into flames and crash into the sea.

"He then turned back toward Wewak, and I turned with him. Tonys were all over the sky. I made another pass at a Tony from about 10 o'clock, but deflection was wrong. I looked behind and saw a Tony closing on my tail, so I dived for the nearby clouds. We were now at about 7,000 feet. When coming out of the clouds I could no longer see the Tony. I climbed to 15,000 feet and called the flight. They all checked in, and we proceeded to Lae and landed there at 1240. Captain Moore destroyed 2 enemy fighters and Captain Dunham 1. Major Gallagher had chased a Zeke into the clouds and was unable to find another enemy aircraft when he came out. We refueled at Lae and returned to Port Moresby.

"Claim 2 Zekes, 2 Hamps, and 2 Tonys."

On October 12 the Fifth Air Force P-38s escorted wave after wave of B-25s and B-24s attacking airfields, shipping, and harbor installations at Rabaul. The enemy was undoubtedly caught by surprise, for the majority of the aircraft destroyed that day were caught on the ground. When the last bomber departed the target area many columns of smoke from the airfields were visible testimony to the destruction they had inflicted.

The Japanese were apparently alarmed by the raids on Rabaul and seemingly believed that an invasion of New Britain was imminent, for they dispatched a large mission from Rabaul on the fifteenth of October against Allied shipping at Oro Bay.

Both the 49th and the 475th fighter groups scrambled to meet the enemy formation of approximately 20 fighters and 25 Val dive bombers. While the Japanese fighters tried desperately to drive off the P-40s and P-38s, the Americans dove down on the Vals in wave after wave, closed on the tails of the dive bombers and shot many of the planes down into the sea. The light defensive armament of the bombers was no match for the concentrated firepower from the fighters. Very few, if any, of the Vals were able to escape the massacre, and the enemy also paid with 18 of his fighters.

The Japanese came back on the seventeenth, and this time his formations of fighters and Lily bombers were cut to pieces again by the 49th and 475th groups, plus the 41st Squadron of the 35th Fighter Group over Buna, Finschhafen, and Morobe Harbor. Lieutenant Tommy McGuire was one of the pilots of the 475th intercepting, and in this violent combat he was shot down and almost killed.

"We were at 23,000 feet when we sighted the enemy at a position of 11 o'clock, slightly above us. (A group of 15 to 20 Zekes.) After we dropped our belly tanks, Lieutenant Kirby, in his capacity as squadron leader that day, led us in to a head-on attack, climbing slightly. I selected 1 Zeke at the right of the formation and began firing. He started smoking and rolled out and down to his right. I followed, firing intermittently, to 18,000 feet, then pulled back up to rejoin our formation.

"I lost my second element and my wingman by this time. My wingman could only drop 1 belly tank, and because of this could not pull out of his dive until he reached 4,000 feet. He saw the Zeke that I had fired on going straight down, still smoking. I pulled up behind Red Flight at 21,000 feet and arrived in time to see 2 Zekes attacking from a position of 4 o'clock high. After I had fired at them in an attempt to drive them away 4 other Zekes started down on me from 6 o'clock high, forcing me to dive to about 1,000 feet. I had begun a climb when I sighted 2 Zekes at 3 o'clock and about 1,000 feet below me. I dived in to attack, getting several shots with no results observed. I was at 18,000 feet when 3 Zekes from 8 o'clock high attacked me. As I was diving out, 1 closed in to very close range, putting about 2 slugs into the cockpit and possibly other parts of the ship. My evasive maneuver in this instance was to increase my dive to vertical, diving to 7,000 feet, then pulling back up to 12,000 feet.

"At that time I saw 7 Zekes in a loose formation and to the rear of a P-38, which appeared to be in trouble. As 1 Zeke began his pass at the P-38 I made my attack on him at 90-degree deflection. I fired a long burst and saw him break into flame. Feeling that I could distract them from the P-38 by making an attack, I pulled up slightly and to the right, getting a direct tail shot. I closed to about 100 feet and began firing. The Zeke immediately started burning and rolled slowly to the left and down. The remaining Zekes attacked me at that time.

"One was about 100 feet behind me and closing. As I started to dive out, my left engine began to burn, my right engine was smoking, a cannon shell burst in the radio compartment, and a 7.7 shell hit my wrist and passed into the instrument panel. Other shells hit at the base of the control column. I received shrapnel in my right arm and my hips. I tried to pull out of my dive but found my elevator controls were entirely useless. I then released my escape hatch and bailed out. I landed in the sea about 25 miles from shore and remained there for approximately 30 minutes.

"I was unable to inflate my life raft due to shrapnel holes in it. I was picked up by a Navy PT boat, *No. 152,* and carried to PT tender *Hilo* in Buna Bay. During the engagement I saw at least 30 enemy fighters and clusters of bombs that had been dropped about 28 miles offshore."

Another attack on Rabaul got off as scheduled on October 18, but the weather was so bad that the P-38s had to turn back. However, the majority of the bombers managed to get through to the target, which they bombed and strafed with good effect.

Three squadrons of Lightnings of the 475th Fighter Group took off on a fighter sweep to Rabaul on the morning of October 23. Their mission was to hit the fighter fields in the area before the enemy could get airborne to intercept the B-24s that would follow. The cloud buildup was such that the P-38s couldn't go down to hit the airfields but were forced to orbit at high altitude, awaiting the arrival of the bombers.

Captain Danny Roberts of the 475th Group's 433rd Fighter Squadron had his unit at 25,000 feet when 10 enemy fighters were observed at 15,000 feet. Initially the 2 other P-38 squadrons were able to take care of the opposition, but another formation, 35 interceptors, appeared. Roberts had his pilots drop tanks, and they dove down to attack. Roberts immediately lined up behind a Zeke and gave it 3 short bursts. As the Zeke banked to the right, the

Lightning pilot put another burst into its wing, setting it on fire. Roberts then turned into another Zeke, hitting him from a quarter head-on pass. This Zeke rolled over, burned, and dove straight down.

A dozen of the Japanese fighters were destroyed before the P-38s hovered in over the scattered flights of the B-24s and headed for home.

The heavy bombers rested the following day while the P-38s took the B-25s back to Rabaul. On that mission the 80th Fighter Squadron got into what was its biggest air battle to that date. Sixteen of their Lightnings came in at 11,000 feet when 40 to 50 Hamps and Zekes were sighted scattered in pairs from ground level to 10,000 feet.

Lieutenant Jay T. Robbins saw a B-25 fall victim to the enemy fighters before he could intercept. The Japanese fighters sought safety in the clouds and down over the harbor, but to no avail. Robbins lined up on a fighter at only 600 feet, and a long burst sent it crashing down in flames. He then turned into another Hamp head-on, and as his slugs tore into the engine of the aircraft, it flamed. A 30-degree deflection shot took the wing off another Hamp. Robbins' final deflection shot flamed his fourth victim of the brief combat.

Lieutenant C. M. "Corky" Smith got no victories that day, but in his encounter with the enemy rated them as the best that he had seen. "The sky was filled with enemy fighters. We stayed in the area about 25 minutes making passes, but I did not get any hits. The enemy fighters were all Zekes and Hamps. I saw no Tonys. The enemy fighters were all painted black and were very good in tactics. They stayed together, and when P-38s made a pass at one of them the P-38 would be attacked by other enemy fighters. There were quite a few clouds, and the enemy fighters took full advantage of them. It was pretty rough. The only way to scare them off was to turn into them, as they didn't like this type of tactic."

What the American fighter pilots didn't know at the time was that the predominance of Zekes and Hamps in the Rabaul area was due to the fact that these were strictly Japanese Navy fighter-type aircraft. The Tonys and Oscars were Army-type fighters, and the Japanese Army air units had all been relegated to New Guinea by this time.

The Lightning pilots claimed 37 enemy fighters that day, while all the P-38s returned to base. Two of the B-25s were lost before the escort could rescue them from the initial onslaught.

B-24s formed up the morning of October 25 for another strike on Rabaul. Major Charles H. MacDonald was leading 8 P-38s of the 432nd Fighter Squadron to the target when he heard the lead fighter squadron call that the weather looked too bad, and they turned back. "The weather to the east of the target was bad," reported MacDonald. "Rather than let the bombers go on alone I took my 7 men very high and covered the lead bomb squadron of the 90th Group, so that the enemy seeing us would be discouraged and perhaps figure there were lots more of us. We figured to be mostly moral support.

"Off Cape Gazelle the lead bombers were intercepted. We made a dive and scared them off. Then all the squadrons began talking at once that they were being hit. We helped them out mostly through scaring the enemy, who weren't too eager. Over Vunakanau I shot a Zeke who burst into flames—witnessed by all the flight and some bomb crews. Flak was terrific over the harbor. We stayed over the target 45 minutes. The flight was attacked on at least 2 occasions, but we kept weaving and covering the rear men so that none of the attacks were pressed home."

This action on the part of MacDonald and his squadron undoubtedly saved many B-24s from enemy fighters that fateful day.

The first phase of the Bougainville invasion operation took place on the morning of October 27, when troops of the New Zealand 8th Brigade Group went ashore on Stirling Island in the Treasury group. No opposition was met on Stirling and only limited resistance was met on Mono Island.

To cover the landing, General Nathan Twining, commander of the Thirteenth Air Force, had 16 P-38s of the 339th Fighter

Squadron flying top cover, with P-40s and P-39s from the 18th and 347th fighter groups down below. At 3:15 P.M. 4 P-38s led by Lieutenant Shubin sighted enemy aircraft below. The Lightnings intercepted a force of Val dive bombers just as they were making their run on a destroyer. In the encounter Lieutenant Shubin got 2 of the Vals, while Lieutenant Howie scored 3 times. At about this time a second section of 8 P-38s arrived on the scene led by Lieutenant Bill Harris. Lieutenant Harris managed to down one of the dive bombers, and 2 of his section teamed up to dispose of a Kate-type bomber before the surviving enemy planes scurried for home.

Seven of the enemy fell to the guns of the 339th Squadron in the combat, but not before the Japanese bombers managed to score 2 hits on the destroyer, causing it to retire from the scene.

General Kenney sent the bombers and fighters of the Fifth Air Force back to Rabaul on October 29. The Japanese attempted to intercept the bombers over the target with 35 to 40 fighters, but the P-38s broke their attacks effectively. The Lightnings scored 17 times, while the bombers pasted the airfields once more.

In order to reinforce Japanese air strength at Rabaul, Admiral Koga, chief of the Imperial Fleet, ordered the planes of the Third Air Fleet off the carriers onto the airfields there. These 173 aircraft—82 Zekes, 45 Vals, 40 Kates, and 6 reconnaissance planes—joined the 200 of the Eleventh Air Fleet, which was operating from Rabaul and its satellite airfields at the time. These reinforcements arrived at Rabaul on November 1 as U. S. Marines were hitting the beach on Bougainville off Cape Torokina.

While the 3rd Marine Division was landing on the beaches, air cover was provided by the fighter planes of COMAIRSOLS. Eight P-38s of the 339th Fighter Squadron were flying at 23,000 feet when 20 Zekes arrived for an early-morning attack against the fleet. Seven of the Zekes were downed by the Lightnings without a loss.

Throughout the day the enemy continued to break through the invasion fleet, but the bombs that were dropped by the Val dive bombers missed their targets. The AAF and Marine Corps fighters broke up each attack in the area of the beachhead.

That night an enemy task force of cruisers and destroyers came down to break up the landing fleet in Empress Augusta Bay, but U. S. Navy forces intercepted them and sank a Japanese light cruiser and a destroyer before the enemy broke off the sea battle and sped back to Rabaul.

The Fifth Air Force was prevented from taking the pressure off the invasion of Bougainville by attacking Rabaul due to bad weather on November 1. However, the narrative of the historian of the 475th Fighter Group vividly describes the job that the pilots of "Satan's Angels" performed on November 2, 1943, when they went to Rabaul.

"At last, at 11 o'clock in the morning of the second, 37 of our pilots set out for Rabaul. Their assignment was to protect B-25s during a low-level strafing and bombing attack on the enemy shipping in Simpson Harbor. The weather was bad. Almost all the way the ceiling was well below 4,000 feet altitude. Bombers and fighters roared low across the sea. En route the escort was weakened when 2 fighter pilots snafued and went home with 1 escort. In St. George's Channel, a Japanese battleship and cruiser blazed away at the striking force. The element of surprise had been lost. The enemy would be warned and ready. Fighters and bombers continued on nevertheless, circled to the north of the target, and then came in. Danny Roberts with 12 planes of the 433rd Squadron provided close cover. Leading his flights, he flew beneath a 2,000-foot overcast at treetop level, slipped over the mountaintops, and then roared down over the harbor into a blizzard of ack-ack.

"Just before reaching the harbor, 9 planes of Hades Squadron (431st) ascended to 7,000 feet, then made a long, slanting dive across the target. Thirteen planes of the 432nd Squadron climbed to a scant 4,000 feet altitude to meet Japanese fighter attacks. The time was 1335.

"Ack-ack almost blotted out the harbor as the entire fleet and shore batteries hammered at the Mitchells and Lightnings. Overhead more than 100 enemy fighters circled, dropped aerial burst bombs, then peeled down through rifts in the overcast to attack the raiders. Deliberately Danny Roberts kept his flight low, warding off fighter attacks, weaving through ack-ack, staying with the bombers to help them although he sacrificed to the enemy fighters the tremendous advantage of superior altitude.

"The 9 planes of Hades Squadron dived again and again to the rescue of the bombers, scorning the scores of Japanese that sought to kill them from behind. When Marion Kirby saw 3 enemy fighters working over a crippled B-25, he went after the enemy alone. The first foe fell to his gunnery, then he tackled the others. As he sent the second Zeke spinning to destruction, the third swung in behind him and opened fire. But even as the enemy moved, Fred Champlin was turning to his teammate's aid. He had the skill to do it. Before the enemy could make his kill, Champlin had shot him down.

"A swarm of Japanese were diving on a group of B-25s, and the bombers called for assistance. Single-handedly, Lowell Lutton engaged the foe. He set 1 Zeke ablaze, but 2 others came at him from astern. Ed Wenige and his lean, tall wingman, Franklin Monk, went after the 2 Japanese, Wenige knocking down the first and Monk forcing the other to break away. The 3 Lightnings weaved back and forth above the bombers firing and blocking enemy attacks. The enemy then turned on the Lightnings. Two Zekes dived on Lutton from 1 o'clock high. Again Wenige and Monk met them, with the same results. A third Zeke followed the first pair in, but as Weinge opened fire, his guns ran out of ammo. Unable to fight, he ducked under the attack while Monk met the enemy and shot him down. Lutton was still in the thick of the fight and heavily outnumbered. With his useless guns Wenige dived at the enemy while Monk teamed with him to break up attacks. Five more Japanese boxed them in but failed to bring them down.

"Meanwhile, scissoring in and out of the clouds, the 432nd Squadron fought to break up the diving attacks from above. Enemy

Navy fighters circled overhead waiting to pick off any plane which became separated in the overcast. The 4 planes of White flight lost their squadron, moved to the edge of the combat, and began to engage enemy fighters as they came into the clear. One fanatic failed in a desperate attempt to ram Howard Hedrick and John Rundell. As they dodged the enemy, Leo Mayo flashed down on a Zeke at terrific speed. Closing rapidly, he opened fire. The enemy plane exploded as Mayo's flight came up behind him. To their horror, a flying mass of wreckage sheared off the wing of his plane. As it hurtled down, he jumped and his parachute flared out. Fogarty and Rundell circled their friend as he dropped toward the sea, blocking the Japanese who sought to strafe him. Hedrick, alone, stayed up to cover them. Four Japanese dived down upon him, shot out 1 engine, then tried desperately for the kill. Slipping, skidding, and turning, Hedrick dodged their fire. One of the enemy passed in front of him, and Hedrick shot him down. Finally the rest gave up the chase and left him. Giertsen of the 431st was shot down but escaped into the jungle. Two other P-38s were lost. For 40 minutes the Lightnings held off the Japanese and sent 19 to destruction. At last, 54 miles south of Rabaul some 60 enemy fighters gave up the chase and turned home.

"Somewhere, more than 200 miles to the south, lay the tiny island of Kiriwina, the closest landing field for the men of the 475th. The weather had grown worse. To the east a towering front paralleled their course. The ceiling ahead had lowered to 2,000 feet, and a thickening haze dimmed their vision. North of Kiriwina another front forced them to consume precious gas in a detour. From 3 to 4 o'clock that afternoon the P-38s straggled in to Kiriwina. When they landed some had only 10 gallons of fuel left. Lieutenant Lutton never arrived. In his gallant fight over Simpson Harbor he had used the gas he needed for the long flight home. The rest of the planes refueled and flew back to Dobodura."

Mayo, too, was lost forever, despite all the efforts to get him down safely.

The over-all claims for the day by the Fifth Air Force were 40 enemy fighters downed by the Lightnings and 26 by the B-25 crewmen. Eight B-25s and 9 P-38s had been lost in the fierce air fighting.

Planes from Navy carriers struck at Rabaul on November 5, and the Fifth Air Force cooperated with them by dispatching a group of 27 B-24s escorted by 58 P-38s from the 8th, 49th, and 475th fighter groups to attack the wharf area. A number of enemy aircraft were seen in the vicinity of the target, but Captain Dick Bong was the only Lightning pilot to score that day. Bong dived down on the tail of a formation of Zekes and downed 2 of them before fuel shortage forced him to break and start the long flight home.

The poor weather that had been so prevalent in the area between New Guinea and Rabaul made its presence felt once more on November 6, but the next day the heavies set out to hit Rapopo Airdrome. The job turned in that day by the 80th Fighter Squadron is indicative of the continuing brilliance of the performances by the Lightning pilots.

The fronts on the way to the target were so bad that 7 of the original formation of the 80th Squadron's 16 P-38s had turned back. Before the target was reached, Major Edward Cragg decided to fly a fighter sweep over the area in an attempt to keep the enemy below the level of the bombers. The 9 P-38s of the 80th Squadron went on ahead, leaving the other Lightning units to escort the bombers.

The 80th came in at 27,000 feet, and Major Cragg sighted the enemy below—at least 100 Japanese fighters in the area and only 9 P-38s. Major Cragg let down slowly, and as the Zekes and Hamps started to climb, the battle was joined. The P-38 pilots attempted to stay together, but the enemy came in from all directions, and violent evasive maneuvers were necessary.

During the early part of the battle Major Cragg and Lieutenant Allen Hill forced an entire formation of 16 enemy fighters to split-ess. Lieutenant Cy Homer dived through a formation of approximately 30 fighters on his first pass. Homer fired at 2 planes, missed, and fired on a third. His tracers entered the cockpit of the plane, which pulled up gradually and fell off to the right. Lieutenant Homer was then attacked by 6 Zekes, which forced him to break violently. Recovering from his dive, he climbed back to altitude and went back down through a large enemy formation with his guns blazing. Six more passes split the Japanese fighters up further, and on his last pass he had the satisfaction of shooting pieces off a Zeke, which went down out of control.

Lieutenant Allen Hill scored with a head-on pass at a Zeke, which caught fire after falling several hundred feet.

None of the other pilots scored, but all made passes at the enemy and kept at least 50 of them occupied and away from the bombers. The 9 Lightnings prevented the bombers from being attacked in force over the target, and all of the B-24s returned to base safely. None of the 80th's P-38s were lost, although 2 of them returned on single engine.

Back in New Guinea, the 36th Fighter Squadron, which had done yeoman duty in P-39s for many months, got into combat for the first time flying their new P-47s. While on patrol over Nadzab 4 of the Thunderbolts encountered 12 enemy bombers escorted by an equal number of Oscars flying northeast at 18,000 feet. Lieutenant Edward L. Milner picked out an Oscar and sent it down in flames. Lieutenant Joe Clements downed a Sally bomber, and Lieutenant W. K. Giroux attacked 2 bombers after they had completed their bombing run across Nadzab Airstrip. His tracers were seen to enter the enemy aircraft, and both fell out of formation, burning badly.

While the P-38s of the 5th Fighter Command had been devoting most of their attention to Rabaul shortly after the Bougainville invasion, it was still necessary to hit the enemy airfields at Wewak,

Madang, and Alexishafen in New Guinea to prevent buildups of enemy aircraft in the theater.

On such a mission the 5th Fighter Command lost one of its early aces and outstanding aerial leaders. Captain Danny Roberts led his 433rd Fighter Squadron to escort B-25s in the Alexishafen area on November 9 when 15 to 20 Tonys, Zekes, Oscars, and Hamps were encountered.

Roberts blew up a Hamp low over the water, and as the P-38 pilot gathered his brood to continue on his way, he sighted a Zeke that was racing for home. Apparently, Roberts' wingman, Lieutenant Dale Meyers, sighted it at the same time. Meyers pulled in behind Roberts as Lieutenant William Grady slipped into the No. 2 position.

When the Zeke reached his strip at Alexishafen he banked sharply to the right. Roberts racked his P-38 over hard to stay with him, and Lieutenant Meyers attempted to do the same, but he was unable to maneuver quickly enough. His plane collided with Roberts'. Debris from both Lightnings flew through the air as both of the aircraft plunged to their destruction in the jungle.

The Hamp that he had downed early in the combat was Roberts' fifteenth victory. During the 37 days that he had commanded the 433rd Fighter Squadron it had been credited with 55 enemy aircraft for the loss of 3 American pilots. The loss of such leadership would be sorely felt.

For the balance of November the primary efforts of the Fifth Air Force were concentrated on keeping the Japanese air strength beaten down in the Wewak area; at the same time strikes began in the area of Saidor and at Cape Gloucester in New Britain. With U. S. Marines making good progress on Bougainville, the eyes of the Allied high command were cast toward the invasion of New Britain, which would be the final step in the reduction of the primary Japanese base at Rabaul.

The Japanese sent a heavy raid down the Ramu Valley on November 15, directed at Gusap. They were intercepted by P-40s of the 8th and 35th fighter squadrons, who downed 18 planes. Lieutenant Richard West, in his second aerial encounter, accounted for 4: 2 fighters and 2 bombers.

The month of December 1943 saw the completion of a number of movements by units of the 5th Fighter Command. As these squadrons were shifted up the coast of New Guinea it put all of them in position for the landings that would be taking place. The 49th Fighter Group completed its movement to Gusap, and the P-47s of the 348th Fighter Group departed Port Moresby and took up new station at Finschhafen.

Colonel Neel Kearby, who had given command of the 348th Group up to Lieutenant Colonel Robert Rowland in November, came down from 5th Fighter Command headquarters on December 3 to lead a flight of 4 P-47s into the Wewak area looking for a fight. Kearby, in his white-tailed Thunderbolt *Firey Ginger,* was flying about 20 miles northwest of Wewak when his wingman sighted over 20 Tonys and Zekes below at 22,000 feet heading southeast along the coast.

The P-47s attacked in a high-speed dive out of the sun. Kearby closed on a Zeke from the rear and opened fire from about 1,500 feet. As he closed, strikes were observed, and the Zeke rolled over as flames came from the left wing and fuselage. Kearby quickly turned slightly to the left for another stern attack on a Zeke, but 4 enemy fighters were observed turning in toward him from the left.

Kearby turned into the attack and opened fire on the lead aircraft. Good strikes were observed, so Kearby quickly moved the lead to his wingman, on whom hits were also scored. Kearby nearly collided with the No. 4 in the formation as they met. Looking back, Kearby saw flames coming from one of the Zekes as it went down. The other had gone in and was seen burning in the water. In view of the superior numbers of Japanese aircraft, the Thunderbolts formed up and high-tailed, but not before Kearby had taken 3 of their number out in quick succession and Captains F. G. Oksala and Meade M. Brown had downed singles.

Early on the morning of December 15, 1943, men of the 112th Cavalry Regiment were landed on Arawe Peninsula on the south coast of New Britain. Eighty-two P-38s of the 8th, 49th, and 475th groups plus 46 P-47s of the 348th Group covered the landings during the day, but the fighters scored little against the 2 raids the Japanese mounted in opposition to shipping offshore.

For the next 2 days P-47s of the 348th Group and P-38s of the 475th Group continued to patrol the area of Arawe with good results. The Japanese sent bombers escorted by fighters down from Rabaul, and the Americans continued to take their toll.

During the week before Christmas both the fighters from the Fifth Air Force and those from the Thirteenth Air Force began to really mix it up with the enemy. The Fifth still patrolled Arawe and escorted bombers to the Cape Gloucester area in preparation for the invasion there, which was scheduled for December 26. To take pressure off the forthcoming landing at Cape Gloucester, the fighter planes of COMAIRSOLS began to escort bombers striking Rabaul. Each day both Marine Corps and Thirteenth Air Force planes went out against airfields and shipping in the Rabaul area.

Around noon on December 21 the 432nd Fighter Squadron was on patrol over Arawe when the controller reported a large flight of enemy airplanes coming in from the northeast. Colonel Charles MacDonald was leading the squadron of 18 P-38s that sighted the enemy flying in heavy cumulus clouds only 500 to 1,000 feet over the water. The dive bombers broke for the clouds when the Lightnings arrived, while the escort came up to intercept.

MacDonald took his flight down after the bombers. Just as he began to close, a Zeke closed in on the rear man of the second flight. MacDonald put a deflection shot into the Zeke; the Zeke seemed to go out of control, but the enemy pilot recovered just above the treetops in time to be hit again and finished off by 2 other P-38s.

The flight of Lightnings then caught up with 6 Vals right over the trees. MacDonald got 2 of them, while his flight accounted for the other 4. The enemy dive bombers were caught right on the deck before they had a chance to take evasive action, and their escort failed to sight the Lightnings over the jungle background before it was too late.

Later that afternoon 7 P-47s of the 342nd Squadron under the leadership of Captain William D. Dunham were on patrol over Arawe when the Japanese attempted to misdirect the Americans from the area. In flawless English the enemy directed the Thunderbolts to the east as they came in to attack from the west. Captain Dunham was on the alert for such tactics, and when he received a call from shipping in the area he had positioned his flight for an attack.

Due to bad weather over the area Dunham split his flight. While Dunham took his formation of 3 down to the deck, the other 4 Thunderbolts intercepted dive bombers at 20,000 feet. In the engagements 8 of the Val dive bombers were shot down, 3 by Dunham and 2 each by Lieutenants Robert Gibb and Randall Hilbig.

The 5th Fighter Command flew a number of fighter sweeps to the Wewak area on December 22 and encountered enemy fighters in great numbers. The 16 P-38s of the 80th Fighter Squadron were flying close formation due to poor visibility caused by light rains when the rear flight was hit by the enemy from behind and above.

The last man in the last flight was hit hard and headed south with flames coming from his left engine. The rear element of the third flight went back to cover him, but on the way home his right engine burst into flames and he crashed into the ground.

A second P-38 was badly shot up and the pilot was forced to ditch the aircraft, but not before he downed one of the enemy fighters.

When the Japanese were first sighted, Major Ed Cragg turned into a Tony, which did a snap roll and evaded him. The flight behind Cragg shot this Tony down. The enemy pilot bailed out and his parachute became entangled in Major Cragg's right propeller and was ripped to pieces.

Shortly afterward Cragg and his flight met 3 Tonys and a Zeke head-on. Cragg fired at 250 yards down to 50 yards before his Tony went down. As he looked back, all 3 Tonys were flaming, and the Zeke dove for cloud cover.

On December 23 the fighters of COMAIRSOLS were up in force to escort the bombers to Rabaul. The P-38s of the Thirteenth Air Force were flying high cover at 22,000 to 24,000 feet. One of the flights, led by Major Robert Westbrook, made contact with the 20 to 30 Zekes that put in an appearance.

Westbrook and his wingman, Lieutenant R. M. Fouquest, spotted a lone Zeke and dived on him at high speed. Fouquest pulled up to 15,000 feet and found himself alone and on the tail of a Zeke.

This Zeke pulled up in a loop in an effort to get on the tail of the Lightning. Fouquest pulled up and gave the Zeke a burst, whereupon it rolled over and made a head-on pass. Its guns were no match for the concentrated cannon and machine-gun fire of the P-38, and at 75 yards the Zeke burst into flames. Fouquest broke sharply to the right to miss flying through the debris.

Meanwhile, Westbrook discovered that the original Zeke hadn't been alone. Westbrook suddenly found himself tailed by another Zeke. This pilot suddenly broke off the combat without doing any damage. Pulling up to rejoin his formation, Westbrook encountered another Zeke and shot it down.

The next day the P-38s of the 44th Squadron went back to Rabaul with the B-24s. Seventeen of the P-38s mixed with the Japanese fighters, getting 8 of them without loss. This time the enemy tried dropping chemical bombs on the Liberators from above but did no damage. Lieutenant J. E. Parker had his left engine knocked out by a 20mm shell from a Zeke pilot who added insult to injury by pulling up alongside and grinning at him before he split-essed and left the area.

Following several days of intensive bombardment, U. S. Marines were landed on the beaches of Cape Gloucester, New Britain, on the morning of December 26, 1943. Once more the Japanese chose not to meet the invasion on the beach but pulled into the dense jungle growth to oppose the Marines. The enemy did not attempt to attack the task force that morning, but between 2:30 and 3:10 P.M. dive bombers escorted by fighters from Rabaul arrived on the scene.

A flight of 19 Thunderbolts of the 342nd Fighter Squadron of the 348th Group were at 12,000 and 18,000 feet when they sighted 15 enemy bombers and 3 fighters headed in for the cape. Fourteen Bettys were destroyed before they could make their bomb run, and 2 of the 3 fighters were downed in the encounter. Lieutenant Lawrence F. O'Neill accounted for 4 of the bombers. The concentrated firepower of the Thunderbolts played havoc with the enemy. Asked why he didn't get more than one of the bombers, Captain Walter Benz stated, "There weren't enough to go around." Without escort the Japanese bombers had little chance against the American fighters.

The P-47s of the 36th Fighter Squadron engaged a bevy of Japanese fighters and Val dive bombers and downed 5 of them for the loss of 2 of their own, but recovered one of the pilots.

The 80th Squadron first sighted enemy Val dive bombers and fighters about 4 miles west of Borgen Bay at 2:45 P.M. The P-38s were stacked up to 19,000 feet, while the enemy dive bombers were at 10,000 feet. The Lightnings attempted to keep the escort engaged while the P-47s, P-40s, and other P-38s went after the dive bombers, but in the ensuing air battle many of the 80th's P-38s were forced to break away and execute individual attacks.

Major Ed Cragg took his flight down to the level of the dive bombers while the rest of the P-38s remained at altitude. Lieutenant Ladd, flying Major Cragg's wing, reported that his leader flew right into a flock of Vals. Cragg was not seen again until Lieutenant Adams saw him shoot down a fighter, after which Cragg headed for the clouds with another enemy fighter on his tail. Lieutenant Adams made a head-on pass at the attacker pursuing Major Cragg and shot it down. It was then that he saw Major Cragg's plane fall out of the clouds in flames. Marines on the ground reported seeing a pilot bail out of a P-38 and drift behind Japanese lines, but Major Cragg was never seen again.

Under Major Cragg's able leadership the "Headhunters" of the 80th Squadron had downed over 160 planes in 9 months. The fighter that he downed on that December day was his fifteenth victory. His ability and energy were reflected in his record and that of his squadron.

Captain Tommy McGuire was one of the P-38 pilots who got into the formations of Vals at low altitude that day. Four of them fell before his guns.

Altogether 22 of the 25 Val dive bombers, 14 Betty bombers, and 26 Japanese fighters were downed by the aerial umbrella over Cape Gloucester.

The following morning the enemy came back again, and this time his formation was cut to ribbons by P-47s of the 340th and 341st fighter squadrons. The 340th intercepted 12 fighters and 10 to 15 Val dive bombers and accounted for 8 Vals, 7 Zekes, and 1 Tony without loss. Lieutenant Myron exploded 2 Vals on a single pass and then sent a Zeke spiraling down on a head-on pass.

The 5th Fighter Command had its last air battle over New Britain on December 31, when P-47s of the 348th Fighter Group intercepted an enemy formation over Arawe. Once more the hapless Vals took a beating, losing 8 of their number, while 4 of the escorts were downed.

The new year of 1944 found Allied troops on the move north in New Guinea once more. A landing was made at Saidor on the coast opposite Cape Gloucester on the morning of January 2. It had been anticipated that the landing would be opposed by 60 to

100 Japanese aircraft from the Wewak area, but this failed to materialize. A small force of 9 Helen bombers escorted by 15 to 20 fighters were broken up by P-40s of the 7th Fighter Squadron. Men and equipment were unloaded throughout the day, and ground troops fanned out in search of the elusive enemy.

COMAIRSOLS bombers and fighters struck at the air bases surrounding Rabaul throughout January and into February. The P-38s of the force did suffer a bad day on January 17. Nineteen Lightnings took off from Stirling Island and rendezvoused west of the Taiof Island with 48 Douglas SBD dive bombers and 18 Grumman FBFs. The fighters were at 17,000 and 15,000 feet when they arrived over Simpson Harbor.

The bombers began their dive-bomb runs from 9,000 feet. At that moment Japanese Zekes put in an appearance. Initially 8 of them were sighted at 19,000 feet; then a second formation of 40 to 50 swept in. The Zekes came down in a diving pass while the P-38s were scissoring for mutual support. As the main body of the enemy struck, the Lightning formation broke up for individual fights, and some flights became separated in the cloud layers.

During the running fight that stretched from Simpson Harbor to Cape Gazelle 3 of the Lightnings were seen to crash in the water. Another 5 didn't return to base.

Captain C. B. Head, a flight leader, got 3 Zekes that day. At Cape Gazelle he did his utmost to rally the remaining fighters, but things were so hectic that many of the pilots made a run for home individually.

The next day Captain Head and 13 others made a return trip to Rabaul. The mission had called for 70 COMAIRSOLS fighters to be airborne, but when the others were tied up by a takeoff accident the Lightnings under Head wound up as sole cover for 34 B-25s.

The P-38s went in on the deck with the bombers and were jumped right afterward by 20 to 30 Zekes. Six of the enemy fighters were downed, but Captain Head got an engine shot out and had to leave the fight.

The P-38s scissored back and forth over the Mitchell bombers, feinting and jockeying the Japanese out of their runs. The B-25s assisted by pulling off the target into a fast, tight formation immediately after rendezvous.

Unfortunately, Captain Head didn't make it home.

Strikes against Rabaul continued on into February, and gradually Japanese fighter strength was whittled down. A carrier strike on the Japanese base at Truk caused the enemy high command to order the surviving aircraft from Rabaul to fall back and reinforce Truk. The intensive attacks of COMAIRSOLS and the earlier missions of the Fifth Air Force coupled with the landings on the western tip of New Britain had served to bypass the strategic Japanese base of Rabaul. From February 19 on, Rabaul served no good purpose in the Japanese chain of bases.

THE ADMIRALTIES AND HOLLANDIA

In order to cut off Japanese reinforcements from Truk into New Guinea and New Britain it was decided that the next island step would be taken against Los Negros and Manus in the Admiralty Islands. This chain of small islands lay to the northwest of Rabaul and almost directly due east of the Japanese base of Hollandia in Netherlands New Guinea.

While Allied ground forces proceeded to build up and gather supplies and equipment for the next move, the 5th Fighter Command continued to strike at the Japanese Army Air Force in the Wewak area in New Guinea. The several airfields surrounding Wewak presented direct threats to the invasion of the Admiralties unless the airfields could be neutralized by Allied airpower. On a fighter sweep over the area on January 18, 1944, a large force of Japanese fighters was intercepted and 14 of them were downed.

The enemy was encountered again on the twenty-third when the fighters returned to Wewak, this time to escort B-24s. Fifty to 60 Japanese fighters were airborne when the American force arrived, but only 20 to 25 of the enemy planes had sufficient altitude to be in a position to attack the bombers.

The enemy attacks were very aggressive and favored head-on attacks, which were pressed dangerously close, as described by Lieutenant Cy Homer of the 80th Fighter Squadron.

"I could not lead element as my right turbo either gave me nothing or 60 inches of manifold pressure. I saw P-40s diving ahead of us over the target, and looking to the right about 10 to 12 enemy fighters coming down at us from the rear. I called squadron leader and then peeled off to the right into them and got a few shots but no results observed. I then tried to join other P-38s but enemy got in between. A lone P-38 was trying to get in a pass at a fighter but pulled off as I continued after it. It took me directly over Boram Strip at about 7,000 feet, where I blew it out of the air from a range of 150 yards. I ran through heavy ack-ack getting away. This plane was an Oscar, and I don't think the pilot saw me, as he took no evasive action.

"I continued about 4 miles from Boram out over the water, climbing to about 16,000, and saw a Tony at my level going seaward. I swung in on a 60-degree deflection shot and hit him around the engine. As I closed to about 200 yards he started flaming around the cockpit. At that instant there was a terrific explosion, which I just barely cleared, and as I went over the top the blast threw me over on my back. When I recovered, oil was on my windshield and nose and pieces had dented the leading edges of my wing. I turned left and was very surprised to see the elevator and rudder assembly of a P-38 intact spinning down along with a conglomeration of wings and engine. I had not seen the P-38 before but assume he had been making a head-on pass at the Tony as I came in from the side. I had wondered why the Tony had not turned into me. Earlier in the fight I had seen a lone P-38 set an Oscar on fire and its pilot had bailed out in this same area. . . .

"As I circled, looking at the P-38 and Tony parts falling, another Tony jumped me from the rear. The first indication I had was when shells hit my right wing. I immediately pushed over, but even then the Tony skimmed over my canopy not over 10 feet from me. As he passed over his draft gave my ship a violent bump. He climbed away and rolled over and headed for home, thinking I was badly hit. This Tony was all silver with red roundels and a large red spinner. My ship was O.K. but minus aileron trim control.

"I turned back and tried to join 3 P-38s coming head-on at about 45 degrees when a lone Oscar dived on the tail of the rear P-38. I called them and dropped maneuver flaps trying to get around, but the rear P-38 turned into me and dived, with the Oscar about 200 feet behind him. I split-essed but could not catch them, having to pull out due to my ship buffeting. The P-38 was smoking badly. As I came around I saw a huge splash in the sea and an explosion and the Oscar heading off for Boram Strip. I gradually pulled up on the Oscar and caught him about a mile and a half from Boram at about 2,000 feet. He turned slowly to the left as I fired, then rolled over and went straight into the water burning. I fired from about 250 yards. To my knowledge the first 2 P-38s never knew they lost the third man. The P-38 hit the water about 7 to 10 miles east of Boram.

"I then climbed to 5,000 and was jumped by a silver Tony as I tried to join some P-40s to the west. I saw him coming and turned into him. He made no attempt to break away but I don't think he fired his guns. I barely cleared him by pulling up.

"The Tony pilots are too determined in a head-on pass and press too close, making one think they don't intend to break. Seemed very fast. All the Tonys were silver throughout with red spinners. Quite a few Oscars were silver also with their engine cowls painted red and some blue. Others were camouflaged green and brown."

No further air battles developed until the B-24s returned to Wewak on February 3. On this mission a formation of 16 P-47s from the 340th Fighter Squadron were attacked by 40 enemy fighters, which dove down upon them from 25,000 feet down to 20,000 feet. A Tony dove under Captain Michael Dikovitsky, who split-essed and fired. The Tony exploded in midair. Dikovitsky's second pass was at a Hamp, which rolled over and crashed. Four other enemy aircraft were felled by the Thunderbolt pilots before the Americans left the scene.

In February 1944, Captain Dick Bong had returned to the Southwest Pacific and was assigned to 5th Fighter Command headquarters at its new base at Nadzab, which was located northwest of Lae, along with another top fighter ace, Major Thomas J. Lynch. At that time Bong had 21 victories, and Lynch had pulled his score up to 18. Colonel Neel Kearby, also assigned to headquarters, had 21 victories to tie Bong. These were the 3 top fighter aces of the Fifth Air Force at that time.

Bong and Lynch teamed up for a short while in what they called their own little "flying circus." The 2 took off together on the afternoon of February 10 to fly a sweep over the airfield at Tadji, southeast of Hollandia. As they arrived, about 6 single-engine aircraft were sighted taking off. Just as they became airborne, a twin-engine aircraft took off in the opposite direction. The 2 Lightning pilots dropped their tanks and started diving from 15,000 feet.

The 2 overtook the Lily bomber at 1,000 feet about a quarter mile from the strip. Lynch led the duo, so he pulled in, fired a short burst, and the right wing of the bomber burst into flames and the plane went straight down. Bong had missed out on the action. All that he could do was confirm that the plane crashed in the water some 200 yards offshore.

Action the rest of the month of February was concentrated in escorting bombers to the Admiralties when the weather permitted and the continuation of fighter sweeps over Wewak. P-40s of the 8th Fighter Squadron and the 40th Fighter Squadron mixed it up with a number of fighters over Wewak on the fifteenth of the month and downed 9 of them.

American troops went ashore at Los Negros on the morning of February 29 against limited opposition. By March 4 capture of the island was assured. All aerial operations over the beachhead were canceled due to bad weather by midmorning. The 475th had sent its P-38s out early; unfortunately, 4 of them failed to return after being separated from the formation under ceiling zero conditions.

Major Tommy Lynch and Captain Dick Bong had another successful sweep to Tadji on the afternoon of March 3. Just as they approached the strip they sighted a Sally bomber taking off. Lynch dropped his tanks and pulled in on its tail. The right engine of the bomber began to smoke after taking hits from Lynch, who overran and peeled off. Bong came in right behind him and put the Sally into the trees.

As the 2 proceeded back to the Tadji area, Bong sighted 5 fighters over the sea offshore and started to attack. The enemy turned back into Lynch and a fighter started a head-on attack, but instead of pressing, it pulled up into a climbing turn to the right. Lynch delivered a short burst and it began to burn. The pilot bailed out.

Lynch then dived down on a Tony and it started smoking, lost altitude, and crashed near Tadji Strip. Another Tony half rolled over Lynch, who pulled up sharply and made a quick shot head-on without results. As the Tony swung around to get on his tail, Lynch slammed the throttles forward and climbed away from him.

Leveling out, Lynch sighted 2 bombers under the clouds and called for Bong to follow him. Lynch made a tail-on pass on 1 and observed hits on the fuselage and engine, but then ran out of ammunition. Bong followed the bomber, put another burst into it, and watched it crash.

In the late afternoon of March 5, Colonel Neel Kearby, perhaps taking his cue from the operations of Lynch and Bong, teamed up with Captain William D. Dunham and Captain Blair of the 348th Fighter Group for a 3-plane fighter sweep to the Wewak area.

"We were over the target at 1710, flying at 22,000 feet and patrolled up the coast for 10 minutes, at which time Colonel Kearby saw 1 Tony approaching Dagua Strip," reported Captain Dunham. "The Tony was landing, so we did not go down after him. Approximately 3 to 5 minutes later, we sighted 3 bombers coming in from the sea. We started our let down and started firing as the bombers were flying parallel to Dagua Strip at 500 feet and 100 yards inland. Colonel Kearby fired on the leading bomber and set it on fire. He then fired at the right wingman but did not knock him down.

"I made a run on the left wingman, knocking him down in flames, and then made a pass at the same one Colonel Kearby had fired at, but did not get him. I immediately made a sharp turn to the left. Captain Blair attacked the third bomber at this time and sent him down in flames.

"As I completed a 180-degree turn, I saw Colonel Kearby with an Oscar on his tail. I immediately swung into position and met the Oscar head-on. My first burst struck the engine and fuselage. The Oscar broke off the attack and turned into me. I held my fire on him and set him on fire. As I passed him the canopy flew off and the ship crashed in the same area the bombers went in. Captain Blair saw all the ships hit the ground.

"As I turned left after firing at the Oscar, a P-47 went past me headed for the hills. I joined him and we came home. As we left the area, we saw where a plane had crashed on the opposite end of the strip from the place the 3 bombers and Oscar had hit. The bombers were Nells."

Dunham got to the Oscar on Colonel Kearby's tail just a bit late. The Oscar had already put his telling shots into Kearby's Thunderbolt. Another outstanding leader and fighter ace was lost to the 5th Fighter Command.

Ironically, it was only 4 days later that Tommy Lynch, who had just been promoted to lieutenant colonel, was killed. He and Bong had returned to the Tadji area, and when they couldn't find any aerial opposition they went down to strafe 3 Luggers, which were motoring along right off the coast. The ships appeared to be carrying fuel drums, which should have made excellent targets.

Lynch led the pass down, and the first run was made. Just as the 2 P-38s pulled up, Bong saw one of Lynch's propellers fly off, and the engine began to smoke. Lynch immediately made for the shoreline, and as he approached it he bailed out. At almost the same instant the P-38 exploded. Just a ball of fire and flaming debris briefly marked the area in which Tommy Lynch had met his death.

The day before Allied troops landed on Manus in the Admiralties, the fighters went up to Wewak once more to make sure the enemy hadn't moved in any aerial reinforcements. The 340th Fighter Squadron tangled with 30 Japanese fighters over the latter's home base and destroyed 14 of them for no loss of their own, although 3 P-47s were damaged.

As the P-47s proceeded to drop the Oscars one after the other, the Thunderbolts began to get low on fuel. Lieutenant Lloyd H. Zaage had downed his Oscar and was flying along at about 4,000 feet when he suddenly felt bullets hitting his aircraft. He turned to the left and dived. His engine was running so rough that he couldn't read his instruments because of vibration. Zaage got down just off the water and began to trim the airplane when a black Tony slid up off his wing. The Japanese pilot looked at him for a long time and probably saw that he was hurt and then got on his tail and proceeded to put more holes in the Thunderbolt. All that Zaage could do was skid slightly, but after a while the Tony finally quit shooting. Perhaps he ran out of ammunition or figured the American pilot couldn't make it home. Regardless, Lieutenant Zaage did manage to make a wheels-down landing at Saifor with only 10 gallons of gasoline left.

Major Hervey B. Carpenter, who got 2 Oscars in the combat, related, "The Japanese pilots were very aggressive and determined. It seems that they had a patrol out to sea about 23,000 feet when we arrived over the target and were waiting for us to lose our advantage of altitude by attacking the fighters on the deck, whose primary mission was to draw us down. Their teamwork was excellent. I am of the opinion that we all mixed it up too much with the enemy, 3 of our ships being damaged as a consequence. However, after committing ourselves on the first attack it was impossible to do otherwise. Another point of interest was the fact that on several occasions the enemy fighters passed up our planes which had no white tails or white markings. This ties in with the statement of my element leader who saw 2 enemy planes with wings similar to a P-47, which he believed to be Tojos. The enemy might have mistaken our unmarked P-47s for friendly Tojos."

Ground troops went ashore at Manus the next morning against limited opposition. By March 17 they had occupied the airfield there and had broken the primary enemy resistance. Air opposition in that area was such that the Fifth Air Force was able to divert its attention elsewhere.

In preparation for the operation of gaining air supremacy over Hollandia and providing long-range escort against the bases there, a number of P-38s had been modified at the depots in Australia. This had been accomplished by installing 110-to-120-gallon tanks in the leading edges of the wings of the P-38Js. In addition there were a number of P-38Js already in New Guinea that could be modified. Specially trained crews were sent up, and the task was accomplished in record time. As the modifications were completed and the new aircraft were moved up from Australia, it was decided to assign all the long-range P-38s to the 8th and 475th fighter groups, while the 9th Fighter Squadron of the 49th Fighter Group exchanged its P-47s for the older P-38s.

The Japanese attempted a final try to reinforce their base at Wewak on the fifteenth of March. However, reconnaissance aircraft caught the convoy of 3 supply ships a day out of Hollandia and damaged 1 so badly that it had to return to port. The other 2 managed to slip into Wewak but were caught at sea by B-25s and A-20s. Neither survived. This was the last attempt to reinforce Wewak. On March 16 all Japanese fighter aircraft were withdrawn from the strips around Wewak and assigned to the bases in the Hollandia area.

Photo reconnaissance in late March revealed that Hollandia was housing approximately 265 serviceable aircraft. It was imperative that air strikes be initiated against these airfields so the invasion of the area could take place in late April of 1944.

A few night missions were flown by B-24s before the first big daylight strike was scheduled for March 20. That morning a force of 75 B-24 Liberators laden with 20-pound fragmentation bombs or 120-pound fragmentation clusters was airborne. They were escorted by 59 long-range P-38s of the 8th and 475th fighter groups flying from Nadzab.

Captain Jay T. Robbins was leading the 23 planes of the 8th Group's 80th Fighter Squadron when 7 Japanese fighters were sighted at 18,000 feet preparing to dive on the bombers. Robbins called in the planes to the 2 P-38 squadrons of the 475th Fighter Group, dropped his tanks, and took off after an Oscar. A direct tail shot rang true as the Oscar rolled out of range. Going down through light anti-aircraft fire to drive off several other enemy fighters, Robbins got numerous hits on another Oscar, which burst into flames and crashed.

Robbins took his flight back up to 12,000 feet to take on another formation of the enemy. Once more he got on the tail of an Oscar, which again half rolled very far out of range. Robbins made a fast diving turn to the left and got on its tail again. In his attempt to dive away from Robbins, the enemy pilot waited too long to recover and went right on into the ground.

The B-24s deposited their bombs on the dispersal points of the airfields and returned to base without loss. The P-38s scored 7 victories and suffered no losses on the mission.

The following day an almost identical force returned to Hollandia. The 80th Squadron met about 25 enemy fighters, as did the 431st Squadron. The 80th scored 6 times, while the 431st added another 7 to the tally. Captain C. M. "Corky" Smith sighted a single plane some 5,000 feet above him, and by pushing everything to the firewall he managed to overtake and shoot down a Dinah twin-engine reconnaissance plane. Heavy black smoke began to emit from the Dinah just as 8 Oscars arrived on the scene. Smith turned into them, but apparently they wanted no part of the

38. The Kawasaki Ki. 61 "Tony." When first encountered over New Guinea, some identified it as a German Messerschmitt. (Oba Collection via Izawa)

39. Captain James A. Watkins (left) poses with his ground crew and his P-38 *Charlie Jean* in New Guinea toward the end of his first combat tour. (Watkins)

40. Colonel Neel Kearby, who won the Congressional Medal of Honor for his feat of downing 6 enemy fighters on October 11, 1943. (USAF)

41. Captain George Welch, who scored his initial victories over Pearl Harbor, became one of the top-scoring pilots in the Southwest Pacific. (USAF)

42. A great fighter pilot and top ace of the Thirteenth Air Force was Lieutenant Colonel Robert B. Westbrook. (USAF)

43. Mitsubishi A6M3 "Zeke" fighters aligned at Rabaul. The Japanese Navy Zeke pilots on Rabaul were some of the very best encountered in the Pacific War. (Izawa)

44. *Porky II* was one of the personal aircraft of the great 80th Fighter Squadron ace, Major Edward Cragg. (80th Fighter Squadron Association)

45. The Mitsubishi A6M2 was the first-line Japanese Navy fighter for the majority of the war. This one was based at the bastion of Rabaul. (Izawa)

46. Colonel Dick Rowland took command of the 348th Fighter Group following Colonel Neel Kearby's promotion. (Grant)

47. Major Tommy Lynch was one of the first Pacific aces and gained great repute as a combat leader in the 35th Fighter Group. (Tansing)

48. The nose of Captain Dick Bong's aircraft when he was at the 25-victory mark. (Haislip)

49. Lieutenant James Haislip of the 9th Fighter Squadron when the unit was flying P-47s in early 1944. (Haislip)

50. B-25 Mitchells slug it out with enemy fighters over Timor Island during the Hollandia campaign. (USAF)

51. Twenty-two-victory, 80th Fighter Squadron ace, Major Jay T. Robbins. His airplane's name, *Jandina*, literally stood for Jay and Ina, his wife. (Weatherill)

52. B-25 rakes Japanese warship with fire in low-level attack. (USAF)

53. 342nd Fighter Squadron ace Captain Marvin Grant and *Racine Belle*. (Grant)

54. P-38Ls line up for takeoff on mission to escort the bombers. The P-38s did a tremendous job of keeping the Japanese fighters off the bombers throughout the war in the Pacific. (USAF)

55. B-24 Liberator *Betsy* of the 90th Bomb Group, Fifth Air Force. (USAF)

56. Thirty-sixth Fighter Squadron ace Captain W. K. Giroux with his crew chief. Giroux not only downed a bevy of enemy aircraft over the Philippines, he also sunk an enemy tanker off the coast of Borneo. (Giroux)

57. Major Tommy McGuire (center) discusses a mission with Charles Lindbergh (left) during the time the great pioneer of aviation was in the Pacific teaching cruise control. (Hill)

58. Three aces of the 475th Fighter Group: left to right, Lieutenant Colonel M. M. Smith, Captain H. L. Condon, and Captain F. J. Lent. (Forester)

59. Pilots of the 9th Fighter Squadron that made the long-range escort mission to Balikpapan, Borneo, in October 1944. (Haislip)

60. Left to right, Major Wally Jordan, Lieutenant Colonel Jerry Johnson, and Major Dick Bong after the Balikpapan show. (Haislip)

61. P-38s of the 475th Fighter Group patrol over Leyte Gulf in the Philippines. (USAF)

62. "The Wheels" of the 49th Fighter Group late in 1944. Front (left to right), Major Robert DeHaven, Major Wallace Jordan, and Major James A. Watkins; back (left to right), Major George Laven, Lieutenant Colonel Gerald Johnson, and Lieutenant Colonel Clayton Tice. (Watkins)

63. *Pudgy IV* was Major Tommy McGuire's aircraft at the 25-victory point. (Mitchell)

64. Captain Marvin Grant's last P-47, *Sylvia,* in the Philippines. (Grant)

65. Major Dick Bong, America's ace of aces, was credited with 40 victories in the Pacific before General Kenney sent him home. (Haislip)

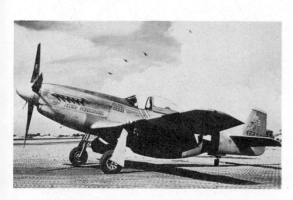

66. Major William A. Shomo's aircraft *Flying Undertaker* in the Philippines. The plane was so named in view of the fact that the pilot had been a mortician in civilian life. (Hill)

67. Captain William A. Shomo, who downed 6 Tonys and a Betty bomber in one combat to win the Congressional Medal of Honor. (Hill)

68. A 165-gallon drop tank fitted with bomb fins for use as a napalm bomb. (Watkins)

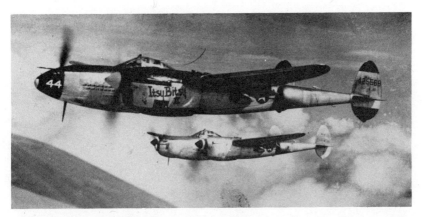

69. Major George Laven of the 49th Fighter Group and *Itsy Bitsy* venture out from Okinawa in 1945. (Watkins)

70. Lieutenant Colonel Clayton Tice and *Elsie*. Tice became commander of the 49th Group late in the war. (Watkins)

71. P-51s of the 348th Fighter Group on Okinawa returning from a fighter sweep over Japan. (USAF)

combat, for they split-essed and dove away. Smith pulled up and around to check on the Dinah once more, but by that time it was in a flaming dive toward the sea.

These 2 missions against Hollandia, coupled with some harassment bombing by night, destroyed over 200 enemy aircraft in the area. The fragmentation bombs dropped by the nocturnal B-24s had played havoc with the enemy aircraft sitting in their revetments, and the enemy reacted by flying the majority of the bombers from their Hollandia bases.

Weather prevented strikes the next 2 days, but on April 3 the P-38s escorted the Liberators to the targets in the Hollandia area once more. This time the bombers were loaded with 1,000-pound high-explosive bombs, which wrecked the enemy's installations.

The B-24s were followed by a second attack wave composed of 96 Douglas A-20 attack bombers, which swept in at treetop level, strafing and dropping parafrag bombs.

To culminate what was one of the most successful missions ever flown by the Fifth Air Force, a third wave of bombers came in to finish up. Seventy-five B-25 Mitchells bombed and strafed everything in sight. On their departure the Japanese aerial strength at Hollandia was finished.

Twenty-four P-38s of the 80th Fighter Squadron escorted the first wave of B-24s in to the target. Lieutenant Cy Homer was leading the third Copper Blue Flight over the target at 17,000 feet when 3 Oscars were sighted above the flight and directly over the target. "One Oscar dove away while the other two started a gentle turn into me as I climbed under them," stated Homer. "I fired a 10-degree deflection shot at the rear enemy fighter and hit him when he half rolled. I rolled down with him and got in a direct tail shot as he leveled off. Black smoke poured from the engine, and a few seconds later this Oscar caught fire and dove into the mountain north of the target. He carried a bomb under his right wing.

"I then saw 2 Tonys in range behind 2 P-38s firing. I called the P-38s, but they continued in a gentle climb. As I was out of range, I could do no good. The first P-38 half rolled with his left engine smoking badly. The second P-38 followed with his right engine smoking. The Tonys continued level flight until they saw me. They began a gentle dive toward Cyclops Strip. My wingman, Lieutenant Fletcher, and I followed, closing into range very gradually. Three thousand feet from the ground I caught the rear Tony, closing to 75 yards before firing. When I fired, the smoke from this Tony was so bad I could not see him and had to pull up as he fell off to the left. I continued and both Lieutenant Fletcher and I fired at the first Tony, which all this time had been trailing quite a bit of smoke. I caught him with a burst as he tried to enter a cloud, whereupon he fell to the left and dived straight into the ground.

"I made a 180-degree turn and dived over the other Tony, which had hit a small hill and created quite a fire. When I next looked back my wingman was gone. As I turned back I saw an Oscar about 100 yards from his tail. I forced this Oscar to break away but scored no hits. More Oscars dived on us and I saw Lieutenant Fletcher set one aflame about 400 yards to the rear of me. Six more P-38s joined us as about 10 Oscars dived on us. I caught 1 Oscar with a 60-degree deflection shot. This enemy fighter was about 300 yards behind a P-38. It started smoking and half rolled. As it recovered I put in a 3-second burst tail shot from about 300 yards. It rolled to the right, pulled up once, then dived into the water northwest of target area about 40 miles.

"As I pulled off him I looked back to find a Tony directly behind firing at me. I pushed over and did vertical reverses, going straight down till I attained 400 miles per hour. I pulled out just over the water and flew due north, gradually outdistancing the Tony. After 5 minutes he turned back, so I turned and followed him until he joined about 5 enemy fighters.

"Being alone and having 2 holes in my left wing, I turned for home, climbing to 20,000 feet and continuing to Buriu in a gentle letdown, where I picked up Lieutenant Dwinell, who had his right engine feathered. I escorted him back to Nadzab. All Oscars I observed were camouflaged brown and green. Red roundels with white outer rim. Some had two white stripes where tail joined fuselage. Some, about 2 I remember, had yellow rings on leading edge of engine cowling."

Lieutenant Dick Bong was flying with the 432nd Fighter Squadron covering the A-20s when Oscars made an attempt to intercept. Bong initially got in some deflection shots, which were ineffective, before he got onto the tail of one of the Oscars and put enough bullets into it to send it crashing into a hillside.

Following the mission to Hollandia on April 3 the air over the area belonged to the Americans. There was a brief resurgence on April 11–12 when the Japanese staged a small fighter force to Wewak, where they intercepted and downed 3 P-47s of the newly arrived 58th Fighter Group.

To insure that the enemy was not moving in a new and large force back into Hollandia, the Fifth Air Force dispatched the B-24s to targets in that area on the morning of April 13. Major Dick Bong joined the 80th Squadron for the mission, flying with the last flight in the unit.

The 2 confirmed victories that he got that day were his twenty-sixth and twenty-seventh, which surpassed the record of 26 victories gained by Captain Eddie Rickenbacker in World War I. The same day General Kenney pulled Bong out of combat again after promoting him to the rank of major. Once more the cherub-faced Michigander was to be returned to the United States. Some weeks later, after Allied forces took Hollandia, divers would check the exact spot where Dick's "probable" had gone in that morning. It was found where he had pinpointed it. Victory No. 28 was officially confirmed.

The bombers that day added to the devastation of the airfields at Hollandia, and the P-38s had downed another 9 enemy fighters. The spark of aerial resistance in the area had been snuffed out.

Coordinated missions continued against Hollandia, but with the absence of enemy air opposition. The bombers became so confident that they began to make individual runs over the target areas, dropping their bombs at will. Weather proved to be the biggest problem. April 16, 1944, will always be known as "Black Sunday" to the men of the Fifth Air Force.

On that day 58 B-24s, 46 B-25s, and 118 A-20s escorted by P-38s carried out another successful attack against ground installations at Hollandia that all but wiped out the fixed defenses in the Humboldt Bay area. On their way home, however, the planes ran into a front that had moved in quite suddenly across the Markham Valley to blanket Nadzab and the other fields in the area with low clouds and rain.

Fighter planes in particular were running low on fuel, and they desperately tried to get into the field at Saidor. Flight patterns were ignored, and soon confusion reigned as the pilots attempted landings with their last few drops of gasoline. When the final total was added, 19 bombers had been lost and 5 P-38s of the 433rd Fighter Squadron had gone down, along with 2 reconnaissance aircraft. The Fifth Air Force had lost 16 men killed, and 37 more were missing from the turbulent weather that had spawned "Black Sunday."

Carrier planes from U. S. Navy Task Force 58 hit the airfields at Hollandia on April 21, the day before invasion, but encountered little enemy air opposition. The next morning ground forces went ashore following another bombardment and strafing of the area. Air strikes were canceled due to lack of air opposition.

The infantrymen met with limited resistance and immediately pushed inland toward the landing strips. The engineers were supplied by air drops despite bad weather, and by April 28 they had the Hollandia strip usable. On May 3, P-40s of the 49th Fighter Group arrived to take over the task of combat air patrol. By May 15 the P-38s of the 9th Fighter Squadron of the 49th Group and the P-38s of the entire 475th Fighter Group were on the ground at Hollandia ready for further operations.

XI

WRAPUP IN NEW GUINEA

The final phases of the New Guinea campaign saw a series of "leapfrog" movements by Allied forces as they moved northward up the coast on into Netherlands New Guinea. The new bases at Hollandia in Netherlands New Guinea proved to be quite a disappointment, as the dust was so bad on the fighter fields that visibility was cut to a minimum and each takeoff of the units based there presented hazards that oftentimes proved fatal.

It had been hoped that 2 of the Hollandia bases could be made all-weather strips in order to move the heavy bombers forward. Construction was started on these facilities as quickly as possible, but then the rains came early, and it became obvious that these bases were unsuitable for heavy bomber operations. The occupation of the island of Biak north of New Guinea, which was serving the Japanese as a vital island outpost in their defense perimeter of the Philippine Islands, became essential.

Before the invasion of Biak could take place, it was necessary that another advanced base be made available for the fighter planes that would cover the landing and support the operation. Surveys indicated that the best locale up the coast would be the Sarmi area, some 96 miles north of Hollandia, and Wakde Island, off the coast of New Guinea. Only a single Japanese air base was in operation in the area, but the enemy had sizable ground forces in place. Air opposition was believed to be quite weak, as the Japanese were in the process of rebuilding their air strength with reinforcements coming down from the Philippines, Japan, and Truk.

Throughout the month of May the bombers of the 5th and 13th Bomber commands carried out missions against Wakde, Noemfoor, and Biak. Enemy air opposition was limited and ineffective. On the morning of May 7, American ground troops landed on the New Guinea coast unopposed between Sawar and Sarmi. The next morning the infantrymen landed on the island of Wakde, where they met intense opposition from some 800 enemy troops who were dug in and prepared to fight to their death. Douglas A-20s and North American B-25s flew close ground support as the infantrymen rooted the Japanese from their emplacements. By late afternoon all organized resistance on the island had ceased.

Aviation engineers went to work on the strip at Wakde immediately, and by May 22 the ground echelons of the 348th Fighter Group moved in but found the island so crowded with men and equipment that they set up their camp on the small island of Insoemanai, some 300 yards away. Four days later the air echelon flew in its P-47s and began combat operations.

Following the conquest of Wakde the attention of the bombers of the 5th and 13th Bomber commands was turned to Biak. Weather prevented the 5th from striking with the desired intensity, but the 2 B-24 groups of the 13th hit targets on Biak practically every day for 2 weeks before the invasion.

P-38s of the 9th Fighter Squadron of the 49th Group provided escort for the bombers, but opposition in the air over Biak was nil. However, the P-38s did tangle with a handful of Tojos while escorting the 380th Group B-24s, which had flown from their base in northwestern Australia to bomb Manokwari Airdrome in Netherlands New Guinea. Four of the Tojo fighters were downed with no loss to the Lightnings.

In the early morning hours of May 27 American troops landed on the island of Biak under a formidable aerial shield. There was little opposition on the beaches and there was initial hope that the airfields would be taken easily. The Japanese had other thoughts about this. The enemy commander chose not to meet the Americans on the beaches, but had concentrated his troops around the area of the airfields and had set up ambush emplacements in the cliffs that overlooked the road that ran from the village of Bosnek, where the troops had landed, to Mokmer Airfield.

The initial enemy air opposition appeared in the form of 8 fighter planes, which came in on the deck late in the afternoon. These were intercepted by P-47s of the 342nd Fighter Squadron, which downed 5 of them but lost a Thunderbolt.

Ground forces found the going very difficult against the determined Japanese, and it was immediately apparent that the conquest of the forces on Biak would require reinforcements and close ground support from aircraft. To prevent enemy air raids, the P-38s of the 5th Fighter Command continued to escort the bombers to air bases in Netherlands New Guinea and against a Japanese base on Jefman Island off the coast of that area.

On June 3, P-38s of the 9th Fighter Squadron took the B-25s to the airfield at Babo on New Guinea, where they downed 12 enemy fighters but lost their squadron commander in the encounter. The enemy planes shot down plus the damage done by the bombers against grounded aircraft and installations virtually eliminated Babo as an important base.

The Japanese decided that the landings on Biak did, indeed, present a vital strategic problem, for once American bases became operational from this location the Philippines would be next to come under attack. This was, in fact, the first real invasion of that defensive domain.

A Japanese task force was assembled and plans were made to steam south with reinforcements for the garrison at Biak. The early sighting of the task force and an erroneous report that an American force supported by aircraft carriers was in the Biak area caused the enemy to call off his initial plan of reinforcement.

It was later decided that 6 destroyers loaded with 600 troops would make the dash for Biak. This force was sighted on the morning of June 8, and B-25s of the 17th Reconnaissance Squadron escorted by P-38s of the 432nd Fighter Squadron caught the force near Amsterdam Island shortly after noon. Three of the Mitchell bombers were downed, but not before they had sunk a destroyer and damaged 3 others. The enemy ships withdrew, regrouped, and started for Biak again that night, but they were met by American destroyers, which broke up the group and sent it scurrying northward. Later a larger force, including 2 battleships, made preparations for another run to Biak, but the American invasion of the Marianas Island to the east ended all hope for the garrison at Biak being supplemented.

In one of the more sizable attempts by the Japanese to bomb American positions on Biak, a formation of Kate-type aircraft were set upon by P-47s of the 342nd Fighter Squadron on the morning of June 12. Captain Popek downed 3 of the Kates in short order. "We were covering the convoy off Biak when they told us a plot was coming in at 15,000 feet," Popek reported. "I turned my flight and started climbing. I spotted five Kates directly in front of us headed south. They were beginning their bombing run. We dropped our tanks and turned to the attack. I couldn't drop my right wing tank as we closed on the Kates. Grant, Overbey, and I took 1 ship each, and they burst into flames and crashed. I pulled up in a climbing turn and saw another to the right of me. A 10-degree deflection burst blew him up, and I turned on another. I closed on him, and after a short burst he fell in flames."

The invasion of the Marianas Islands to the east had prevented further aerial reinforcement for the 23rd Japanese Air Flotilla, but their complex at Jefman-Samate still presented a threat to the Biak area. An all-out strike by B-25s against the airfields there was planned for June 16. The Mitchell bombers were fitted with bomb bay tanks to permit them to make their longest-range mission to date. The B-25s staged into Hollandia and the P-38s of the 8th and 475th groups moved up to Wakde early on June 16 for refueling before taking off on the long haul.

Some of the P-38s became separated while skirting thunderstorms en route, but the majority made their scheduled rendezvous with the B-25s. Major Tommy McGuire took over the lead of the 431st Squadron after Colonel Charles MacDonald had to return to base due to electrical failure. As he led his squadron of Lightnings over the target area at 6,000 feet, enemy aircraft were sighted taking off from the airstrip at Jefman. McGuire dropped his tanks and went down after the single-engine Sonia attack aircraft that were taking off.

McGuire got a good burst into his first target, but excessive speed caused him to overrun the aircraft. However, his element leader, Lieutenant Gronemeyer, shot down the Japanese plane. McGuire's second pass put him on the tail of another Sonia, which he downed with a couple of short bursts.

Finding himself with only his wingman, McGuire turned into an Oscar that was making passes at the bombers. A few short squirts set the enemy fighter to smoking, and when the Oscar reversed his turn, this placed McGuire on his tail. All it took was another burst and the Oscar blew up.

Lieutenant Richard L. West of the 35th Fighter Squadron had fallen behind his unit to protect his wingman, Lieutenant Alsop, who ran out of fuel from his left belly tank. After several attempts, Alsop finally got his left engine started, and he and West struck out together. The 2 P-38s caught up to a flight of 6 other Lightnings and went into the target area with them. On arrival West sighted 5 or 6 Zekes attacking the B-25s that were working the airfield over with strafing attacks.

West got a 90-degree deflection shot at a Zeke. Alsop watched the enemy fighter absorb some of the lead, and then he put another burst full into him. The Zeke went straight down and splashed in the sea below.

West pulled in on the tail of another Zeke and fired until the canopy flew off and the pilot bailed out.

While orbiting the area, West sighted a sail boat in the bay. Amidship there was what appeared to be a bale of cotton or some such material, and the boat was manned by 2 people in the bow and 1 in the stern. West made a pass at the vessel, the crew dove over the side, and the bundle burst into flames. For good measure West strafed a barge on the way home with the rest of his ammunition.

The P-38s alone claimed 25 enemy aircraft downed, while the bombers claimed a dozen. In addition, the Mitchells had destroyed numerous planes on the ground and left the strip on Jefman Island and the one at Samate on the mainland in shambles.

On June 28 the Japanese 23rd Air Flotilla headquarters retreated from Sorong on the Vogelkop Peninsula to Amboina on the island of Ceram. All organized Japanese air strength in New Guinea had been defeated.

Ground echelons of the 49th and 8th fighter groups had been dispatched to Biak early in June with the prospect that the Japanese air bases on the island would fall quickly to the Americans. The men of the 49th were unloaded on June 5, and due to the situation it was necessary to crowd them into a small camp area under adverse conditions. These conditions proved to have another tragic feature when on the twelfth of June a Japanese bomber dropped 4 bombs into the area. Nineteen of the 49th's men were killed and 29 were injured. It was late June before enemy resistance was reduced to small pockets holed up in caves. The enemy's destruction required another month's ground action.

The men of the 8th Group were kept on board the LSTs until June 12–14, when they were debarked at Bosnek. After spending several tense nights expecting Japanese infiltrators they were ferried to the island of Owi just south of Biak on the eighteenth to make preparations for the arrival of the air echelon.

Unfortunately, an epidemic of scrub typhus broke out among the ground echelons of both groups, and before it ran its course over 200 men had been stricken, some of them fatally.

The first 2 squadrons of the 8th Fighter Group flew in to Owi on the twenty-first and twenty-third of June, and they were joined by the third unit on July 1. In addition, a detachment of the 421st Night Fighter Squadron arrived along with some P-39 Airacobras of the 82nd Reconnaissance Squadron.

When difficulties were encountered in the conquest of Biak, General Douglas MacArthur decided another landing must be made in the northern area to insure that airbases would be available for the future scheduled movement toward the Philippines. The island of Noemfoor was selected, as the Japanese already had some airfields there, and its position some 81 miles west of Biak and 45 miles east of Manokwari on the Vogelkop Peninsula of Netherlands New Guinea lent itself to thwarting moves from the north by the enemy.

Fifth Air Force bombers went to work on the island on June 20, and in the absence of air opposition they worked it over thoroughly while the fighters circled overhead uncontested. The landing was made on the island on the morning of July 2 against slight resistance. This was one of the few occasions of island hopping in the Pacific where enemy troops were encountered who had been bombed to the point where they were literally "punch drunk." A number of prisoners were taken the first day, which was most unusual for the Japanese.

One of the prisoners reported that there were 5,000 Japanese on the island, which caused the American command great concern, as this was over twice the number of the enemy that had been estimated. As a result the 503rd Parachute Battalion had 1,424 of its troopers dropped on July 3 and 4. Due to a smoke screen that had been laid to shield the drop, a large number of the troopers were injured when winds spread the smoke over the island. No resistance was encountered by the troopers, and a third drop was canceled.

By July 7 the enemy remnants had been pushed into the interior of the island, and the engineers were able to get to work on the airfields. These fields were found to be surfaced with sand and clay, which limited their future use. However, they were suitable for basing transport aircraft and to stage fighter aircraft through for future operations against the Halmaheras Islands, northwest of New Guinea.

In early July, Mr. Charles A. Lindbergh, the famed American flier, arrived in the New Guinea area, and there he was greeted by General Douglas MacArthur and General George Kenney. Lindbergh discussed at length with General Kenney the performance—or lack of it—that the pilots of the 5th Fighter Command seemed to be getting from the P-38. With proper power settings the pilots could get much greater range from the craft.

General Kenney was quite impressed with this and had Mr. Lindbergh check in with the 475th Fighter Group, where he spent some time teaching the pilots of the unit cruise control on the P-38. The extraordinary consumption of fuel by the P-38 on combat operations had been causing the pilots to have to make refueling stops at advanced bases on their return from missions before returning to home base. Lindbergh taught the men that through manipulation of the rpm controls to a lower setting, then coordinating the manifold pressure (throttle) setting to conform to the setting of "Maximum Economy of Operation," and with mixture setting in automatic lean, that no pilot should suffer any fuel problems.

The one thing that did upset the pilots initially was his statement that by utilizing this method of cruise control there was no reason that the P-38J should not be able to fly 10-hour missions. The thought that missions this long would be forthcoming was not welcomed in any quarter.

However, Lindbergh did prove his point on July 9, when the 475th went all the way to Samate Airdrome in Vogelkop, Netherlands New Guinea, to escort the B-24s. This mission of 8 hours, 15 minutes was at that time the longest mission that had been flown by fighter pilots of the Fifth Air Force.

There was no aerial opposition, so the pilots were forced to spend their offensive punch upon barges and small freighters in the area. One barge was sunk off Cape Sansapor and another barge was left burning.

On July 27 the P-38s of the 475th and 8th groups teamed up to take the Liberators against airfields in the Halmaheras Islands. The bombers completed their run over the target unmolested, and as they headed for home the fighters began to look for targets. Major Tommy McGuire had his P-38s drop their tanks and let them down to strafe Lolobata Airstrip. Several passes were made shooting up enemy aircraft on the ground. McGuire encountered an Oscar fighter in the air; he promptly shot the plane down.

Lieutenant W. K. Giroux was leading an element of the 36th Fighter Squadron when an Oscar was sighted flying low along the coast. Giroux's flight leader and his wingman made passes at the enemy fighter but missed. Giroux made his pass, but just before he hit the trigger the Oscar pulled up, preventing him from getting enough lead to fire. Before Giroux could rack his plane around for another pass Lieutenant Dunaway, the flight leader's wingman, came in for a second pass and shot the Oscar down.

Giroux and his wingman, Lieutenant Randolph, then flew toward Lolobata Airstrip, where 2 more Oscars were sighted. Randolph peeled off first, made a pass, and pulled up. Giroux dove and closed on the Oscar to 200 yards and fired until he was within 50 yards. The Oscar did a split-ess from 400 feet and crashed into the trees at the end of the strip.

Giroux then ran into a real "old pro" while chasing the second Oscar. In the course of the chase 2 more Oscars were sighted, and Giroux wound up in a turning contest with 1 of them. Even though he made 5 passes at the enemy, the Japanese pilot would either outturn him or try to draw him across the strip into the anti-aircraft fire. Giroux had been around too long to be suckered into the latter maneuver. He headed for home.

There is no official record, but it is said that Mr. Charles Lindbergh flew this mission with the 475th Group and in the ensuing air battle over the Halmaheras Islands strips downed a Sonia-type enemy aircraft. The daring of his *Spirit of St. Louis* days had not deserted him.

On the morning of July 20, 1944, American ground forces landed in the Sansapor area of the Halmaheras Islands. Opposition was light, and ground fighting never developed beyond minor skirmishes. Infantrymen moved inland immediately and took the desired airfield sites and Sansapor village.

Following the big air battles over Rabaul in January and February 1944, the pilots of the 13th Fighter Command found themselves left in the backwater of the war. The bombers of the Thirteenth Air Force joined the bombers of the Seventh Air Force in attacks on the Marianas Islands in the Central Pacific, but the range was too great for the Thirteenth Air Force fighters to provide escort.

Upon the seizure of the airfields at Sansapor it was decided that the fighter units of the 13th Fighter Command would be moved forward as quickly as possible. The ground echelons of the 347th Fighter Group and a detachment of the 419th Night Fighter Squadron were shuttled into Sansapor by mid-August, and the air echelons flew into the strip of Middleburg Island just off Sansapor later in the month.

Sansapor was the final step in the leapfrog movement up the coast of New Guinea. It was now time to consolidate positions and begin the buildup of men and equipment for the next steps forward. By the end of July 1944 the squadrons of the 13th Fighter Command were on the move and getting situated at their new bases at Sansapor and on Middleburg Island. The units of the 5th Fighter Command were trying to make things more livable at their crowded bases at Biak, Noemfoor, and Owi. New aircraft and equipment began to trickle in, but as usual, there was nothing new for the men in the way of better rations and comfort. C-rations, canned beef, and dehydrated vegetables continued to compose the bulk of the menu, while bad weather, insects, and poor living conditions did little for morale.

Mr. Charles Lindbergh remained with the 475th Fighter Group for several weeks while teaching the pilots cruise control, and his presence generated a number of interesting stories and events. One of the more repeated stories that was passed from one unit to another had to do with one of the missions that Lindbergh flew. Shortly after takeoff, the P-38 pilots jockeyed for position in the formation, and looking back over his shoulder, one of them sighted Lindbergh struggling to catch up. Glancing back once more, the pilot noted that Lindbergh had not retracted his landing gear. Radio silence was broken with the caustic comment, "O.K., Lindy, that ain't *The Spirit of St. Louis* you're flying. Get your gear up."

To further prove the effectiveness of cruise control on the P-38, Lindbergh accompanied Colonel Charles MacDonald, commanding officer of the 475th Group, Lieutenant Colonel Meryl M. Smith, and Captain Danforth P. Miller on a raid on the Palau Islands 600 miles north of Biak on the morning of August 1.

The foursome arrived over the islands at 15,000 feet. Cloud cover prevented them from getting a good look, so MacDonald led them down to about 8,000 feet below the cover. Not another plane was in the sky, so the Lightnings peeled off for strafing runs. As they climbed upward from their first pass 2 Rufe float planes were sighted.

MacDonald headed for one that sought to get back into the clouds, while Smith broke down for the one that headed for the deck. The enemy pilot never made the clouds, for MacDonald flamed him quickly.

As MacDonald broke off this pursuit, he glanced over his shoulder, and there was Lindbergh with an enemy fighter on his tail. Immediately, he told Lindbergh to break, and he sped toward the intruder. The Japanese pilot sighted MacDonald at the same time and broke for the clouds. This time the Lightning pilot couldn't catch up. The Japanese pilot made good his escape.

In the meantime Colonel Smith had taken care of his Rufe down on the deck, and the 4 P-38s set course for home. En route to base MacDonald sighted a Val torpedo bomber hugging the water; he promptly dove upon the plane and sent it crashing into the sea.

When General Kenney found out that Lindbergh had been on another combat mission and had nearly been shot down, he was most unhappy. While he deeply appreciated the teaching of this outstanding aviation pioneer, he knew that combat was still a young man's game. He ordered Lindbergh to cease combat missions at once and advised him to go home. These Lindbergh did in the latter part of August.

As for Colonel MacDonald, he was dealt the worst punishment a young combat commander could be given. He was ordered back to the United States on leave. With the invasion of the Philippines in the foreseeable future, this was punishment, indeed, for MacDonald.

The Fifth Air Force sent its bombers against the airfields on Ambon, Boeroe, and Ceram Islands in the Netherlands East Indies primarily during the month of August, but much to the disgust of the fighter pilots, the enemy refused to put any opposition in the air.

One exception was on August 17, when the P-38s of the 80th and 35th squadrons escorted B-24s to Haroekoe Airdrome. South of Liang Airstrip on Amboina Island, 15 enemy fighters were sighted. Major Jay Robbins took his flight down for the first pass, and when it was seen that there were no more enemy fighters overhead, he ordered the other 3 to join in the fight.

Robbins got on the tail of an Oscar and apparently hit the pilot with his first burst, for the aircraft careened wildly until it crashed. A 90-degree deflection shot sent another enemy fighter diving for the trees. Here the plane was chased and boxed in by Lieutenants Lloyd and Ravey. Lieutenant Lloyd finally chased it into a valley and destroyed the enemy fighter, but Lieutenant Ravey was killed when he crashed into a hillside attempting to block the enemy's route of escape.

Lieutenant Kenneth Pool and Lieutenant Rolland T. McMillen took Oscars out of the Japanese formation on the first pass by the 35th, and a real free-for-all dogfight followed after their destruction. Lieutenant Gail C. Loveless raked the fuselage of an Oscar, which rolled over and went into the water. Loveless then cut his throttle and lowered his flaps to kill his speed in order to line up on a second Oscar, which he put into the sea with a scoring burst into its fuselage and elevator.

As the Lightnings formed up to head for home, a Sally bomber was sighted down low, coming in for a landing. Lieutenant William A. Gardner closed in fast and opened fire. As he cleared the top of the twin-engine craft, it burst into flames.

En route to base the P-38s ran into a solid front of rainstorms, which caused the formation to scatter. Most of the planes made it through the front, but others were forced to land at Noemfoor and didn't get back until the next day. Once more the weather presented as great a challenge as the enemy fighters.

The first few days of September saw the Fifth Air Force bombers begin to strike at airfields in the vicinity of Davao, the second-largest city in Mindanao. These strikes were aimed at knocking out Japanese air power before the proposed invasion of the island. However, strikes by U. S. Navy fast carrier forces encountered so little enemy air opposition in their missions against targets up the island chain of the Philippines it was proposed that the invasion of Mindanao be bypassed and that the initial landing be made at Leyte.

Before landings could be supported by land-based aircraft at Leyte it was essential that a landing be made on the island of Morotai, the northernmost island in the Halmaheras chain. When ground troops went ashore on Morotai on the morning of September 15, they were unopposed, and very little resistance was encountered throughout the campaign. When the island was declared secure on October 4, only 111 casualties had been taken by the ground forces.

The aviation engineers went to work at once on 2 airstrips, and although there were unforeseen delays, the P-38s of the 8th Fighter Group moved up on October 4 while the P-61s of the 418th Night Fighter Squadron arrived the next day. B-25s moved onto the bomber strip on October 6, and the same day 2 squadrons of P-47s of the 35th Fighter Group moved into the fighter strip.

Since 1942 Allied leaders rued their inability to hit the enemy-occupied and -operated oil center and refineries at Balikpapan in Borneo. A few strikes had been made by bombers of the 380th Bomb Group back in 1943, but these had not been sizable enough to appreciably damage the installations there.

In the summer of 1944 General George Kenney had done his best to obtain the loan of 2 B-29 groups from the 20th Bomber Command to utilize in striking the installations at Balikpapan, but he had been unsuccessful.

It was decided that at the earliest opportunity the heavy bombers of the Fifth Air Force and Thirteenth Air Force would fly the long route some 1,080 nautical miles from Noemfoor to Balikpapan. Initially the 2 heavy bomb groups of the Thirteenth Air Force, the 5th and the 307th, led the way to the Borneo targets unescorted.

Seventy-two B-24s were airborne for the first mission on September 30, 1944, but through mechanical failure and other causes only 46 of them made it over the target. Interception was made by Japanese fighters, and they harassed the bombers constantly in the target area. Four of the big Liberators were lost either to the enemy fighters or to anti-aircraft fire.

The first mission proved that the heavies could make it to the target with sufficient fuel to return and with good bombing results. A second mission was airborne for Balikpapan on October 3. This time the enemy fighters were up and waiting. Unfortunately, the 307th Group went in over the target in a loose javelin-down formation, stepped down from 15,000 to 13,000 feet. The Japanese fighters attacked them unmercifully, and 7 of the 307th's 20 attacking Liberators fell victim to their guns.

The 5th Group came in flying a close formation with sections in line abreast and lost none of their craft. The 307th was quick to change its formation after their disaster over Balikpapan.

Battle formation was not the only thing that the B-24s needed. It was necessary that fighter escorts be provided if the bombers were to attack the refineries in greater numbers. When word got around that the heavy bombers of the Fifth Air Force would be going to the oil targets, General Kenney was determined that the long-range cruise controls that had been learned by the pilots earlier be put to the test. Ground crewmen had found that a 310-gallon tank could be mounted under a wing of the new-model P-47s and P-38s and a 165-gallon tank under the other wing. With this additional fuel the fighters could make it to Balikpapan from Sansapor or Morotai with a bit to spare.

When the big attack came on October 10, first over the target were 16 P-47s of the 40th and 41st fighter squadrons to sweep the area before the B-24s arrived. Enemy planes were sighted taking off from Manggar Airdrome, and the Thunderbolts formed up to meet them.

Captain John R. Young of the 40th Squadron took his flight down from 19,000 to 9,000 feet and pulled up under a formation of 5 Zekes. Young quickly shot down the 2 aircraft in the rear of the formation.

Lieutenant William R. Strand and Lieutenant Hilton S. Kessel made a pass out of the sun on a flight of 4 Oscars. Lieutenant Strand shot the No. 4 man from dead astern, and the plane rolled over and the pilot bailed out.

Strand and Kessel each took an Oscar out of a formation of 5 on the second pass. They climbed into the sun again and joined up for another pass. This time a flight of 4 Oscars got in their way. Strand jumped the leader and shot his wing off for his third victory of the day. In the pass Kessel became separated from Strand. Despite repeated calls to Kessel on the radio, he failed to join Strand and was never seen again. His was the only P-47 lost, while Strand and his fellow pilots cost the enemy 12 fighter planes.

The Fifth Air Force B-24s were next over the target. After the excellent work of the P-47s it had been hoped that things would be a bit easier for the Liberators, but the first 2 groups had to fight off determined attacks to hit their targets. One B-24 was lost to an air-to-air phosphorus bomb, while 3 more went down as a result of air attacks and anti-aircraft fire.

When the Thirteenth Air Force groups of heavies came over the target, they were escorted by 11 P-38s of the 9th Fighter Squadron. The Lightnings accounted for a further 6 victories, 2 of them falling to Major Dick Bong for his twenty-ninth and thirtieth tallies.

The mission of October 14 was virtually a repeat of that of the tenth, but this time the fighters got more kills, and still better, only a single B-24 was lost over the target. The mass formation of Fifth Air Force bombers hit a refinery with excellent results, and Thirteenth Air Force bombers plastered the paraffin and lubricating oil works.

The Thunderbolts of the 40th and 41st squadrons swept the area first, with excellent results. Nineteen enemy fighters were downed for the loss of only a single P-47 to enemy action. One Thunderbolt was shot down by a P-38 in the heat of battle, but the pilot managed to make it out to sea, where he bailed out and was picked up by a Catalina aircraft, which had followed all of these missions for rescue purposes.

Once more determined Japanese pilots mixed it up and attempted to bomb the Liberators with phosphorus missiles. Major Tommy McGuire, who flew the mission with the 9th Fighter Squadron, downed 3 of the enemy and reported, "The Japanese pilots seemed eager and experienced, although their attacks were not coordinated. Besides the bunch we fought there was another bunch of 15 to 20 dropping aerial burst bombs from above us and the bombers. I saw 2 parachutes and about 30 aerial bomb bursts."

Forty-two P-38s of the 13th Fighter Command started out from Middleburg and Sansapor to escort the mission, but due to mechanical difficulties and lack of fuel, only 6 Lightnings of the

68th Fighter Squadron made it over the target. These pilots immediately pitched into the scrap over the target area and accounted for at least 2 of the enemy fighters.

After the fight the P-38s joined up with the Lightnings of the Fifth Air Force and went back as far as Morotai with them, where they landed and refueled. Then they had to make the final leg of their 1,873-mile trip back to Middleburg. Nine hours of flying time had expired for these weary men when they made it home.

The fifth and last mission in the Balikpapan campaign was completed by the 2 Thirteenth Air Force bomb groups alone. The weather was so bad that the escort was unable to get through, and the Liberators that did get over the target area had to drop their bombs by radar.

While the strikes on the refineries had done extensive damage, no permanent destruction was accomplished. The Japanese were able to have the installations back in operational order shortly. The men of the Fifth Air Force and the Thirteenth Air Force got in a lot of long-range experience, which would be of value to them in the Philippine campaign. The return to the islands would be their next objective, and all eyes turned to the north for its accomplishment.

XII

LEYTE

In early October 1944, the U. S. Seventh Fleet assembled the force that would invade the island of Leyte in the Philippines. The Third Fleet, which included Task Force 38, the fast carrier striking force, was working its way southward for the greatest landing the Pacific had ever seen. Strikes were flown by the carrier planes against the Japanese bases at Formosa, where many enemy aircraft were destroyed on the ground and in the air.

For 3 days before the invasion of Leyte the carrier aircraft hit the island of Luzon. Japanese airfields and aircraft received the brunt of the attacks in an attempt to diminish the defensive airpower that the invasion fleet was sure to encounter during and shortly after the landing. In the fleet air strikes on Formosa and Luzon during the period between the tenth and the eighteenth of October, the carrier pilots claimed the destruction of 655 airborne and 465 grounded aircraft.

During this time the fighter planes of the 5th and 13th fighter commands were hard at work bombing, strafing, and escorting bombers of their respective air forces against targets on the islands of Mindanao and Negros. The enemy had not had time to rush reinforcements down to the Philippines, so aerial opposition was practically nil.

On the morning of October 20, 1944, the Americans returned to the Philippines in force. Troops of the 1st Cavalry Division and the 24th Infantry Division landed on the northern beaches near Tacloban on the island of Leyte, while the southern force, composed of the 7th and 96th infantry divisions, went ashore in the vicinity of Dulag. The invasion was made without undue difficulty. The immediate objectives were the airstrips at Tacloban, which fell the first day, and the field at Dulag, which was taken the following day. It was imperative that land-based aircraft be made available to cover the ships in the harbor, which were laden with men and supplies waiting to go ashore. Ground crewmen of the 5th Fighter Command began landing on the morning of October 24 to ready the airfields.

The invasion of Leyte had caught the Japanese off balance, and their naval forces were not in position for immediate reprisal, but plans for a counterattack were set in motion swiftly. In the meanwhile the invasion fleet and beachhead were subjected to sporadic though vicious air attacks.

The enemy course of action was to send a task force built around his surviving carriers down from Japan to attempt to draw the main American fleet north to intercept. Two other forces, without carriers, would strike the invasion fleet in Leyte Gulf.

The great naval battle in Leyte Gulf of October 24–25, 1944, resulted in the death of the Japanese fleet. Four aircraft carriers, 3 battleships, 10 cruisers, and 9 destroyers were sunk, and many more ships were damaged. The beachhead on Leyte had been saved, and some of the ground echelon of the Fifth Air Force fighter groups had a hand in the naval battle when aircraft from escort carriers that had been sunk came into Tacloban Airstrip for refueling and rearming.

As the Japanese rushed their forces from Formosa, Borneo, and the home islands to counter the invasion, the P-38s of the 13th Fighter Command continued to protect the front to the south of the Philippines by striking at enemy installations in the Celebes. On October 23, 16 P-38s of the 339th Fighter Squadron flew a fighter sweep over the Macassar area. Three Lightnings aborted, but 13 made it on to the target. Lieutenant Colonel Robert Westbrook led his section of 6 aircraft in strafing Boeloedowang Airdrome, while Major Endress led the remaining P-38s against Limboeng Airdrome. A total of 6 enemy fighters were destroyed in the air and 6 on the ground, with no losses to the P-38s.

On October 26 the 7th and 9th squadrons of the Fifth Air Force's 49th Fighter Group were sent up to the island of Morotai, northwest of New Guinea, in preparation for their movement to the Philippines. Their ground crews already at Tacloban worked side by side with the aviation engineers throughout the day and night to lay the steel matting in preparation for their arrival. The airstrip at Dulag presented greater problems for the engineers, and it would not be ready before mid-November. Shortly before noon on October 27, the last matting was laid on the 2,800-foot strip at Tacloban, and a few minutes later 34 P-38s roared overhead and came in to land.

As quickly as the planes could refuel, some of them were back in the air over the strip. Major Dick Bong took off with Colonel Robert L. Morrissey and Major Gerald Johnson that afternoon to intercept a reported flight of enemy aircraft, but the pilots were unable to locate them. As they headed back to the strip, 2 Oscars were encountered head-on 15 miles from base.

Bong fired a short deflection burst at one of the aircraft, and then Major Johnson got on the tail of the Oscar. Colonel Morrissey got on the tail of the other, and both Oscars crashed into the water. Bong sighted another Oscar down on the deck, which he went after and flamed right above the sea. While he was chasing the Oscar, Major Jerry Johnson shot down a Val dive bomber that strayed into the area at the wrong time.

Bong added 2 more victories to his score on October 28 when he downed an Oscar over Leyte and another over Masbate Island. Bong had joined up with Colonel George Walker, commanding officer of the 49th, and Colonel Morrissey after he downed the Oscar over Leyte, and on a patrol over Masbate the 3 pilots broke up a formation of some 17 Oscars that were laden with drop tanks and bombs. The enemy fighters dropped their loads, and in the ensuing fight Bong got strikes on 2 of the enemy aircraft, but none of the P-38 pilots was able to chalk up a victory. Bong was hit in the left coolant radiator and Colonel Walker had a fighter get on his tail that had failed to fire, apparently the victim of a jam, so the Americans were glad to break off the combat and head for home. Regardless, they had broken up a large formation of enemy aircraft and prevented a bombing raid on American naval or ground installations.

The P-38s of the 8th Fighter Group, still on Morotai, still had the job of cutting the Japanese supply line to its fuel supply in Borneo. On October 30, Captain W. K. Giroux led the 36th Fighter Squadron against the airfield at Sandakan on the northern tip of Borneo. "The enemy were using it as a refueling station for the planes they were sending in to reinforce the big oil center of Balikpapan," stated Giroux. "When we got there we found only 6 planes on the ground. We knocked them out in a hurry. There were a couple of tankers a little way out in the harbor, so I took my squadron and went in on them. I singled out one and made a run on it. I came in pretty low, just skimming the water. I started shooting at about 300 yards and then pulled up over it. I must have hit a depth charge or some other high explosive because just as I got over the tanker the explosion caught me. I was traveling around 400 miles per hour and it blew me about 50 feet and a lot of debris damaged my plane. After I had passed over I found my plane would still fly and when I looked back the tanker was burning. It had broken in 2 parts and was starting to go down. I made a couple of passes at the second tanker, and all the rest of the guys got a shot at it. We left it burning badly and listing."

The 8th Fighter Squadron came up to Tacloban to join the rest of the 49th Group on October 30, and the following day half a dozen P-61 Black Widow night fighters of the 421st Squadron arrived.

There was no rest for the weary at Tacloban. All were kept awake during the night by continuous red alerts as enemy aircraft seemed to be overhead constantly. Each night took its toll of personnel and aircraft. Despite the rain, heat, and bombardment, the ground crews seemed to have enough fighters serviced, repaired, and ready to take to the skies each morning to cut deeply into the Japanese attackers.

On November 2 the men of the 49th Fighter Group downed 26 enemy aircraft. The Japanese were going for broke, and all available reinforcements were being sent to Luzon to carry out attacks against the Americans on Leyte. A number of new types of aircraft were encountered. Among them was the Jack fighter. This new plane with its big radial engine was an excellent performer, and with a seasoned pilot at its controls it was a real challenge to down one of them.

Captain Robert M. DeHaven, veteran ace of the 7th Fighter Squadron, got one of the new Jacks on the afternoon of the second. DeHaven was in one of several P-38s flying top cover for other Lightnings dive bombing shipping at Ormoc Bay. An enemy fighter was called out, and DeHaven went after it.

"The bogey was about 16,000 feet and even at a distance was easily identified as a new Jack-type fighter," reported DeHaven. "I used full gun trying to reach his altitude and he started climbing, also making a slow right turn. I kept turning in behind him and was gradually catching him in the climb when he decided I was too close, so he started a shallow dive toward Poro Island. At the time, I was at 18,000 feet and directly behind him, so I kept full gun and began to close very slowly, going downhill in about a 20-degree dive. At 15,000 feet I was indicating 400 mph and slowly catching him. He must have been using water injection, for there was a faint trail of dark smoke behind him. About 13,000 I was in range to shoot, so opened fire from dead astern and nearly point-blank range. After the second burst, he started letting out heavy gray smoke, and after the third burst, he came all to pieces. I flew through the wreckage, denting my wings and throwing oil all over my plane. What was left of him crashed on Poro Island."

DeHaven flew through so much debris in downing this fighter that his own was a total washout on his return. On dismantling his P-38 they found a fragment of the map that the enemy pilot had been carrying.

Captain Elliott Dent, also of the 7th Squadron, became separated from his flight that afternoon and fell victim to 4 Zekes. ". . . four Zekes came out of the clouds from the right and I turned into them," Dent related. "Evidently my flight had lost me in the clouds because I never saw them after that. I made a head-on pass at the 4 enemy, firing a burst at the lead ship. The outside man of the flight chandelled to the outside of the formation while the 2 center men split, 1 going up and the other down. From then on, for at least 15 or 20 minutes, which seemed like forever, my memory is very hazy as to individual passes, but during the entire time, I was either attacking or being attacked. As I would go in for a pass on 1 Zeke I'd see 1 or 2 others coming in on me. Firing short bursts, I was able to chase 1 and pull into another before the second one could do any harm. On 2 occasions, to save myself, I had to split-ess at fairly low altitude, 1 time pulling out just over the water as my plane buffeted severely. This continued until only 1 Zeke was left, 2 of the others had gone down in flames, while the third crashed into a mangrove swamp.

"At about 1,000 to 2,000 feet, as I closed on the fourth Zeke from the stern, he passed over a Japanese destroyer and turned to the left. As I was just ready to fire, I must have been right over the destroyer, because my right engine was shot out by what sounded like machine-gun fire. I was blinded by the smoke and couldn't see even after my canopy was jettisoned. Because of the slipstream, I had a difficult time getting out, being pushed back in the cockpit several times. I finally recovered enough to realize I was going too fast, so I chopped the throttles and succeeded in laboriously forcing my way out. Just after the chute opened, the fourth Zeke made 1 pass at me without scoring any hits. I landed on the water about 1 mile offshore from Tolingon. I seemed to be exhausted, and it was several minutes before I could extricate myself from the parachute harness. This was about 5:50 P.M. Luckily, my rubber raft wouldn't work, because I think I would have been picked up by the Japanese had it been visible. Only 1 side of my Mae West would inflate. I saw a coconut floating about 10 yards away and swam over to it, placed my head alongside, and hoped the 2 objects looked alike.

"Within the next 5 minutes an enemy destroyer came within 200 feet of my position but turned away. A little later, a Sonia, flying about 50 feet off the water, came over me but I was lucky again, it kept going. Still later, another destroyer headed for me and came so close I could make out features of Japanese on the deck, but it turned away. They were heaving stuff, possibly garbage, off the deck of this destroyer.

"I gradually tried to edge my way toward shore, swimming slowly, and just before the sun went down I heard voices, and a few minutes later, I saw two Filipinos in a boat."

Dent's rescuers turned him over to guerrilla forces, who got him back to base.

Lieutenant William Huisman of the 9th Fighter Squadron had destroyed 2 Zekes and was coming in to land when another P-38 from another squadron approached from the rear. The propellers of this plane chewed the tail of Huisman's aircraft, causing it to slide down the runway into some heavy equipment. The pilot of the other plane was killed outright, and a number of men working in the area were injured.

In an extraordinary show of heroism, Technical Sergeant Howard G. Harclerode and Sergeant Alfred H. Robinson of the 9th Fighter Squadron braved the flames to pull Huisman from the aircraft. Sergeant Ventriglia and Private Howard A. Darby jumped into an ambulance and roared in to the crash scene amid exploding ammunition to pick up the badly burned pilot and rush him to the hospital. Despite the efforts of these men, Lieutenant Huisman died of his burns a few days later.

In an effort to beef up the fighter strength, the 432nd Fighter Squadron was brought up to Tacloban on November 2, and the P-40s of the 110th Tactical Reconnaissance Squadron were moved in the next day.

On Morotai, the men of the 35th and 36th fighter squadrons still had their hands full escorting bombers attacking the Japanese air bases on Negros.

Captain W. K. Giroux led the fighters of the 36th on November 2 when they met 15 enemy fighters coming up to intercept the bombers. Captain Giroux lost no time in downing an Oscar, which crashed offshore from Alicante. As Giroux started to climb he got an Oscar on his tail, but one of his squadronmates came to his assistance and opened fire with a beautiful deflection shot. The Oscar started to burn immediately. Giroux later learned that this excellent shooting display had been put on by Lieutenant John S. Dunaway.

Giroux then sighted an Oscar diving into a cloud formation, waited for him to come out, and chased him down on the deck, where he shot him up and sent him crashing into the trees. A third Oscar was downed in a turning contest that finally saw the plane crash south of Alicante.

Two days later Captain Giroux led 15 P-38s up to Negros once more to strafe the Japanese airdrome at Fabrica. Fifteen enemy aircraft were sighted, and the squadron split into elements and climbed to the attack. Lieutenant Dunaway put on another exceptional show of deflection shooting, which accounted for 2 Zekes, a Tony, and a Kate bomber. Giroux downed a Tony to mark up his seventh victory in 4 days.

The Thirteenth Air Force fighter groups were too far back to get in on the Philippine action, and they continued to concentrate their efforts against targets in the Celebes. A fighter sweep against airdromes in the Macassar area on November 7 by Lightning pilots of the 339th Squadron met with great success.

Three Nick-type fighters were downed and another 17 enemy aircraft were set afire and destroyed on the ground. Lieutenant Donald Coe caught his Nick as it tried desperately to get in to land. The enemy craft went into a steep dive and managed to get into clouds, but Coe picked it up again as it came in on its final approach to land. The Lightning pilot gave it a short burst from out of range as the Nick touched down. For some strange reason it took off again. Lieutenant Coe then closed on it when the Nick was 50 feet in the air. Coe raked the twin-engine craft from tail to nose, which caused it to nose over and belly in.

When the Lightnings finished strafing the enemy planes on the ground, 17 were ablaze, while 5 others were shot up and apparently did not burn due to empty fuel tanks. The P-38s began to run low on gas and were forced to set course for home. Fortunately all of them made the 785-mile trip back safely, although the engine of 1 P-38 went dead after landing for lack of fuel before he was able to taxi off the runway.

Lieutenant Joseph M. Forester of the 432nd Squadron prevented a strafing run on the strip at Dulag on Leyte on the morning of November 8. He and his wingman had just pulled up off the field when they noticed 3 flashes, denoting a red air raid alert. An Oscar was sighted at an altitude of 500 feet coming in with the evident intention of strafing the planes that were parked on the side of the landing strip. Lieutenant Forester called the controller to stop the anti-aircraft fire that was bursting around the enemy aircraft. He then gave chase and caught the Oscar in the vicinity of Catmon Mountain, where he set it afire with a series of short bursts. The Oscar crashed in flames while the pilot bailed out.

In another attempt to reinforce their ground forces on Leyte, the Japanese sent a convoy down from Manila on November 8, which was sighted late on the afternoon of the ninth off Ormoc. B-25s, P-38s, and P-40s attacked viciously, and although none of the ships was sunk, many troops were killed, and much equipment was destroyed before darkness came.

The 432nd Squadron had a great day on November 10, in 2 engagements. The first fight occurred when 12 P-38s were scrambled at 8:15 A.M. to intercept enemy aircraft over Ormoc Bay, where the reinforcing convoy was fleeing northward. An Oscar and a Zeke were sighted flying over Ponson Island. Colonel Charles MacDonald, who was leading, destroyed the Oscar, and the Zeke escaped by ducking into the clouds.

MacDonald and his wingman were low on fuel, so they returned to base, leaving Lieutenant Perry Dahl to take over the remaining formation of 10 P-38s. About 5 minutes later, 12 Tonys were sighted flying in a tight "V" formation. The Lightnings were on the same level as the enemy, so Dahl took them into a high climbing turn to the left in order to get in an attack position from 6 o'clock high.

The enemy was apparently unaware of the presence of the P-38s until the Tonys were fired upon. In the short but spirited fight, 9 of the Tonys were definitely destroyed, and 2 were chalked up as probables. However, the fight had its tragedy. Lieutenant Perry Dahl, the formation leader, collided with Lieutenant Grady Laseter. Dahl's right wing and tail boom were torn off, but by some miracle he was able to bail out of the flaming wreckage. Lieutenant Laseter died in the crash.

After landing safely in the water, Dahl found himself in the center of the Japanese convoy of 4 destroyers. One destroyer fired at him in his rubber dinghy and then pulled up alongside his raft. Dahl had remained in the dinghy but slumped forward in the hope that they would believe him to be dead. Due to his burns, which had blackened his body, the Japanese apparently deemed him to be so. They were so close that Dahl could hear them talking, but suddenly they revved up their engines, and the ship steamed on out of the area firing its anti-aircraft guns. Dahl then ventured to look up and observed that the ship had come under attack by B-25s.

Later in the day Dahl was subjected to a strafing attack by a Tony, which made a pass and sped on to the west. Shortly afterward more Japanese shipping passed close by, but Dahl resumed his game of playing possum and was not bothered.

At dusk his raft passed close to land, and Filipinos came out in canoes to pick him up.

During this period rainfall had played havoc with the airstrips on Leyte. Each takeoff and landing was a gamble. The steel matting became covered with mud, and accidents were numerous. The 432nd Squadron stayed mired in the mud on Bayug Airstrip from November 13–21, held to the ground.

Camp areas for the men were barely livable. All referred to the camp areas as "swamps." "Ten in one" rations were warmed in the cans over smoke pots and small gasoline stoves. Any bathing had to be done from helmets filled with rainwater. Strict blackouts were in effect, and every night the enemy came over to send the men scurrying to their slit trenches, which were usually half filled with rainwater. The one advantage of the dampness was its effect on incendiary bombs; they sputtered harmlessly and went out in the mud.

Four P-38s of the 431st Squadron, which had arrived on Leyte on November 9, were airborne from Dulag Airstrip on the afternoon of November 12 when they sighted 4 Jack-type fighters escorting a Lily bomber, heading toward their base. As soon as they were sighted the Jacks split into elements, one to the left and one to the right. Major Tommy McGuire and his wingman, Lieutenant Hudnall, took off after the Jacks, splitting to the left while Captain Robert Cline and Major Rittmayer went after the right-hand pair.

The Jacks climbed up to meet McGuire and his wingman head-on. McGuire's initial short burst was ineffective as they passed, so he used dive flaps to turn inside one of the Jacks, which he set on fire. McGuire then scared a Jack off his wingman's tail with a deflection shot before both McGuire and Hudnall had to speed to Major Rittmayer's rescue. McGuire broke off his pass on the Jack on Rittmayer's tail, but Lieutenant Hudnall, firing all the way, pulled through with the Jack and it dove straight down into the ground.

McGuire caught the last Jack as it attempted the run for home and hosed it down from dead astern. The Jack's tail assembly went to pieces, whereupon it crashed and exploded.

The men of the 35th and 36th squadrons continued to escort the Liberators up to Negros, and it was on the mission of November 14 that Major Jay T. Robbins, commanding officer of the 80th Squadron but flying with the 36th that day, had a most unusual combat experience.

"The assignment for Agate (36th Squadron) was roving top cover for 2 groups of B-24s, which were to strike Alicante Airdrome, Negros Island," Robbins reported. "After approximately an hour, 5 Agate planes had 'snaffued,' reducing the squadron to 11 P-38s and Blue Flight to 3 planes.

"Headed north at 16,000 feet over Alicante we sighted 1 Zeke and 3 Oscars at 8,000 feet at 10 o'clock position. They probably had just finished a patrol or had been warned that we were in the vicinity and were attempting to land before we sighted them. As we started our dive we were sighted, and the enemy separated into 2 elements of 2 planes each. This prearranged teamwork took 1 element to the right and 1 to the left. I followed the 2 that broke to the right. With my throttle completely chopped, I came almost within firing range when the wingman in the element made a moderately sharp turn to the right. I believe this was a planned maneuver, the leader expecting me to follow the wingman, thus putting him in position for a tight turn onto my tail. So that he might think his ruse had worked, I deceptively started to turn after the wingman, calling at the same time to my wingman and telling him to take the enemy wingman. Then I made a shallow dive and went underneath and to the outside of the enemy leader's gradual right turn. Giving my plane the throttle, I drove up to within 150 feet before opening fire. My maneuver made the enemy flight leader lose me, and he continued his turn without further evasive action. My first burst knocked pieces out of his rudder and left wing, and my second burst hit the canopy, which blew off, barely missing my plane. Black smoke and flames came from the left side of the plane. The pilot attempted to bail out. His chute hit the tail of his plane and either ripped or failed to open, as both the pilot and plane fell to the ground several miles northeast of Alicante Airdrome.

"It is my opinion that the Japanese fighter pilot has a very well-defined blind spot when you come in low and behind him. In the destruction of my last 9 enemy planes, I used this approach on 6 of them, and in each case I was able to approach to an extremely close range without detection and without encountering the evasive half roll that detection usually brings."

The old veteran fighter pilots of the Fifth Air Force were not being fooled by the Japanese at this late date.

On the ground at Leyte, American infantrymen had driven the Japanese across the island, and they continued to press them into a beachhead sector from Ormoc in the north to Baybay to the south. The enemy had tried desperately to get reinforcements to Leyte, but most of his attempts had been stymied. Allied air power and naval power were beginning to tell. If the Navy didn't destroy Japanese shipping in the harbors of Luzon, airplanes caught Japanese convoys either en route or in coves and inlets, where the Japanese attempted to hide during the day. The relentless bombing and strafing of the Americans cost the enemy dearly in equipment and troops.

Early on the morning of November 24 Japanese planes came to attack the strip at Tacloban while the crew chiefs were warming up the planes and pilots were preparing to take off. Fragmentation bombs were dropped, but many failed to explode.

In spite of the dawn raid, the 8th Fighter Squadron had 4 planes airborne after sunrise to patrol Carigara Bay. Captain Robert Aschenbrener had only twelve hours logged in a P-38, but when enemy fighters were encountered over the bay, he turned in a really fine account of himself by downing 4 of them.

November had been a month of momentous events in the Philippines. The Americans were on Leyte to stay, and the Japanese were holding out to make one more desperate stand. The pilots of the 49th and 475th fighter groups had real "field days" in the air battles over Leyte. It was a month that had seen the scattering of veteran aces increase their scores, and many young replacements had chalked up their 5 and more victories on the scoreboard to become aces. The men on the ground had outdone themselves to keep the airplanes in the air despite untold hardships.

The airfield situation on Leyte had been most disappointing. Of the 5 strips on the island, Dulag and Tacloban had to take the entire brunt of air operations. Bayug was a fair-weather fighter base, although by the end of November it had a short steel surface. Both San Pablo and Buri dromes had to be given up when the heavy rains came.

On the night of November 28 another Japanese convoy came down from Manila under the cover of foul weather, and once more the reinforcements were intercepted. Two of the vessels were sunk by American torpedo boats, but supplies and men were unloaded at Ormoc from several ships before they came under attack from P-40s and P-47s the next day.

Although their forces were not built up to the desired strength, the Japanese were still determined that their scheduled offensive to break the back of the American forces on Leyte would take place. But the men and planes of the Fifth Air Force were ready.

On the afternoon of December 6, Japanese twin-engine Topsy transports left Angeles Field on Luzon loaded with paratroopers to be dropped on Leyte. Two transports approaching Tacloban were shot down, and 2 others crashed on Dulag. The 5 paratroopers who managed to bail out over Dulag were quickly disposed of.

Successful drops were made at the deserted strips at San Pablo and Bayug. Little damage was done, but it did take time to hunt down and dispose of the infiltrators. The greatest effect that the paratroopers did have was to cause a great deal of excitement and cause a lot of trigger-happy sentries to be posted around the airfields for several nights.

The nightly raids of the Japanese had also caused the Air Force's 421st Night Fighter Squadron to be replaced with Marine Corps F6F Hellcat fighters. The big P-61s just couldn't intercept the Oscar fighter-type aircraft and chase them at the speeds the Oscars flew.

On December 6, the 475th Fighter Group did a tremendous job of fighting off Japanese kamikaze suicide attacks on Navy ships that were sweeping the Surigao straits for mines prior to the passage of the invasion convoy carrying the 77th Infantry Division. The division's task force left Leyte Gulf late on the evening of December 6, destined for Ormoc Bay on the northwestern coast of the island of Leyte. The 77th Division, which had arrived at Tacloban in late November, hit the beach 4 miles to the south of Ormoc town on the morning of the seventh.

Their landing coincided with the start of the northward push of the 7th Infantry Division, which had driven to the west coast of Leyte in the vicinity of Damulaan. The 7th was to link up with the 77th and close all but the extreme northwestern area of Leyte to the enemy for points of reinforcement.

As fate would have it, the Japanese had chosen the seventh of December to land troops on San Isidro Bay, some 18 miles north of Ormoc. The convoy was attacked by Marine Corps F4U Corsairs, which had just arrived at Tacloban. The gull-winged fighters sunk several of the ships, but not before 4,000 fresh enemy troops had been landed.

Fifth Air Force fighters were kept busy all day on the seventh fighting off the attacks of the determined kamikaze pilots. Sixteen P-47s of the 348th Fighter Group's new 460th Fighter Squadron were covering the task force that morning when a formation of Japanese bombers was sighted beginning their bomb run on an American destroyer in Ormoc Bay. The Sallys were flying at 5,000 feet as 2 P-47s dove down on them from above. Both Lieutenant Thomas M. Sheets and F/O William Aswill opened fire from dead astern, and each attacked Sally burst into flames and crashed into the sea.

Two other Thunderbolts attacked a single Nick fighter over Poro Island, southwest of Ormoc Bay. The element leader attacked first, but overshot after scoring a few hits. The Nick managed to make a circling turn over Ormoc Bay where it dropped a bomb, but it would not escape the second P-47. Lieutenant George R. Grace closed from astern, and a long burst set both of the Nick's wings on fire. The Nick crashed into the water.

Shortly before noon, Colonel Charles MacDonald, commanding officer, and Lieutenant Colonel Meryl Smith, deputy commanding officer of the 475th Fighter Group, intercepted 3 Jack fighters approaching the task force. MacDonald attacked the leader of the enemy flight from astern and set him on fire. Lieutenant Colonel Smith attacked the other 2 bomb-carrying fighters and put 1 of them in the water. MacDonald then got in a heated dogfight with the other Jack. Neither pilot could seemingly get an advantage and bring his guns to bear on the other, but Lieutenant Colonel Smith came back and shot the Jack down in flames.

Major William Dunham was leading 9 P-47s of the 460th Fighter Squadron over the invasion shipping at 1:45 P.M. when he sighted 13 Zekes coming in at 12,000 feet. The enemy was flying in flights of 4, so Dunham took his flights down in a line-abreast stern attack.

Dunham closed on the leader, fired a short burst, and the enemy pilot bailed out as he went over him. Dunham then banked left and attacked another Zeke from astern as the enemy pilot chased a P-47. This Zeke burst into flames and went into the water.

Some 15 minutes later Dunham was circling over the San Isidoro area when he sighted 4 Oscars at 16,000 feet. He and his wingman pursued them south and closed from astern. One Oscar broke down and to the right while the other 3 flew straight ahead. Dunham closed on the right-hand Oscar and set him on fire. Dunham then turned left and attacked the next Oscar to the left from astern. This plane also burned and crashed.

Dunham, who had downed 4 enemy fighters in the brief combat, stated, "The enemy pilots seemed inexperienced but willing to engage in combat. The Zekes carried aerial burst bombs, which they dropped as we went in on the initial attack."

Colonel Charles MacDonald, 475th Group commanding officer, got into his second fight of the day early in the afternoon. He mixed it up with Jacks again and shot down 2 of them. However, when the fight was over Lieutenant Colonel Meryl Smith was missing. After scoring his eighth and ninth victories, Lieutenant Colonel Smith's plane disappeared in an overcast with both engines of his P-38 smoking. He was not seen again.

Major Dick Bong, who was flying with the 431st Fighter Squadron that day, scored his thirty-eighth victory, while McGuire pulled his score up to 30 that afternoon. The 2 were in the same fight, with Bong leading the formation when Bong called in a bogey. "As I did not see the enemy, he [Bong] took us into the rear of the Sally and shot her down in flames on the northeastern tip of Bohol Island," stated McGuire. "We then resumed patrol northwest of the convoy, and at 1540 I sighted a Kate north of the convoy and led our flight in to the attack. The anti-aircraft from our convoy was heavy, so I took 1 good burst at the Kate, getting some hits, then broke away to avoid the A/A. Major Rittmayer, my wingman, followed through the A/A, and as a result of his attack, the Kate went into a spin and crashed into the water.

"We resumed patrol, and at 1610 I sighted 5 Tojos flying in from the north and just under the overcast at approximately

2,500 feet. We started for them just as the convoy opened their defensive fire. I felt it was necessary to break up the Tojo's attack so, despite the A/A barrage, I led the flight in. I singled out the Tojo to the left, fired from astern, and the Tojo crashed to the rear of the convoy. Major Rittmayer made a rear attack on a Tojo, which flew down 1 lane of shipping. That Tojo crashed into the bay. I made a pass at 1, but lost him in a turn, directly over an LST, at low altitude, and Lieutenant Fulkerson latched him, causing the Tojo to explode near the shipping. As there were no more Japanese around, I climbed up to the left and to the north of the convoy. At this time I saw a Tojo crash into the water after Major Bong hit him on a head-on pass. Lieutenant Fulkerson then joined me, and we resumed patrol."

The American fighter pilots didn't call it quits until dark that day of December 7, and a weary bunch they were. Seventy-five Japanese planes had fallen before their guns that day as they flew dawn-to-dusk missions. The Navy lost several ships to kamikaze attacks, but it was through no fault of the 5th Fighter Command and the Marine Corps Corsairs pilots, who constantly braved enemy attacks and friendly anti-aircraft fire to chase and down the Japanese planes.

There was an absence of enemy aerial activity until December 10, when supply convoys of the enemy from Luzon to the Ormoc Bay area set out. The P-47s of the 460th Squadron caught a formation of Sally bombers escorted by Tony fighters and downed 4 of the bombers and 2 of the fighters. A flight from the 432nd Squadron encountered 3 Jacks and a Zeke and got hits on 1 of the Jacks before they broke off the combat to escort a wounded Thunderbolt pilot home.

On December 11 both sides put up all the air power they could muster in attempts to reinforce their forces in the Ormoc Bay area. That morning a 4-plane flight of P-38s from the 8th Fighter Squadron led by Captain Robert Aschenbrener sighted a Japanese convoy of 8 destroyers and 3 transports between Masbate and Panay. Approximately 30 enemy aircraft were stacked up from the deck to 24,000 feet covering the convoy. Captain Aschenbrener took his flight in to meet them and came out after destroying 2 of the enemy and probably destroying 2 more while taking no losses, although 1 of the Lightnings came back on a single engine.

To counter the enemy planes coming down from the north, Major William Banks and Major Walter Benz of the 342nd Squadron, which had moved up to Tacloban on December 1, arranged for a fighter sweep over the air bases on Cebu, where the enemy would be most likely to stage aircraft to protect his own shipping and to attack the American supply vessels.

After 15 minutes of flying over Cebu, 3 Zekes were sighted flying 2,000 feet below. As the Thunderbolts dove down, 1 of the Zekes broke downward, but Major Banks downed 1 of them while Major Benz attacked the other. Benz got a short burst in before this Zeke dove for cloud cover.

The P-47s returned to base, refueled, and went back to the same area. This time a lone fighter was sighted and downed by Benz. Immediately after his kill 7 more enemy fighters were sighted below. Benz and Lieutenant Gerald Sheely dove down to attack a flight of 3, and Sheely took the end man out on the initial pass. The other 2 Oscars fled. Another 7 planes were sighted after this attack, and Major Benz came down out of the sun for a pass, but this time his guns jammed. Lieutenant Sheely was out of ammunition, so the Americans broke off the combat and returned to base.

Another flight of Thunderbolts from the 342nd were overhead providing top cover for P-40s and F4Us that were attacking a Japanese convoy when 8 Zekes were sighted down below. The P-47s dived to attack, but the enemy planes broke and ran. Captain Robert LaBounty gave chase and shot down 2 of them.

On December 12, 8 P-38s were pulled up in a half circle on the base at Tacloban for a decoration ceremony. Dick Bong, in faded and wrinkled khakis, faced General Douglas MacArthur to receive the highest honor that could be bestowed upon him. The general in a brief speech inducted the shy young fighter pilot "into the society of the bravest of the brave, the wearers of the Congressional Medal of Honor of the United States."

By this date naval forces were assembling for the assault on Mindoro, the next move in the Philippines. The last enemy attempt to reinforce Leyte had been broken up, and the aerial threat to supply convoys to Ormoc Bay was over. From then on the ground forces continued to move forward on the island of Leyte without interruption.

XIII

MINDORO AND LUZON

In the few days preceding the landing of American ground forces on the island of Mindoro on December 15, the fighters of the Fifth Air Force and the Thirteenth Air Force hit all Japanese bases in the area from which counter missions could be flown against the task force moving north.

Major William Dunham of the 460th Fighter Squadron led an early-morning fighter sweep over the Japanese airdromes at Negros and found little enemy activity in the area. He and his flight did catch 2 Sally bombers flying in the Talisay Airdrome area, both of which were downed by Dunham and Lieutenant Dewitt Searles.

The 340th Fighter Squadron of the 348th Fighter Group under the command of Captain Meade M. Brown had just moved in to Tanauan Airdrome on Leyte when they were assigned their first mission from their new strip. Brown led his P-47s on a sweep to Negros; he shot down a Tony en route.

While the P-47s were on this mission approximately 50 enemy planes of a variety of types were sighted well dispersed in revetment areas and dispersal lanes around Silay Airdrome. The Thunderbolts hurried back to base, where they were refueled and loaded with 500-pound bombs. The P-47 pilots returned to Silay, put their missiles down on the target, and accounted for 6 twin-engine bombers and 4 fighters. Three strafing passes were made following the bombing, and an additional 5 bombers and 5 fighters were destroyed. The strip was rendered temporarily unserviceable by 4 bomb hits in the center of the runway.

Eleven P-47s of the 40th Fighter Squadron intercepted an unescorted flight of 13 Helen bombers and a Sally bomber laden with bombs and torpedos en route to the American task force on the morning of December 14, and in a beautiful display of shooting wiped out the entire force. This was poetic justice for the men of the 40th, who had missed out on all the air action over Leyte. They had moved into the Philippines with their Thunderbolts in mid-November. The P-47s had just sighted the bomber force when 10 Navy F4Fs from one of the carriers in the task force came in the area. The Thunderbolt commander checked in with them, and the Navy flew top cover while the Air Force pilots went after the bombers.

The Thunderbolt pilots reported that the Japanese pilots seemed confused and gave each other no mutual gun support. P-47 flights broke off in individual passes and were able to get to all of the bombers in this manner.

Four of the P-47 pilots made numerous passes on the bombers after their P-47s were out of ammunition, while another plane would shoot. This seemed to draw the top turret fire away from the Thunderbolt that was actually firing.

Lieutenant Robert F. Steffy was the top scorer, with 3 Helens, and Lieutenants Ellis C. Baker, Jr., William L. Colsh, James E. Meeks, Jr., and Warren G. Wycoff each got 2 bombers apiece.

The infantrymen of the 24th Division and the 503rd Airborne Regiment went ashore on Mindoro on the morning of December 15 almost unopposed, but the Japanese were not absent from the skies. As would be customary each day for a considerable period, the kamikaze attacks were aimed directly at naval vessels in the area. The P-38s and P-47s downed 8 Zekes over the area that day, but the attackers managed to get through and crash into 2 LSTs which sunk, carrying with them the majority of the equipment belonging to the 8th Fighter Group and the 418th Night Fighter Squadron.

The demise of the men in the advance echelon of the 80th Fighter Squadron is described by its historian. "On the morning of the fifteenth, D-Day, fireworks broke loose. LST 738 was out 5 miles from shore, while our task force started shelling Mindoro. At about 0845 hours the enemy began coming over. No one had a clear idea of how many Japanese planes there were because of all the excitement going on.

"LST 738 became the target for a Japanese plane, which approached it from the starboard side. It was thought that the plane would make its pass and then zoom up. However, the enemy was a member of Radio Tokyo's boasted Kamikaze Special Attack Corps of Suicide Pilots. He dove his plane directly at the ship and crashed into it amidships. Fires broke out on deck among the trucks, and the abandon-ship order was given about 30 minutes after the ship had been hit. A destroyer pulled alongside and attempted to put out the fire with its hoses, the water system of the LST having been damaged. Lines and ladders were lowered for the men to go over the side. Most of the men left the ship in an orderly manner; however, some men jumped over the side, and others left by climbing down the anchor chain. There were PT boats, LSTs, and destroyers nearby to pick up survivors, who were brought to shore in a couple of hours and taken to the 310th Bomb Wing on Mindoro. Later it was learned that 13 enlisted men were hospitalized aboard the hospital ship U.S.S. *Brooks*, while 12 officers and enlisted men returned to Leyte on a destroyer. The men who had been brought ashore slept in the fields that night, as all equipment had gone down with the ship. A couple of days later they moved in with the 307th Airdrome Squadron, where they were supplied with a change of clothes, cigarettes, and other odds and ends. . . ."

Major Dick Bong scored his fortieth and last victory over the Mindoro beachhead on December 17. He had downed No. 39 2 days before over Negros. While on a fighter sweep 2 Oscars were sighted, and when the P-38s dropped their tanks they made 180-degree turns and headed due north. Bong gave chase and closed on the enemy leader, who had dived to the right away from his wingman. Bong gave the Oscar a long burst from directly astern and the Oscar caught fire, disintegrated, and dove straight down into the ground. Bong then watched his wingman, Major Rittmayer, shoot down the other Oscar.

On reception of the report that Bong had achieved his fortieth victory, General Kenney issued an order for Bong to fly his plane to Tacloban and leave it there. He was to fly no further combat, for he was to be returned to the United States as soon as possible. Bong's pleas to remain and try for 50 fell on deaf ears.

Twelve P-47s of the 342nd Fighter Squadron were patrolling the beachhead over Mindoro on December 20 when they were attacked from above by 8 Zekes. The P-47s evaded attack in a steep diving turn and saw 12 other Zekes, which were carrying bombs and trying to make a run on the new fighter strip on the island. The Thunderbolts dropped tanks and split up, each element pursuing a flight of Zekes in order to disrupt their bomb runs.

The P-47 pilots soon had the initiative, and in the air battle that took place they downed 10 of the Zekes and probably got another. One pilot, Lieutenant Richard J. Watrous, was unable to drop one of his wing tanks and could not keep up with the rest of the flight. While trying to catch them he sighted a Dinah being pursued by P-38s. They overshot it on their initial pass so, Lieutenant Watrous pulled up behind it and fired until the Dinah's left engine caught fire. The Dinah crashed to the ground.

Another event of December 20 was the arrival of the air echelon of the 80th Fighter Squadron of the 8th Fighter Group at their new base on Mindoro, which had been named Hill Field. After nearly 2 months of chomping at the bit and giving up their aircraft to the 49th Fighter Group at Dulag on Leyte, the pilots of the 80th had come up to make their mark in brand-new P-38Ls.

The next morning they got their chance. Ten P-38s of the 80th had hardly become airborne when 14 enemy planes were spotted at 5,000 feet. The Lightnings attacked and succeeded in destroying 5 Oscars and a Hamp. The 80th, which had been so successful over New Guinea, was back in the thick of things.

By this time there were enough fighters available to provide escort for the B-24s to go against targets on Luzon. These missions were inaugurated on December 22, when the northern suburbs of Manila were attacked. On December 24 the bombers went after targets on Clark Field north of Manila.

Two P-47s of the 460th Fighter Squadron went out in advance of the main force of Liberators with their escort on Christmas Eve. These 2 Thunderbolts sighted the enemy up in force milling around the target area in flights of 2 and 3. The Japanese fighters dropped many phosphorus bombs on the B-24 formation, but these were very inaccurately dropped and did no damage.

The Thunderbolts attempted to restrict their attacks on enemy fighters from above and astern, but as the enemy fighters split-essed and broke for the deck, the American pilots went after them in elements, with one man doing the shooting while the wingman covered his tail. The Zekes and Oscars were certainly no match for the heavy P-47s in a dive. Thirty-three enemy fighters fell victim to the pilots of the 348th Fighter Group, while 3 of the Thunderbolts were lost.

The bombers returned to Luzon on Christmas Day, striking the airfield at Mabalacat. The enemy was up in force once more, and air battles raged all over the sky. Forty-two Japanese fighters fell that day, all of them to P-38s of the escorting 49th and 475th fighter groups. Colonel Charles MacDonald, commanding officer of the 475th, found the enemy "aggressive and extremely clever at aerobatics." MacDonald had downed 2 Jacks and a Zeke when he closed in on another Zeke. The enemy pilot pulled around in a tight turn. MacDonald used dive flaps, got a lead, and fired, but he was pulling too may "G's" for the guns, and they quit firing. As MacDonald pulled out to leave the area he was immediately engaged by anti-aircraft fire from Clark and adjoining fields.

As MacDonald sped across the anti-aircraft pattern he noted that his No. 3 P-38 wasn't there. Immediately he returned and saw the Zeke that had evaded him coming in on the Lightning from astern. MacDonald called his wingman and told him to do the firing as MacDonald led them in on a head-on pass at the Zeke. The enemy fighter broke off and headed for Clark Field while the Americans pulled up and set course for Mindoro.

The 5th Fighter Command continued to take its toll of the diminishing enemy fighter strength the following day when the bombers returned to Clark Field. Lieutenant Sammy Pierce, a veteran who had just returned to the 8th Fighter Squadron, showed that he had lost none of his proficiency by downing 3 Zekes and a Tojo. Major Tommy McGuire ran his score up to 38 by downing 4 Zekes in a brilliant exhibition of deflection shooting.

"The bombers had completed their run and were heading away from the target when, at 1035, I sighted 1 enemy aircraft at 8 o'clock high," stated McGuire. "There were about 5 Zekes coming down on the tail of the bomber formation from above, out of the overcast. We were about 2,000 feet above and behind the bombers. As I started down, I saw 2 enemy aircraft heading south below us. As I started my attack, the first Zeke had finished his pass and the second was driving up the last bomber flight's tail. This was at about 13,000 feet. As the enemy was pressing his attack, and I could see no return fire from the bomber, I opened fire from 45 degrees' deflection from about 350 to 400 yards' range, getting hits right in the cockpit. The Zeke started to burn, but as he was still on the B-24's tail, by then about 50 yards behind it, I closed to within 100 feet, firing another burst. The Zeke rolled over and burst into flames. Captain Weaver, my wingman, saw the Zeke burst into flames and explode.

"I shot at the third Zeke in the string, shooting in about 70 degrees' deflection, but observed no results. Turning to the left and down, I shot 2 bursts into another Zeke at about 60 degrees' deflection. The enemy plane started burning, and Captain Weaver saw him crash in flames.

"About 3 more had come, so I turned on 1, shooting a burst from 30 degrees' deflection, then another good burst from about 45 degrees' deflection and got hits around the cockpit. The enemy started down and crashed in a dry stream. Lieutenant Herman, my element leader, who had broken off to clear himself from another Japanese, saw him crash, going down from 5,000 feet.

"I was then by myself, as my wingman had lost me on that pass. I saw another Zeke heading down, so I turned on it and caught it at about 1,500 feet. I fired 2 bursts from about 40 to 60 degrees' deflection, getting hits around and behind the wing roots, and the Zeke started burning, then crashed near the dry stream. Lieutenant Herman saw the Zeke burn and crash.

"As I was on the deck, I started climbing, and at about 6,000 feet I saw an enemy aircraft diving down quite a distance in front of me. The enemy plane pulled up, so I gave chase, but another flight came down from above to attack him. As the Japanese started for the clouds, it was hit and burst into flames just before reaching the clouds. I saw Lieutenant Pierce, leader of the 8th Fighter Squadron flight, destroy this aircraft."

McGuire had become known in the theater as "8 behind McGuire," for try as he might, it seemed that he was always 8 victories behind Dick Bong. Now that Bong had returned to the United States, McGuire's golden opportunity had arrived, or so he thought after his 4 victories on December 26. However, General George Kenney saw otherwise. Bong was on his way home to be greeted as the leading American fighter ace of World War II, and Kenney feared that if McGuire remained in action Bong would be No. 2 when he arrived for the red-carpet treatment. McGuire found himself grounded until after the first of the year.

The big event of December 26 came at night. At 4 P.M. a Navy patrol bomber sighted a Japanese task force consisting of a heavy cruiser, a light cruiser, and 6 destroyers only 100 miles west of Mindoro speeding toward the American invasion fleet. There were no American warships to be rushed into the gap to intercept the enemy, so it was up to the small force of AAF planes and Navy PT boats to engage. The Air Force effort was made up of P-38s of the 8th Fighter Group, P-47s of the 58th Fighter Group, whose prior action had been restricted to ground-support operations, P-40s of the 110th Tactical Reconnaissance Squadron, and B-25s of the 17th Bomb Squadron. All available aircraft that could be pressed into the night attack on the enemy task force were put in the air. Before the night was over the entire flyable strength of 44 P-38s, 28 P-47s, 20 P-40s, and 13 B-25s would have pressed their attacks on the warships.

The 80th Squadron was one of the P-38 units in the brunt of the battle that night, and its activities are vividly described by its historian. "The evening of the twenty-sixth of December was one that will long be remembered. At 1900 that evening a meeting of all squadron personnel was held, and we were informed that a Japanese task force was approaching Mindoro. Plans for evacuating the camp and taking to the hills were laid down. Engineering, armament, and ordnance men were sent to the line to bomb up and prepare the planes for an aerial attack on the task force. All available planes on both strips were sent into the air: P-38s, P-47s, B-25s, P-61s, and P-40s. Our ships took off at 2120 hours. From camp the flashes of explosions and patterns of tracers could be seen. Only 4 of our planes were bombed up, 2 of them secured 4 near misses on 2 enemy destroyers. Two of our pilots were forced to bail out that night, Lieutenant Kenneth B. Lloyd had completed 5 or 6 passes on a destroyer when his left wing either hit the water or was hit by flak. The left wing was curled up at a 45-degree angle and the prop was bent back over the engine. Lieutenant Lloyd managed to get 2,000 feet of altitude and get back to the field. He bailed out rather than risk a single-engine belly landing in the dark; he was picked up and brought back to camp uninjured.

"Lieutenant Orland J. Harris underwent a harrowing experience that night, one that was almost unbelievable. He came in to strafe a destroyer from the side when he received a jolt that threw his head up against the gun sight, stunning him momentarily. On recovering from the shock, he became aware that his left engine was on fire and his plane below the superstructure of the destroyer, which he had evidently hit on his pass. He pulled back on the stick trying to gain altitude. Because of blood running into his eyes from the cut on his forehead and the dizziness he felt, he had no idea of his altitude until he heard a voice in his earphones saying, 'His right engine is on fire, but he's high enough to bail out.' Lieutenant Harris figured they were talking about him, so he trimmed up his ship and bailed out. That's when his worries began; he landed in the middle of the Japanese task force. After disengaging himself from his chute, he swam away from the destroyer nearby, taking his rubber raft with him. When he turned on the valve to complete the inflation of the raft, the hiss it made was so clear and loud that he had to shut it off until the ship was out of earshot. He finally got the raft inflated and was about to get into it when he saw another destroyer coming straight at him. This time he believed he was done for, but ducked down behind the raft and waited. Again the ship went right past him, so close that its wake carried him along for several yards. He finally got into the raft and paddled toward shore, not making much headway, as the ocean was very rough. He was picked up by a friendly barge early next morning after 12 hours in the water.

"At about 2030 hours that night the Japanese warships started shelling both strips on the island. Bright star shells, which lit up the entire area, were used to illuminate the targets. Some of the men took off for the hills when the shelling became too much for them. The shelling lasted about 30 minutes and did not accomplish its main objective, which was to render the strips unserviceable. The convoy withdrew under fierce attack by our planes after 3 destroyers were sunk and the cruiser damaged. [These claims were greatly overestimated.] All friendly planes took off with wing lights on and kept them on while in the area to keep from having A/A thrown up at them. Some Japanese planes sneaked in with their lights on and strafed the strip, destroying 1 and damaging 4 of our planes in revetment areas. Nine planes of the 80th that participated in the attack on the task force landed at Leyte at 2400 hours that night; 7 of them took off the following morning to return to base."

Although only a single Japanese destroyer was sunk, and this by a PT boat, the planes had done extensive damage to the enemy warships by demolishing a number of the main batteries and killing a majority of gun crews. Only a single American vessel, a liberty ship that had not taken refuge behind Ilin Island as directed, was sunk.

The American warplanes had done a tremendous job of attacking under blackout conditions. Most had to turn on navigation lights to keep from running into each other. This set them up as excellent targets for anti-aircraft fire from the ships. The naval bombardment kept many of them from returning to their base at Hill Field to refuel, and they were forced to fly through darkness and bad weather to seek refuge at Leyte.

All told, the little force had suffered the loss of 3 B-25s, 7 P-38s, 10 P-47s, and 6 P-40s. This was a tremendous casualty rate for the attackers, but they had accomplished their mission. The task force broke off the engagement and sped off into the night.

Following this battle the fighter and bomber strength on Mindoro was built up as rapidly as possible. The primary limitation of operations from the bases there became the shortage of fuel and bombs that resulted from the loss of tankers and supply ships to kamikaze attacks. This situation would not be remedied until shortly before the invasion of Luzon on January 9.

The P-61s of the 418th Night Fighter Squadron on Mindoro were active again on the twenty-seventh. Lieutenant Bertram C. Tompkins was one of the pilots who was airborne that evening. "Approximately 1½ hours after becoming airborne the GCI controller vectored me onto a bogey approaching from the northwest," Tompkins reported. "F/O Wertin made radar contact with bogey at 0010 at a distance of 6 miles and altitude of 10,000 feet on heading of 280 degrees. He directed me to 2,000 feet directly behind and below bogey and I obtained a visual and identified it as a Tony. I closed to 150 feet and fired 1 short burst. The Tony exploded and fell burning into the water approximately 20 miles west of base. No evasive action was used by enemy aircraft.

"Immediately GCI vectored me onto second bogey, which was 20 miles southeast of me. F/O Wertin made radar contact at 6 miles and directed me to 3,000 feet, directly behind and slightly below the bogey, where I got a visual. I closed to 300 feet and fired 1 burst, and enemy aircraft exploded and fell to the water burning. Kill was made approximately 5 miles west of Mindoro coast. E/A was identified as a Tony. Violent evasive action was used."

In preparation for the move on Luzon, the bombers of the Fifth Air Force and the Thirteenth Air Force continued to pound airfields on the island, and then during the first week of January 1945, the Third Fleet's carrier squadrons got in their licks. One of the more destructive Air Force missions was flown on January 7, when P-38s from the 49th Fighter Group on Mindoro covered a massive raid by A-20s and B-25s against Clark Field. One hundred thirty-two bombers deposited nearly 8,000 parafrag bombs on the airfield, and no enemy fighters challenged the escort, although half a dozen Hamps attempted to hit a B-25 formation with their customary phosphorus bombs.

After this destructive mission even kamikaze attacks against American shipping fell to almost nil. When American troops went ashore on the morning of January 9 at Lingayen Gulf, there was practically no enemy air opposition.

While the attack against Clark Field was under way on January 7, other P-38s were flying neutralizing strikes against enemy air bases on the island of Negros. It was on one of these missions that America's No. 2 fighter ace, Major Tommy McGuire, was killed. He was not downed by enemy action but lost his life when he violated one of his own cardinal rules and attempted to maneuver with a Japanese fighter at low speed close to the deck. His final mission is described by Captain Edwin R. Weaver: "I took off as No. 2 man in a flight, led by Major McGuire, of 4 P-38s of the 431st Fighter Squadron. We climbed on course for Fabrica Airdrome on Negros Island, leveling off at 10,000 feet. West of Leyte, cloud coverage became 10/10ths at 6,000 feet and remained so to the target area. Over Negros we descended through the several layers of stratus clouds, breaking out below the overcast at 1,700 feet, 10 miles northeast of Fabrica strip. We proceeded to that strip, arriving at 0700, and circled it at 1,400 feet for about 5 minutes. Major McGuire then set course, at this altitude, for the strips on the western coast of Negros. At about 10 to 15 miles west of Fabrica I saw a Zeke "52" coming directly toward us 500 feet below and 1,000 yards ahead. By the time I radioed this information and the leader had seen the enemy, he was directly underneath us. Major McGuire, followed by his flight, made a diving turn to the left for an attack. The Zeke immediately dived to the left also and came around on the tail of No. 3 man, Lieutenant Thropp, who had previously been instructed by his element leader, Major Rittmayer, to change positions with him. The enemy was on the inside of this very tight turn at 300 feet and fired at Lieutenant Thropp. I radioed that the Zeke was directly behind us, and Major Rittmayer, in No. 4 position, fired a burst sufficient to make the enemy turn even more tightly and lose Lieutenant Thropp. That put the Zeke in range and inside of me, in No. 2 position. I radioed Major McGuire that I was being attacked and increased my turn, diving slightly. The enemy stayed with me, but I was now inside and a little below my leader. At this time Major McGuire, attempting to get a shot at my attacker, increased his turn tremendously. His plane snap-rolled to the left and stopped in an inverted position with the nose down about 30 degrees. Because of the altitude of my plane, I then lost sight of him momentarily. A second later I saw the explosion and fire of his crash. The Zeke broke off his attack just before Major McGuire's crash and climbed to the north. It is my opinion that the enemy did not at any time change his attack from me to my leader. I believe his crash was caused by his violent attempt to thwart my attacker, although it is possible that the major was hit by ground fire, which had now begun.

"When the Zeke broke away to the north, I also turned in that direction and joined the remainder of the flight as No. 3 man. We chased the enemy, and Lieutenant Thropp, in No. 1 position, got in a burst just as the Zeke climbed into the overcast. A second later, as we turned toward the south, the Zeke reappeared to the east and headed toward us. It got a burst at Lieutenant Thropp from 10 o'clock high, and I saw a slight amount of smoke come from Lieutenant Thropp's left engine. Pulling up my nose, I got a short burst from 30 degrees below. Then I followed Major Rittmayer, the No. 2 man, in a 180-degree turn to the right to pursue the Zeke, who swung around and again attacked from 10 o'clock high as we jettisoned our auxiliary tanks. I saw hits on Major Rittmayer and again pulled up my nose, turning to the right for a burst from 30 degrees below. The Zeke, also being closed on by Lieutenant Thropp, who was now above, behind, and to the left of me, made a diving turn to the right and attempted to get on my tail momentarily. I pulled from him and headed north. Lieutenant Thropp had continued his right turn and started home with a bad left engine. The Zeke swung on to his tail and fired just as Lieutenant Thropp entered the overcast. I was too far out of range to fire, as the Zeke also climbed into the overcast, breaking off toward the south. I circled the bottom of the overcast for approximately 3 minutes, waiting for the enemy to show himself again. Thinking he might be above, I climbed up through the overcast and looked for him there for a few minutes. Lieutenant Thropp radioed that he was all right and on his way home. I then gave up the hunt and set course to my base at 0715, landing at 0805."

A posthumous award of the Congressional Medal of Honor would be made to McGuire for his outstanding actions over the Philippines during late December.

Another Congressional Medal of Honor would be won over the Philippines in 1945. When the 82nd Reconnaissance Squadron arrived on Mindoro in late December 1944, they were flying brand-new North American Mustangs. These aircraft were new to the theater, and their pilots were eager to put them in action after flying over-age P-39s and P-40s for many months. On the morning of January 11, Captain William A. Shomo and his wingman, Lieutenant Paul M. Lipscomb, took off on a reconnaissance mission to Aparri in northern Luzon. They sighted a Betty bomber escorted by 12 Tony fighters just south of Baguio. The formation was some 2,000 feet above them when first sighted.

Shomo pulled back on the stick, shoved the throttle forward, and climbed up to attack, with Lipscomb on his wing. The Japanese either didn't see the climbing Mustangs or took them for more Tony fighters coming up to join them. At a distance the American in-line engine fighter somewhat resembled the enemy fighter.

On the first pass the Betty bomber and one of the Tonys were left spinning down to their destruction. The enemy fighters broke but could never seem to get together on any type of tactics to counter the Americans. Shomo and Lipscomb were in and out of the enemy formation, with guns blazing. When all was finished 9 of the Japanese fighters had been downed, along with the Betty. Shomo had accounted for 6 of the Tonys and the Betty, and Lipscomb felled 3 of the Tonys. Shomo's destruction of 7 enemy aircraft in something less than 15 minutes was recognized with the Congressional Medal of Honor.

The war in the air over Luzon was all but over during January 1945. The few Japanese airplanes that were sent down to reenforce the shrinking enemy air force were quickly disposed of, and the American fighter pilots had to settle for ground support and strafing of enemy ground targets and installations.

As the ground troops drove eastward and southward, airstrips were begun immediately in order to move the Army Air Force planes forward. By January 17 the P-38s of the 18th Fighter Group of the Thirteenth Air Force and the P-40s and P-51s of the 82nd Reconnaissance Squadron were in place at Lingayen Airstrip. The veteran 35th Fighter Group and the P-51s of the new 3rd Air

Commandos of the Fifth Air Force arrived at Mangaldan Airstrip on January 22.

February 1945 saw more ground-support missions by the fighter planes, and the use of napalm was inaugurated. Tanks ranging from 75-to-165-gallon capacity were filled with the mixture of napalm gel and gasoline and dropped on enemy installations all over the island. Although gasoline alone had been used at times against enemy troops in dug-in positions, the napalm proved to be much more effective, as the flames lasted much longer and penetrated deeply.

February also saw the 1st Cavalry Division race southward toward the city of Manila, while the 11th Airborne Division landed on the south coast of Luzon and drove toward the city from their new beachhead. The liberation of Manila was imminent.

The assault phase of the liberation of Luzon was complete early in February. The tedious job of rooting the Japanese out of their dug-in positions and disposing of them throughout the island would take months, and the fighters were primarily restricted to bombing and strafing operations. The only diversions where they would still engage the enemy in the air would come on the missions to Formosa and French Indochina, escorting the bombers that continued to cut the enemy's lifeline from the south.

XIV

FORMOSA, INDOCHINA, AND
NORTH TO VICTORY

Missions against industrial installations on Formosa had begun by
Fifth Air Force bombers in the form of night strikes in early January of 1945. By the end of the month the bombers were attacking
by day escorted by P-47s and P-38s of the 5th Fighter Command.
During January and February the 348th Fighter Group turned in
its Thunderbolts and received P-51s, which were utilized on the
missions to Formosa and southern China. Some of these strikes
covered 1,400 to 1,600 miles and kept the pilots in the cramped
cockpits of their new Mustangs for up to 8½ hours. The biggest
obstacle that the pilots encountered on these missions during February was weather. Out of 9 shipping strikes scheduled for the
348th Fighter Group, 4 were aborted due to fronts that were encountered en route.

Captain Perry J. Dahl led a typical P-38 fighter sweep of the
432nd Squadron from Clark Field over Formosa on the afternoon
of March 5, 1945. The P-38s were about two thirds of the way up
the western coast of Formosa when the squadron went in string to
strafe targets on the water. Several runs were made on fishing
boats, but fire was withheld when it appeared that most were
manned by civilians.

As the formation pulled up to 1,500 feet, a Sally bomber was
sighted plodding along, heading northward. Dahl dove on the twin-
engine craft, which pushed over hard and dove for the deck. Dahl

started firing, set the starboard engine on fire, and managed to put 2 more bursts into it before the Sally crashed on the beach. Five survivors were seen running from the Sally, which had failed to fire the first shot in its defense.

P-38s of the 431st and 432nd squadrons were on an escort mission to Indochina when they encountered a big enemy formation on March 28. A B-25 pathfinder aircraft led the Lightnings to the Indochina coast, where the Mitchell bombers were to attack an armed convoy. On arrival the convoy could not be located, and only after a 45-minute search by the P-38s was the enemy sighted. The force consisted of 11 ships, including 2 destroyers.

Captain Perry Dahl had to take his Lightnings down to 7,000 feet to keep the enemy in sight in the haze, and the convoy began to throw up quite a bit of anti-aircraft fire just before enemy aircraft came in to intercept. One flight of the 432nd Squadron sighted a few enemy aircraft down on the deck before they realized that there were 20 more up above.

Dahl attempted to call this flight in on the radio, but the frequency was jammed. The enemy fighters started to attack by twos from above, but Dahl took his 8 P-38s up into them. After warding off the first pass, Dahl lowered the nose of his P-38 to gain a little speed and then pulled up into the next 2 diving fighters. An attack was being initiated by a Hamp on the No. 4 man in the flight whom Dahl had been protecting, so Dahl ordered Lieutenant Kimball and his flight down after him.

Lieutenant Kimball's guns jammed, so his wingman, Lieutenant George Wacker, pulled inside, fired a short burst, and the Hamp broke off in a violent roll to the right and split-essed. Lieutenant Wacker followed and closed to 300 yards, let go another burst, and the Hamp flamed.

Captain Dahl constantly had to maneuver to ward off the attacks on the flight of P-38s below them until they became aware of the situation. One time Dahl was able to bring his guns to bear, and he brought a Hamp down with a 60-degree deflection shot.

Finally the flight below saw what was happening and pulled up and into the enemy formation. By this time Dahl and his flight had exhausted so much of their fuel supply that they were forced to break off the combat and leave the area. One of the pilots was unable to make it back to base and had to bail out. One of the P-38s covered him as long as possible while radioing the position to a Navy PBY. Unfortunately, upon its arrival the patrol craft could find no sight of the pilot.

The following day a flight of 4 P-38s under the leadership of Lieutenant Laurence C. LeBaron returned to the same area. This time the Lightnings surprised the enemy. A flight of 11 Zekes was sighted, and on the initial pass from above Lieutenants LeBaron and Harrold Owen scored. Two more Zekes were downed, one by Lieutenant John O'Rourke of the 431st Squadron and a second by LeBaron, before the Japanese pilots realized they were under attack.

Lieutenant Owen's left supercharger burned out, but this did not prevent him from protecting Lieutenant LeBaron in the ensuing dogfight with the Zekes. LeBaron was able to pursue and down a third Zeke as it broke out over the clouds near the China coast.

Lieutenant Laurence Dowler destroyed 2 Zekes, 1 as the result of a head-on pass (at which time both of his props were holed by return fire) and the other as the result of a good deflection shot, which caused the Zeke to burst into flames.

Lieutenant Owen was forced to feather a prop due to the burning out of his supercharger, and he had to make it the entire 850 miles back to Clark Field on a single engine. As though this weren't enough, he discovered that his hydraulic system was out, and he had to pump his landing gear down. After 8 hours, 25 minutes flying time, all planes made it home safely.

The last victories in the south were scored when the P-38s of the 49th Fighter Group escorted the B-24s to Hong Kong. Upon arrival at the target 2 Tojo-type fighters were sighted 10 to 15 miles north of the city. Lieutenant Colonel Gerald R. Johnson led his flight in chase. Diving from 13,000 feet, Johnson made a dead-astern attack on a Tojo and saw slugs rip into the fuselage. The enemy craft went into a spin and crashed in a riverbed. Captain James A. Watkins scored over the other Tojo in the chase.

The 2 fighter groups of the 13th Fighter Command had missed out on the big activity in the Philippines, and they were not destined to get in on any amount of aerial fighting for the rest of the war. They supported the invasion forces going into the western Philippines and were later to take up their final stations in that area. The 18th Fighter Group finished up at Zamboanga, and the 347th Fighter Group's final wartime base was at Palawan. Both of these units did yeoman work in escorting the bombers to Formosa, Indochina, and southward to Balikpapan, Borneo, late in the war.

The 49th Group continued to strike at Formosa into the summer of 1945. On June 23 the 9th Fighter Squadron joined other units of the group in the first napalm attack on Formosa. The mission against the town of Mato was highly successful, and a large portion of the area was left in flames. By dropping the bombs in waves of 4 to 8 planes the target had been completely saturated.

Colonel Clayton Tice led the 49th Group to Formosa on July 17, 1945, on an experimental bridge-busting mission. Dive, skip, and glide bombing techniques were tried against the Soton railroad bridge, using 4-to-5-second delay fuses on 1,000-pound demolition bombs. The 9th Squadron came in first and neutralized the target by hitting anti-aircraft installations with fragmentation bombs, and then the other P-38s went into their bombing routine unmolested.

Following the end of the war in Europe in May of 1945, the fighter groups of the 5th Fighter Command began to receive the new aircraft that they had begged for. The 35th Group received P-51s in the spring of 1945, and the majority of the P-38 units received the latest model of their aircraft.

Following the conquest of Okinawa in the Ryukyus in June of 1945, the greatest airfield construction program in the Pacific got under way. In preparation for the impending invasion of the Japanese home islands as many strips as could possibly be built were begun for the great influx of aircraft that were sure to be needed.

General Ennis Whitehead of the Fifth Air Force had alerted his units and planned to rush them forward just as quickly as possible. Before hostilities ceased, 4 Fifth Air Force fighter groups and 2 night fighter squadrons were operating from the Ryukyus. The 35th Fighter Group flew from Yontan and the 58th from Kadena, while the 348th and the 8th groups took up station on Ie Shima.

First to get into action were the P-51s of the 35th Group, which flew a fighter sweep over Sesabo on the island of Kyushu, Japan, on July 3, 1945. Three Japanese fighters were shot down in the air, but these were to be the only victories by the 5th Fighter Command for the month. The Japanese were hoarding their fighter planes for the invasion, and the fighter pilots had to direct their activities to strafing of transportation, industrial targets, and shipping. This they did with relish, and then they started to enjoy something that was little known in the Pacific—locomotive busting.

At this late date practically all of the pilots of the 5th Fighter Command were replacements for the old-timers, who had long since left for the United States. There were a few of the veterans around to lead, such as Lieutenant Colonel William D. Dunham, who headed up a flight of 4 P-51s from the 348th Group over Kyushu on the morning of August 1, 1945.

While his flight was at 16,800 feet a flight of 16 to 20 enemy fighters was sighted below at from 9,000 to 15,000 feet. They were in no particular formation, but they were making passes at a B-24 formation. Dunham took his Mustangs down from above, and on the initial pass both he and Lieutenant Thomas M. Sheets downed 2 of the Frank fighters. Major Edward S. Popek caught and downed 2 more in the brief action with the Japanese pilots, who were in no mood to mix it up with the Americans.

Medium bombers began to strike Japanese airfields to get the enemy fighters on the ground if they refused to come up and fight. A few began to rise to meet the escorts, and P-51s of the 340th Squadron downed 4 Zekes over Saishu Airdrome on August 6.

The same day a new weapon was unleashed upon the city of

Hiroshima. A B-29 dropped the first atomic bomb. Three days later a second of the devastating weapons was dropped on the city of Nagasaki. While the Japanese considered surrender ultimatum conditions, aerial operations against the home islands were suspended.

While the pilots of the 5th Fighter Command were sitting idle and wondering if the war was soon to come to an end, they received the tragic news concerning America's No. 1 fighter ace. Major Dick Bong, who General Kenney had pulled out of combat to preserve his life, had been killed in the crash of a P-80 jet fighter plane at Burbank, California, on August 6.

The last aerial victories and the last shots of the war by the 5th Fighter Command were fired on August 14, 1945. Five P-38s of the 35th Fighter Squadron were providing cover for 2 rescue planes at a position midway between Kyushu, Shikoku, and Honshu over the Inland Sea at an altitude of 12,500 feet when 6 enemy Franks dove down on them.

Captain Raymond F. Meyer heard the fighters call out over the radio and broke to his right with his wingman, Lieutenant George I. Stevens. They watched the Franks pass overhead and then start back. Closing head-on, Meyer let go a burst from 1,000 feet, which raked the cockpit and engine and started fires in the fuselage and wing. As he pulled up, Meyer looked back and saw his victim spin into the sea.

As he leveled out, Meyer sighted a Frank hot on the tail of a P-38. Meyer dove and fired a burst, causing the enemy fighter to break to the right. Captain Meyer streaked behind him and peppered his rear with fire. The Frank emitted a stream of black smoke and split-essed to eventually crash into the sea.

Lieutenant Stevens also met one of the Franks head-on, and when the enemy broke, Meyer tacked on its tail and held the trigger until the plane burst into flames.

Captain Billy G. Moore sighted a Frank on the tail of a P-38 and drove it off with a short burst. At 9,000 feet the Frank went down in a split-ess, with Moore on its tail. The enemy pilot leveled out at 3,000 feet and made a mad dash for the shoreline. As he sped away, Moore closed the gap and fired a long burst, which shot a piece of the fighter's wing off and seemed to put the fighter out of control. Moore stuck with it until the Frank rolled over and went straight into the water.

Lieutenant Dwight Hollister accounted for the other Frank destroyed that day. Hollister was the first to spot the enemy aircraft, but his mike button stuck and he was unable to warn the formation. He dropped his belly tank and broke toward the No. 3 Frank in the formation. In the head-on pass he poured lead into the engine and canopy of the craft. A small fire spurted from the left side of the cockpit and the enemy fighter rolled over on its back. Hollister closed in a tight right turn and pulled into firing position. Two more bursts caught the Frank in the engine, and it went into a flat spin and into the sea.

The final victories had not been without loss. Lieutenant Duane L. Keiffer had been flying Captain Moore's wing as they were chasing the Frank along the coast. Lieutenant Keiffer fired a long burst at the enemy, overshot, and pulled up in a climb. Ignoring the P-38 on his tail, the Japanese pilot straightened out long enough to put a burst into Keiffer's right engine, which set it to burning. Lieutenant Keiffer was seen to jettison his canopy in an attempt to get out, but his plane spun into the sea before he could get out.

Also on August 14, Lieutenant Joe Ozier led a flight of 12 Mustangs from the 341st Fighter Squadron to bomb shipping on the southwestern coast of Kyushu. The pilots had been ordered not to bomb or strafe shore installations pending word concerning Japan's surrender. Ozier's bomb did not release, so he and his flight orbited while the other planes went in first. Ozier then went in and dropped his bomb, and 2 members of his flight did a bit of strafing over the shipping as they pulled off target. This may well have been the last bomb and the last shots fired in the Pacific.

Eight Mustangs of the 35th Fighter Squadron were off early the next morning to escort rescue craft, but they returned home without incident. Later that morning the word came through that Japan had accepted the surrender terms. For all practical purposes the war was over!

In recognition of its achievements in its long period of combat, the Fifth Air Force fighters were given the honor of participating in the escort of Japanese bombers bearing the surrender envoys to Ie Shima en route to Manila. The American fighter planes contacted the Betty bombers, repainted in white with green crosses, and escorted them to Ie Shima on August 19. From there the Japanese delegation continued to Manila in transport planes.

Fifth Air Force fighters continued to fly reconnaissance missions over Japan while final surrender arrangements were being made. The 49th Fighter Group had 2 P-38s become the first planes to land on the Japanese home islands as a result of 1 of these missions. Colonel Clayton Tice and F/O Hall noticed that they were running short of fuel, and after talking it over they landed on a Japanese field at Nittagahara. There they were greeted with open arms, and the P-38s were refueled. The Lightnings returned to Okinawa without incident.

From a tragic beginning in the Philippines in 1941 the fighter units of the South and Southwest Pacific had fought their way back to the Philippines and then taken the fight all the way to Japan. They had shot down over 3,000 of the enemy's aircraft in the air and destroyed hundreds more on the ground. As strafing platforms they had destroyed untold amounts of equipment, hundreds of installations, and had killed tens of thousands of the enemy's troops. This they had accomplished with a minimum of equipment and personnel.

The fight from island to island, muddy airstrip to muddy airstrip, and dismal campsite to dismal campsite was finally over.

APPENDIX

U. S. ARMY AIR FORCE
FIGHTER ACES OF THE SOUTH AND SOUTHWEST PACIFIC

Rank	Name	AF	GP	Score
Maj.	Richard I. Bong	5	35 & 49	40
Maj.	Thomas B. McGuire, Jr.	5	475	38
Col.	Charles H. MacDonald	5	475	26
Lt. Col.	Gerald R. Johnson	5	49	22
Col.	Neel E. Kearby	5	348	22
Maj.	Jay T. Robbins	5	8	22
Maj.	Thomas J. Lynch	5	35	20
Lt. Col.	Robert B. Westbrook	13	347 & 18	20
Lt. Col.	William B. Dunham	5	348	16
Maj.	Bill Harris	13	18	16
Maj.	George S. Welch	5	8	16[1]
Maj.	Edward Cragg	5	8	15
Maj.	Cyril F. Homer	5	8	15
Lt. Col.	John D. Landers	5	49	14.5[2]
Capt.	Robert M. DeHaven	5	49	14
Maj.	Daniel T. Roberts	5	8 & 475	14
Capt.	Coatsworth B. Head, Jr.	13	18	12
Capt.	Kenneth G. Ladd	5	8	12
Capt.	James A. Watkins	5	49	12
Capt.	Richard L. West	5	8	12
Capt.	Francis J. Lent	5	475	11
Maj.	John S. Loisel	5	475	11
Capt.	Murray J. Shubin	13	347	11
Capt.	Cornelius M. Smith, Jr.	5	8	11
Lt.	Kenneth C. Sparks	5	35	11
Maj.	Robert W. Aschenbrener	5	49	10
Capt.	William K. Giroux	5	8	10
Maj.	Ernest A. Harris	5	49	10
Lt.	Andrew J. Reynolds	5	17 PS & 49	10
Maj.	Paul M. Stanch	5	35	10
Capt.	Elliot Summer	5	475	10

Rank	Name	AF	GP	Score
Maj.	William M. Banks	5	348	9
Capt.	Frederick F. Champlin	5	475	9
Capt.	Perry J. Dahl	5	475	9
Capt.	Grover E. Fanning	5	49	9
Maj.	Joseph M. Forester	5	475	9
Maj.	Allen E. Hill	5	8	9
Lt. Col.	George C. Kiser	5	17 PS & 49	9
Capt.	Joseph J. Lesicka	13	18	9
Capt.	Joel B. Paris III	5	49	9
Col.	Meryl M. Smith	5	475	9
Capt.	Robert H. White	5	49	9
Capt.	David W. Allen	5	475	8
Maj.	Walter G. Benz, Jr.	5	348	8
Lt.	Fernely H. Damstrom	5	49	8
Capt.	William A. Gardner	5	8	8
Capt.	Frank Gaunt	13	18	8
Lt.	Leroy V. Grosshuesch	5	35	8
Capt.	Frederick A. Harris	5	475	8
Capt.	Kenneth F. Hart	5	475	8
Capt.	John L. Jones	5	8	8
Capt.	John G. O'Neill	5	49	8
Capt.	Edward F. Roddy	5	348	8
Col.	Robert R. Rowland	5	348	8
Capt.	William A. Shomo	5	82 TR	8
Capt.	Robert H. Smith	13	18	8
Maj.	Arland Stanton	5	49	8
Maj.	Boyd D. Wagner	5	17 PS, 49 & 8	8
Capt.	Burnell W. Adams	5	8	7
Capt.	Samuel V. Blair	5	348	7
Capt.	George A. Davis	5	348	7
Capt.	Zach W. Dean	5	475	7
Lt.	John S. Dunaway	5	8	7
Capt.	Vincent T. Elliott	5	475	7
Capt.	Jack A. Fisk	5	475	7
Lt.	Marvin E. Grant	5	348	7

Rank	Name	AF	GP	Score
Capt.	William J. Hennon	5	17 PS, 49	7
Maj.	Verle E. Jett	5	475	7
Maj.	Warren R. Lewis	5	475	7
Maj.	John T. Moore	5	348	7
Capt.	James B. Morehead	5	17 PS, 49	7
Lt.	Sammy A. Pierce	5	49	7
Capt.	John E. Purdy	5	475	7
Capt.	Lucien B. Shuler	13	18	7
Maj.	Carroll C. Smith	5	418 NFS	7
Lt.	Richard E. Smith	5	35	7
Capt.	William H. Strand	5	35	7
Capt.	Elmer M. Wheadon	13	18	7
Capt.	Calvin C. Wire	5	475	7
Lt.	Stanley O. Andrews	5	35	6
Capt.	Ellis C. Baker, Jr.	5	35	6
Capt.	Meade M. Brown	5	348	6
Lt.	Edward J. Czarnecki	5	475	6
Capt.	Edwin L. DeGraffenreid	5	8	6
Capt.	Elliott E. Dent, Jr.	5	49	6
Maj.	William C. Drier	5	49	6
Lt.	Hoyt A. Eason	5	35	6
Capt.	Lee R. Everhart	5	8	6
Capt.	Richard H. Fleischer	5	348	6
Capt.	William B. Foulis, Jr.	5	348	6
Maj.	Charles S. Gallup	5	35	6
Capt.	William M. Gresham	5	475	6
Lt.	James P. Hagerstrom	5	49	6
Lt.	Robert L. Howard	5	49	6
Lt.	Lloyd G. Huff	13	347	6
Maj.	James C. Ince	5	475	6
Maj.	Wallace R. Jordan	5	49	6
Lt.	John H. Lane	5	35	6
Capt.	Paul W. Lucas	5	475	6
Capt.	Donald C. McGee	5	8	6
Capt.	Joseph T. McKeon	5	475	6

Rank	Name	AF	GP	Score
Lt.	Henry Meigs III	13	18 & 347, 6 NFS	6
Lt.	Donald W. Meuten	5	49	6
Capt.	James D. Mugavero	5	35	6
Capt.	Paul C. Murphey, Jr.	5	8	6
Lt.	John Pietz, Jr.	5	475	6
Capt.	Horace B. Reeves	5	475	6
Lt.	John C. Smith	5	475	6
Capt.	Thomas H. Walker	13	347	6
Capt.	Ralph H. Wandrey	5	49	6
Capt.	Arthur E. Wenige	5	49 & 475	6
Capt.	Lynn E. Witt, Jr.	5	8	6
Capt.	Ellis W. Wright, Jr.	5	49	6
Lt.	Robert H. Adams	5	8	5
Lt.	Ernest J. Ambort	5	49	5
Capt.	Jack A. Bade	13	18	5
Capt.	Rex T. Barber	13	18	5
Lt.	Truman S. Barnes	13	18 & 347	5
Maj.	Paul S. Bechtel	13	18	5
Capt.	Harry W. Brown	5	475 & 49	5
Capt.	Robert Byrnes	13	18	5
Lt.	Nial K. Castle	5	49	5
Capt.	George T. Chandler	13	18 & 347	5
Capt.	Vivian A. Cloud	5	475	5
Capt.	Harry L. Condon	5	475	5
Lt.	Warren D. Curton	5	49	5
Capt.	William C. Day, Jr.	5	49	5
Lt.	George Della	5	348	5
Capt.	Frederick E. Dick	5	49	5
Capt.	Michael Dikovitsky	5	348	5
Lt.	I. B. Jack Donaldson	5	21 PS, 49	5
Maj.	Francis E. Dubisher	5	35	5
Maj.	Marion E. Felts	5	49	5
Lt.	William Fiedler	13	347 & 18	5
Maj.	Nelson D. Flack, Jr.	5	49	5

Rank	Name	AF	GP	Score
Lt.	Zed D. Fountain	13	347	5
Capt.	Grover D. Gholson	5	475	5
Lt.	Robert D. Gibb	5	348	5
Lt.	Cyrus R. Gladen	13	18	5
Capt.	Cheatham W. Gupton	5	49	5
Lt.	Myron M. Hnatio	5	348	5
Capt.	Besby F. Holmes	13	18	5
Maj.	Alvaro J. Hunter	5	35	5
Capt.	Curran L. Jones	5	35	5
Maj.	Charles W. King	5	35	5
Lt.	Marion F. Kirby	5	475	5
Capt.	Robert H. Knapp	5	348	5
Maj.	Thomas G. Lanphier	13	18	5
Capt.	Alfred B. Lewelling	5	49	5
Lt.	Lowell C. Lutton	5	475	5
Lt.	Jack C. Mankin	5	475	5
Lt.	Milden E. Mathre	5	49	5
Maj.	William F. McDonough	5	35	5
Capt.	Franklin H. Monk	5	475	5
Capt.	Paul V. Morriss	5	475	5
Lt.	Jennings L. Myers	5	8	5
Capt.	Leslie D. Nelson	5	49	5
Maj.	Franklin A. Nichols	5	49 & 475	5
Lt.	Lawrence F. O'Neill	5	348	5
Lt.	Kenneth R. Pool	5	8	5
Lt.	Edward S. Popek	5	348	5
Capt.	C. B. Ray	5	8	5
Capt.	Louis Schriber	5	8	5
Capt.	Richard C. Suehr	5	35	5
Capt.	Charles P. Sullivan	5	35	5
Lt.	Robert C. Sutcliffe	5	348	5
Capt.	John A. Tilley	5	475	5
Maj.	Clifton H. Troxell	5	8	5
Capt.	Robert H. Vaught, Jr.	5	49	5
Capt.	Robert R. Yaeger, Jr.	5	35	5

1. Major George S. Welch's first four victories were scored over Pearl Harbor, Hawaii, on December 7, 1941.

2. Lieutenant Colonel John D. Landers scored his first six victories with the Fifth Air Force. He went on to gain 8.5 victories with the Eighth Air Force flying from England.

The fighter aces of the Fifth Air Force and the Thirteenth Air Force didn't choose to split victories where two or more pilots had teamed up to down an enemy aircraft. They either cut high card or rolled high dice to see who got the victory. For this reason no fractional victories appear on the lists of Fifth and Thirteenth Air Force aces.

VICTORIES OF MAJOR RICHARD I. BONG

Date	A/C Type	Place
Dec. 27, 1942	Val	Dobodura, New Guinea
Dec. 27, 1942	Zeke	Dobodura, New Guinea
Jan. 7, 1943	2 Oscars	Huon Gulf, New Guinea
Jan. 8, 1943	Oscar	Lae, New Guinea
Mar. 3, 1943	Oscar	Huon Gulf, New Guinea
Mar. 11, 1943	2 Zekes	Dobodura, New Guinea
Mar. 29, 1943	Dinah	Dobodura, New Guinea
Apr. 14, 1943	Betty	Milne Bay, New Guinea
June 12, 1943	Oscar	Bena Bena, New Guinea
July 26, 1943	2 Tonys	Markham Valley, New Guinea
July 26, 1943	2 Oscars	Markham Valley, New Guinea
July 28, 1943	Oscar	Rein Bay, New Britain
Oct. 2, 1943	Dinah	Gasmata, New Britain
Oct. 29, 1943	2 Zekes	Rabaul, New Britain
Nov. 5, 1943	2 Zekes	Rabaul, New Britain
Feb. 15, 1944	Tony	Cape Hoskins, New Britain
Mar. 3, 1944	2 Sallys	Tadji, New Guinea
Apr. 3, 1944	Oscar	Hollandia, New Guinea
Apr. 12, 1944	3 Oscars	Hollandia, New Guinea
Oct. 10, 1944	Oscar	Balikpapan, Borneo
Oct. 10, 1944	T/E U/I	Balikpapan, Borneo
Oct. 27, 1944	Oscar	Tacloban, Philippine Islands
Oct. 28, 1944	2 Oscars	Masbate, Philippine Islands

Date	A/C Type	Place
Nov. 10, 1944	Oscar	Ormoc Bay, Philippine Islands
Nov. 11, 1944	2 Zekes	Ormoc Bay, Philippine Islands
Dec. 7, 1944	Sally	Bohol Island, Philippine Islands
Dec. 7, 1944	Tojo	Ormoc Bay, Philippine Islands
Dec. 15, 1944	Oscar	Panubulon Island, Philippine Islands
Dec. 17, 1944	Oscar	San José, Philippine Islands

VICTORIES OF MAJOR THOMAS B. MCGUIRE, JR.

Date	A/C Type	Place
Aug. 18, 1943	2 Zekes	Wewak, New Guinea
Aug. 18, 1943	Tony	Wewak, New Guinea
Aug. 21, 1943	2 Zekes	Wewak, New Guinea
Aug. 29, 1943	Zeke	Wewak, New Guinea
Aug. 29, 1943	Tony	Wewak, New Guinea
Sept. 28, 1943	2 Zekes	Wewak, New Guinea
Oct. 15, 1943	Val	Oro Bay, New Guinea
Oct. 17, 1943	3 Zekes	Buna, New Guinea
Dec. 26, 1943	3 Vals	Cape Gloucester, New Britain
May 17, 1944	Oscar	Noemfoor, New Guinea
May 19, 1944	Tojo	Manokwari, New Guinea
June 16, 1944	Sonia	Jefman, N. New Guinea
June 16, 1944	Oscar	Jefman, N. New Guinea
July 27, 1944	Oscar	Lolobata, Halmeharas
Oct. 14, 1944	Oscar	Balikpapan, Borneo
Oct. 14, 1944	Hamp	Balikpapan, Borneo
Oct. 14, 1944	Tojo	Balikpapan, Borneo
Nov. 1, 1944	Tojo	San Pablo, Philippine Islands
Nov. 10, 1944	Oscar	Ormoc Bay, Philippine Islands
Nov. 12, 1944	2 Jacks	Cebu, Philippine Islands
Dec. 7, 1944	Oscar	Ormoc Bay, Philippine Islands
Dec. 7, 1944	Tojo	Ormoc Bay, Philippine Islands
Dec. 13, 1944	Jack	Tanza, Philippine Islands
Dec. 25, 1944	3 Zekes	Mabalacat, Philippine Islands
Dec. 26, 1944	4 Zekes	Clark Field, Philippine Islands

FLYING THE P-38 IN COMBAT

(As given by Captain W. K. "Kenny" Giroux, a member of the 8th Fighter Group, 36th Fighter Squadron of the Fifth Air Force. Captain Giroux flew the P-39, the P-47, and the P-38 in combat, but scored all of his 10 official victories in the Lightning.)

After 6 months in Panama and about 150 hours in P-39s and P-40s, I was assigned to the Fifth Air Force, 8th Fighter Group, at Port Moresby, New Guinea. The 8th Group consisted of the 80th Squadron flying P-38s, the 35th Squadron flying P-40s, and the 36th flying P-39s and war-weary P-400s. No luck on this assignment: I drew the 36th. It took no time to realize I had a poor combat airplane. It had served its purpose well in Panama, but this was a brand-new ball game. The P-39 had no range to get you where the real action was, poor service ceiling, poor rate of climb, and it wasn't the best in a dive. Consequently, we drew the poorest missions. Strafing for ground support and short-range escort for the transports were our primary duties. After about 30 such missions our war-weary P-39s and P-400s were replaced with new P-47s. From the smallest fighter plane in the AAF to the big 2,000-hp P-47 was quite a transition. At least we had a plane that could take you to where the action was.

Late in January 1944 while we were stationed at Finschhafen, we were told that the squadron would be re-equipped with P-38s. On February 1, 2 Lightnings were assigned us, and the checkouts began. I can't recall ever being as eager to fly or as impressed as I was with the new airplane. I would fly a mission in the morning and spend the rest of the day at the flight line talking to the checkout pilots.

On February 4 I was given a cockpit check and told, "It's all yours." What a feeling! I started the 2 big Allisons. I had flown Allison engine-powered craft before in the P-39s and P-40s, but the sound was different. It's not like the roar you get from the short exhaust stacks on the P-40 or the noise of the gear box and exhaust of the P-39, but a smooth purr as the exhaust from the 12-cylinder Allison is channeled through the superchargers.

I taxied out to the runway and got clearance for takeoff. As in all fighters it's a "do-it-yourself deal," with no instructor pilot riding along. This airplane had a good feeling and I didn't seem to "sweat it out," as with other checkouts. I advanced full throttle, and the purr of the engines changed to a deep-throated, muffled roar. As you went down the runway, building up speed, you could feel the difference. There was no standing on the rudder to compensate for the torque, as in a single-engine plane. The speed built up fast. The big fighter was only halfway down the runway when it became airborne, so I picked up the gear and climbed out. The cockpit was comfortable and not the tight fit of the P-39 nor the deep seat of the P-47. You sat high with plenty of room with excellent visibility except at the 2 o'clock and 10 o'clock positions due to the engine nacelles.

I leveled out at 15,000 feet and started to feel the bird out. I tried stalls with power off and with power on. It reacted very well and broke clean. The plane warned you well ahead of its stall. I leveled out and put it into a high-speed turn, pulling hard on the yoke to get a high-speed stall. The plane again gave warning in its shutters, but you still had control.

It was hard to imagine that this big twin-engine fighter could be such a nimble craft for aerobatics, but after a few rolls, loops, and Immelmanns, I was a believer. It handled like nothing I had ever flown before.

I headed back to the field for my first twin-engine landing. The forward visibility was perfect. I came in "over the fence" at about 90 mph. With no ammunition and just a hundred gallons of fuel it floated a bit, but I held it off and it landed beautifully.

I had checked out in the P-38F. Later I flew the J and L series.

On February 23, 1944, I flew my last P-47. That month I had flown 26 missions, 19 in the P-47 and 7 in the P-38. I really didn't have a dislike for the "Jug." I had some success with it, but like a mother-in-law who stays too long, I was glad to see her go.

The P-38 was used for every type of combat mission: photo recon, bombing, strafing, and fighting. Stripped down for photo work, its speed and service ceiling made it the best in the Pacific. Its performance as a bomber was unbelievable. It could carry 2 2,000-pound bombs or a 2,000-pound bomb and a 300-gallon belly tank.

As bomber pilots we got to be fairly accurate. We would fly in over the target at 8,000 to 10,000 feet, roll over on our back, and split-ess, trying to release our bombs while in position over the target. The bombing run would be followed by strafing, which could do considerable damage. In aerial combat a pilot's skill will keep him alive, but in strafing it's a "luck game." The P-38 increased your odds. Its twin engines, its ability to take punishment, and its concentration of firepower let you do your job and live to fight another day.

As with all AAF fighter aircraft, the P-38 was not a plane to get in a dogfight and slug it out, blow for blow, with a Japanese Zero. A Zero pilot with average flying ability could beat you every time. However, by being alert and using the P-38 to its best advantage the kill ratio was 12 to 1 in our favor.

I believe the success of a fighter pilot depended upon his eyesight, his ability to fly, and the aircraft he was flying. Seeing the enemy first had the battle half won. After sighting the enemy you used your flying ability to "set him up" and take advantage of everything the P-38 had to offer. With the airspeed above 300 mph we made our pass and climbed or dived away. If you missed you used your speed and power to get in position for another pass. If the enemy turned we would stay with him for not more than 180 degrees. A tight turn would kill off the airspeed and you had lost your advantage. No one felt bad because the big, heavily loaded P-38 wouldn't turn with the Zero.

With a late-model P-38J or P-38L with the new hydraulic boost for the ailerons and the maneuverability flap I believe I could have come close to turning with the Zero. I never tried it; the hit-and-run was a sure winner, so why not stay with it?

The two things that bugged the P-38 pilots in Europe were the lack of enough cockpit heat and compressibility in a dive. Although the faults were corrected in later models, they were never a problem in the Pacific. Our missions were not at the great altitudes they used in Europe. We rarely exceeded 25,000 feet. The new foot warmer in the Js kept us comfortable in our suntans. In fact, a little coolness at altitude felt very refreshing after a day in the hot jungles. To dive at the speed of sound or encounter compressibility for us was uncalled for. There was no enemy plane we could not outdive at 600 mph, a safe speed for the P-38.

If the war had lasted a few more years no doubt the P-38 would have had a 1,000-mile range. With Colonel Charles Lindbergh teaching us cruise control (high manifold pressure) and adding more fuel tanks in the leading edge of the wing, the legs got longer. We could reach targets over 1,000 miles away. In less than 2 years we had doubled our range. My longest was 8 hours, 45 minutes. Eight hours is a long time to sit anywhere. However, the old bird would do its best to keep you comfortable. It could be trimmed up to almost fly hands off. The cockpit was large enough so that you could loosen your safety belt and at least stretch a bit.

The abort rate was not high. Personally I aborted 3 times, twice due to a bad fuel booster pump and once for a rough engine due to a bad magneto. The credit for the almost faultless performance goes to my two great crew chiefs, Sergeant Livingston and Sergeant Neal. Over-all, the Allisons were good, tough, powerful engines. Coupled to the twin-boomed airframe it made the P-38 a true fighting thoroughbred. From the E series to the L series at the war's end the P-38 was always "the" airplane in the Pacific.

In my opinion it was the greatest fighter airplane of its time. Yes, I've flown the P-51.

FLYING THE P-40 IN COMBAT

(As given by Captain Robert M. DeHaven, 14-victory ace of the 7th Fighter Squadron, 49th Fighter Group, Fifth Air Force. De-Haven became an ace flying the P-40 and later flew the P-38. This report is extracted from *Twelve to One—Fighter Combat Tactics in the SWPA,* a 5th Fighter Command publication.)

Inasmuch as our combat to date has been confined to the P-40 fighter, our views regarding combat tactics with the enemy will deal solely with that aircraft. However, it must also be remembered that in conjunction with the successful execution of these tactics, we have had on many occasions the cooperation of P-38s and P-47s as high cover, running "interference," etc.

1. Defensive

It has been firmly established that in the P-40 the best defensive maneuver is the split "S" if the attack is in progress, that is, if we have been jumped. The ability to roll a P-40 on its back and gain speed quickly straight down is usually sufficient to evade the fire of the enemy. We have found this maneuver to be effective as low as 5,000 feet. However, in the dive we adhere to the iron-clad rule of never pulling out in the same direction that we go in. Even a half roll is enough to disrupt the enemy fire and confuse him as to our direction of pullout. In the case of the type 3 fighter, Tony, that statement must be qualified to the extent that one must have altitude to dive away. The Tony will dive with a P-40 up to speeds of 400 mph, but it apparently is allergic to sudden high-speed pull-outs, and we have "shaken" it in that manner. We have also found with the Tony that if there is the slightest opportunity for circular combat it is preferable to diving out. We realize that this subject is very controversial, but we have destroyed several Tonys in true circular combat and feel that the P-40 will definitely outturn it.

We have also on occasion used the pushover when jumped by

the Oscar or Zeke because their carburation system will not feed their radial engines on a sudden pushover. However, a steep dive is difficult to attain in this fashion, and the danger of "redding out" makes it more detrimental than beneficial. On top of that, while the P-40 is gaining speed slowly, the enemy may half roll and be in easy position to shoot.

In the event that the enemy is seen starting the attack, it has been our policy to wait until he commits himself definitely as to direction and then turn into him. The Japanese pilot is generally not eager for a head-on pass, and a sudden turn into him will usually delay his attack long enough for us to get out of gun range and gain altitude using a high-speed climb. It has been our experience in combat and against captured enemy aircraft that with a slight distance advantage, a shallow, high-speed climb will pull us away from the Tony, Oscar, and Zeke.

In case the enemy is above us but has not yet committed himself to attack, our practice has been to get out from under, gain altitude, keeping him in sight and then return to make our own passes. Peculiarly, we have found that the enemy is not likely to follow us either singularly or in groups while we are in the process of pulling away and gaining altitude.

The last of the defensive maneuvers concerns being caught on the deck and, needless to say, that's a tough spot to be in. If alone and the enemy is diving for the attack, his speed is too great for us to try pulling away; therefore, the only alternative is to put your foot on the throttle, turn into him, and/or skid the airplane violently. If he is behind and in gun range, pushing and pulling the stick to get a roller coaster effect has often worked safely, but other than that, a "firewalled" throttle quadrant and violent skid is the only choice we have. About that time, a prayer comes in handy, too.

2. Offensive

Inasmuch as no 2 combats are identical, it is difficult to make any set rules governing attack. The only definite advantages we always try to gain are altitude, speed, and position.

In the case of fighters, we naturally like to originate our attacks from above and behind or in the sun. Due to the "flying circus" formation the enemy usually flies, the element of surprise is eliminated; however, being above gives us opportunity to gain superior speed, make a pass to break up their group, and then pull back up to altitude. Originally the conception of P-40s vs. Zeros was to make 1 pass and go home, which is safe but not necessary. We find with an initial altitude 2,000 feet greater than the enemy's, at least 4 passes can be made before we are forced to leave the fight and regain altitude. Sometimes even this is not necessary because the Japanese prefer to fight down low where their maneuverability is greatest; therefore, as we continue to make diving passes, the fight will get progressively lower. In regard to that, our practice is never to get below 5,000 feet on a pass unless we outnumber them and are positive there is nothing above or we have a higher cover. In that case, we keep superior speed and fight right to the deck. Another theory of individual combat that has been somewhat exploded is never to turn with a Zero. It already has been mentioned that circular combat with a Tony is possible, and to a point, the same is true of an Oscar, Zeke, or Hamp. It is a rare occasion when the individual gets a dead-astern shot; therefore, following a Zero's turn for as much as 270 degrees has and does get results. Of course, it's preferable to have a high-speed turn because the greater the speed the greater the diameter of a Zero's circle. We have found that in the initial turn a Zero will "mush" to a great extent and present good opportunity for a high-deflection shot. Also, he has an unusual habit of reversing his turn or rolling; in either case, presenting "cold Turkey." The enemy has also split "S" when attacked by a P-40, and that is welcomed if we're along—providing we have the necessary speed and altitude and there are no enemy above. True, he can split "S" and lose far less altitude than the P-40; however, the Warhawk can roll and get started down just as quickly as a Zero and be shooting all the way. In attacking groups of 2, 3, or 4 enemy by oneself, it's safe to say that they will attempt to "box in" the individual. One favorite maneuver by 3 Zeros is the Prince of Wales, in which the leader does a loop and the wingmen make opposite chandelles. To follow any 1 is to invite the other 2 for Bingo; therefore, we usually take a snap shot at 1, keep going, regain altitude, and try again. In the case of 2 or 4, they will usually be spread out and stacked up. If the opportunity is such that we can hit the top man, we do so; but attempting to attack low men even with superior speed is not conducive to a safe trip home. Of late we have found enemy pilots who will take a head-on pass and, with our greater firepower, it's usually disastrous for them. They do, however, have the trick of coming in head-on, rolling, and firing on their backs; then as they pass under, executing a split "S" and looping up under us. This is easily counteracted by making a tight chandelle as soon as they roll and pass underneath. In 1-against-1 fights, a Japanese pilot who knows his aircraft can—and did—make a fool of 1 P-40 by continuous tight turns into the attack. In such circumstances it is best to bring in another P-40 or let the enemy go before he has a chance to reverse the advantage. In regard to individual tactics on bombers, a frontal pass is the rule, preferably low front quarter. After firing all the way in, pass over and under as close to the bomber as possible to disrupt the fire of the turrets, and then break down and out, skidding violently.

FLYING THE P-47 IN COMBAT

(As given by Lieutenant Colonel William D. Dunham, 16-victory ace of the 348th Fighter Group, Fifth Air Force. This report is extracted from *Twelve to One—Fighter Combat Tactics in the SWPA,* a 5th Fighter Command publication.)

In this theater, the best individual defensive tactic is a hard and fast offensive, regardless of the odds. This tactic used in defense takes full advantage of the superior speed and diving ability of the P-47. It permits a pass at the enemy and a fast dive away with little danger of being shot down.

If you are attacked from above while you are at cruising speed, and the attacking planes have excessive speed, the best defensive maneuver is a sharp aileron roll to the right and down, diving out 180 degrees from the direction of the attack. *This maneuver cannot be started too soon,* but must be executed just before the attacking plane is within range. The slow aileron action of the Japanese fighters at high speeds makes it impossible for them to pull through far enough to get the proper lead, and by the time he can change direction you should have enough speed to easily outdistance him.

If attacked from above when you are on the deck and you do not see the enemy soon enough to turn into him for a head-on pass, the best immediate defensive maneuver is a gentle skid. The average Japanese pilot will not correct for skid unless it is very noticeable. In one case, a Tony expended all his ammunition without a single hit while firing from dead-astern position at a range of 100 yards.

In offensive individual combat there are 2 principles to observe. First, never attack unless you have an equal or greater altitude than the enemy. Second, plan your attack to afford the greatest element of surprise. An altitude advantage of at least 10,000 feet does not guarantee surprise, but it does offer the greatest odds in favor of securing this advantage. While flying 4-ship fighter sweeps with Colonel Kearby, we made it a policy to go in at 26,000 or above. At this altitude they could neither see nor hear us on the ground, while it was easy for us to see the enemy landing or taking off. Our attack was invariably from the stern, with the sun to our advantage. In every case we were firing before the Japanese knew we were around. Excessive speed of the P-47 in such a diving attack permits a rapid recovery of the altitude advantage begun with. At a speed of 350 mph or more, one can easily pull up and hammer-head back down into the fight. IN SUCH AN ATTACK, AND IN ALL ATTACKS ON THE ENEMY, IT IS IMPERATIVE THAT NO TURN GREATER THAN 90 DEGREES BE ATTEMPTED BEFORE BREAKING OFF THE ATTACK.

When attacked from the rear or side, the Japanese will frequently hold his course until you are in firing range, and then turn sharply, making it impossible for you to get a proper lead. A good way to counteract this defensive maneuver is to open up at 500 to 600 yards in order to induce him to make this maneuver in time for you to get sufficient lead. Ninety per cent of the time, the enemy will start his turn at the first sight of tracers, thus giving you time for sufficient leading. In one case a Japanese turned so sharply that I finished the pass head-on.

With additional power afforded by water injection one can attack from an equal altitude and climb away in a high-speed climb until sufficient distance is acquired to make a head-on pass.

COMBAT TACTICS
IN THE
SOUTHWEST PACIFIC AREA
by Captain Thomas B. McGuire, Jr.

Published and Distributed by

Asst. C. of S. A-3, 5th Fighter Command

May 4, 1944

FOREWORD

When one considers just what he should say to a new sport who is reporting in to an operational fighter group, the mind becomes confused in the complex maze of information it is necessary for the new sport to know. All of it is important; most of it vital; and all of it is just too much for one brain to absorb in a few lectures.

Rarely has complexity been reduced to clarify and still include a wealth of information, as has been done in this article by Captain McGuire.

"The proof of the pudding . . ." The fighter group of which Captain McGuire is a part of the team, has destroyed 329 enemy aircraft in 8 months of operations in the SWPA. He describes the tactics of the group, and its successful pilots.

To the new sports . . . don't read this article once. Read it again and again. The more you learn before the fight, the more you'll learn during the fight, and the more chance you'll have to keep on learning.

Charles H. MacDonald
Lieutenant Colonel, AAF

FORMATIONS AND TACTICS

General. The standard formation for P-38s is 16 planes in 4 4-ship flights, the flight being the basic unit for both attack and defense. Each man within the flight takes up a position on a line extending back at an angle of approximately 45 degrees from the

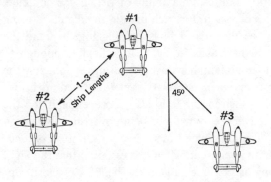

DIAGRAM 1

The Flight Formation

flight leader, the planes being spaced 1 to 3 ship-lengths apart. The wingman flies to the left or right and below the flight leader, the element leader to the left or right and above the flight leader, usually on the opposite side from the wingman. The wingman for the element leader may fly either above or below the element leader, but whatever vertical variations there may be, the 1-to-3 ship-length distance on the horizontal plane and the angle in respect to the flight leader will be maintained.

This flight formation assures a maximum of visibility, a complete coverage of all angles of vision, for each man in the flight, allowing the flight leader to see that his flight is holding together and the others to keep the flight leader in sight. It is flexible enough to permit each man to maintain his throttle setting by playing the turns and crossing over when necessary, yet this freedom brings no decrease in support strength. It is also loose enough for the flight leader to maneuver freely without being overrun by his men or losing them by an unanticipated turn, dive, or climb, a particularly valuable attribute in combat, when it is essential that the flight hold together as long as possible to gain the benefits of close support. A word of caution in this respect: It is entirely the responsibility of the wingman, element leader, and the tail-end Charlie to keep out of the blind spot directly behind the flight leader. Flexibility is not synonymous with sloppiness, and a momentary restriction of the flight leader's line of vision may endanger the whole flight as well as hindering the leader's tactics by making him uncertain as to the disposition of his men in respect to himself. No matter what type of cover is being provided, whether the mission happens to be escort, patrol, or search, the flight formation will hold to the same pattern. This is a purely defensive formation designed for maximum strength, and will never change to line-abreast; nor will it change to line-astern except in combat.

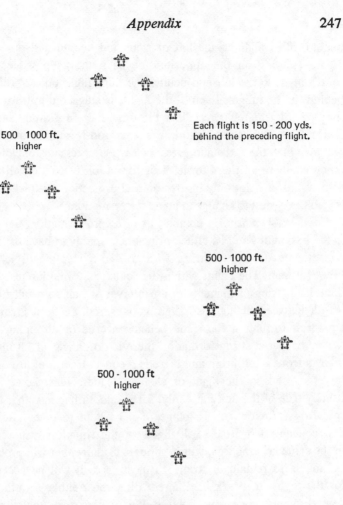

500   1000 ft.
higher

Each flight is 150 - 200 yds.
behind the preceding flight.

500 - 1000 ft.
higher

500 - 1000 ft
higher

DIAGRAM 2

The Squadron Formation

The squadron formation has the same characteristics of flexibility and visibility as the flight formation, with each of the following flights being able to see the squadron leader and all the other flights ahead. The lead flight will be at the lowest altitude and ahead, the second flight will be to the left or right and

behind, third flight to the left or right and behind and preceding
flights (staying on the opposite side as much as possible), the
fourth flight to the left and behind the third flight but not directly
behind the first flight. Each of the flights is staggered upward from
the one immediately preceding, the difference in altitude ranging
from 500 to 1,000 feet. Within the squadron formation the flights
will also play the turns and press over when necessary to avoid too
much changing of the throttle. This formation is used on all types
of missions and not only insures mutual protection if attacked, but
is also the easiest to change to an attack formation.

Combat formation. In combat, as in escort formation, the flight
is the basic unit, and its attack principle is simply to have the flight
constituents drop into string with a 3-to-6 ship-length interval
between them. The flights within the squadron formation also drop
back in a string of flights with an interval of half to a full flight's
length between flights, also slightly staggered. In both flight and
squadron formation the same benefits accrue on dropping back
to the staggered string formation there is no danger of hitting the
man in front when firing and there is a concentration of fire on the
target chosen by the flight or element leader. This, however, is
usually true of the first pass only, for it seldom happens that a full
squadron formation of 16 planes can be kept together after the
first concentrated attack. All flights of the squadron will remain
in the same general area, within support distance, but will probably
be unable to remain in string. In most cases it will be necessary
for the flights to break in different directions, either to attack or
defend against the enemy fighters. It is at this point that the real
value of the 4-ship flight becomes most apparent.

The 4-ship flight must hold together as long as possible, and if
the attack is centered on bombers there is no reason for breaking
formation. Nothing is so embarrassing to a flight leader as when
a small formation of enemy bombers is jumped and the planes go
off individually. It can be more dangerous to encounter a few enemy planes than many if uncoordinated passes cause the lead man

to find himself turning into a stream of tracers from the guns of his own men.

After making a pass, the flight leader will try to hold the line of flight in a shallow dive or climb so that his men can follow through normally and retain their relative positions. For the individual and the 3 others with whom he is flying it offers the best mutual support, the tail-end man watching over those ahead, the flight leader in position to swing around if the tail-end Charlie is attacked.

If the combat turns out to be fighter vs. fighter, then it may be necessary to break up into 2-ship elements, but no further. There is no excuse at all for a wingman to leave his element leader, and the 2-ship element must be regarded as the absolute minimum under any circumstances. The minimum, that is, if the combat is to be successful from our point of view. Ninety-five percent of the men who have been lost in combat have been lost while they have been alone, separated from the rest of their flight. The phrase, "He was last seen at a little distance from the rest of the formation" comes up time and time again in reports of actions in which we have suffered casualties.

An excellent demonstration of some of the points made in the foregoing paragraphs took place over Rabaul a few months ago, when a mission there meant certain interception. Before the target was reached the lead flight had had one snafu, the third flight leader had taken over the position of squadron leader, and there were 2 snafus from the third flight, leaving 9 of an original 12 planes. Just after the B-25s had finished a low-level bombing run and were heading for home, a force of 60 or 70 enemy fighters attacked both the bombers and the escort. Shortly after the first attack the No. 2 man in the first flight became separated from the rest, and the other flights split up into elements, leaving the squadron leader without a wingman. One element, the leader of the second flight and his wingman, saw his danger and stayed with the squadron leader, who had been singled out by the enemy and was subjected to repeated attacks. On the first attack, made from the rear, the leader of the second flight shot down one Zeke while his wingman fired a long burst, which caused the second Zeke to break away. The next attack was made head-on. Again the flight leader shot down one and again the second Zeke broke away. The third attack was made from 11 o'clock low. The leader of the second flight had run out of ammunition by this time, and as the Zeke came on, the leader ducked under and to the left, allowing his wingman to fire a burst, which sent the enemy plane down in flames. Two more Zekes attacked the squadron leader from behind, and the flight leader made a dry run on them, causing them to peel off in opposite directions. Then one of about 5 enemy aircraft in the vicinity made a 90-degree deflection attack from the right. The flight leader pulled up at the Zeke and it half rolled away, frightened off by empty guns.

Had either of the 2 men in the leading element of the second flight broken away to fight on his own, the squadron leader could not have survived this engagement. Sustained close support saved him. Don't sacrifice yourself and the man you are supposed to protect by making a grandstand, lone-wolf play. You might be lucky, once or twice, but don't forget that you are gambling with another man's life as well as your own, and his luck may not last him through the first minute after you have left him. Because it is a temptation for the last man to strike out on his own, having no one following him, it is the general practice in this area for the strongest wingman (and by strong is meant experienced enough to hold his place) to fly the No. 4 position in each flight, and for the first and fourth flights to be the strongest in the squadron. Tail-end Charlie is a mighty important man, and any time you play the part, play it square with the men who are relying on you to play it just that way. It is an obligation, not a courtesy, for you to do so.

TACTICS

Our Tactics Against Enemy Aircraft While Escorting Our Own Bombers

Heavy bombers, close cover. Depending on the number of bombers escorted and the opposition expected, close cover for heavy bombers will usually mean that one squadron is assigned to each of the flanks, one squadron ahead, and one squadron astern. Formations of 24 or less bombers will not require 4 full squadrons as escort, but above that number, fighters will multiply until, with 100 or more bombers, there will be 3 or 4 squadrons as close cover, 2 squadrons as medium and high cover, and a possible additional squadron as top cover for the fighter and bomber formation as a whole. The close cover flies 1,000 to 4,000 feet above the bombers, weaving to keep the true forward speed the same as that of the bombers and being particularly careful, if the bomber formation is ragged, to keep watch over the outer fringe. On return from the target crippled bombers or bombers flying in pairs will make it necessary to have a flight assigned to them for protection.

Heavy bombers, top cover. The job of providing successful top cover for heavy bombers is a difficult one, not because the Japanese make determined attacks, but because those who do attack only do so from the position most favorable to themselves. The squadron which acts as top cover weaves over the whole bomber formation and the escorting close cover, from 4,000 to 8,000 feet above them. The enemy will seldom make a real interception, in the sense that they will try to break up our formation before it reaches the target. On the approach to the target the Japanese fighters will be seen scattered over the area, in no apparent formation, flying singly or in pairs or threes, but during or after the bombing run there will be haphazard attacks by individuals or pairs. Almost always these attacks will come when the enemy pilots have altitude. They will do a half roll and make an overhead pass, diving through the bomber formation, clearing away to the side, then returning to altitude. Since there will be no attack in formation, the only possible countertactic is to break up the top cover into flights and drive off the attacks as they are begun; there can be no general movement of the squadron, for the scattered distribution of the enemy fighters and the impossibility of anticipation leave no alternative but to check each pass as soon as possible after the enemy has committed himself.

The above also holds true to some extent for the close cover. While a number of the enemy will attack from above, there will be others attacking from beneath, particularly against B-24s. At such times the close cover will move down somewhat and will break up into flights to ward off the single passes.

Remember, the favorite enemy target is the target of opportunity. Be most watchful when the target area has been left behind and damaged bombers begin to straggle. A crippled bomber is no match for 5 or 6 eager Zekes, and the best way to forestall such attacks is for the squadron leader to assign flights to each of the stragglers within range of his cover.

Escort of low-level strafers and bombers. The squadron acting as close cover for bombers or strafers on a low-level strike will generally be at slightly higher altitude than when escorting heavy bombers, from 2,000 to 6,000 feet above the bomber formation. The top cover will also go higher, staying at 8,000 to 10,000 feet above the close cover.

Since attack from beneath is virtually impossible, the strategy of our fighters is to break up the Japanese attacks before they are well started, before too many can get within range of the strafers and bombers. Against strafers, the enemy dive down either to or through the formation in as nearly vertical dive and climb as they can achieve. A few make passes horizontally, but the disadvantage in altitude will dissuade all but the most eager. Here again the squadron formation will be broken up to ward off attacks at numerous points and will probably break from flights to elements relatively early in the combat, because the defense will be more a matter of protecting individual bombers at the perimeter than covering the whole formation. It will be a temptation on this kind of mission to attack and give chase to the opposing fighters *after* they have made their passes and before they can regain altitude. This is foolish and futile. It weakens both squadron and flight and defeats the purpose of the escort. Attack is the function of the bombers in this case; you are present to assure them a chance to do their job with as little hindrance as possible from enemy fighters.

TACTICS

Our Tactics When Intercepting Enemy Bombers

The enemy is well aware of the advantage of a tight formation, as well aware of it as we are, and an enemy bomber formation will hold its pattern tenaciously, closing up if one of its number is shot down and making itself as little vulnerable as it can. The answer to this tactic is to make the first pass with 16 planes and break up the enemy formation. This way the highest concentration of our own power is achieved and the enemy is forced to disperse his firepower. Our function is to break up the enemy formation and keep it from reaching the target. Once the formation is broken, the individuals or pairs make much better targets for flights or elements.

Medium bombers. The best way to attack enemy medium bombers is to make a head-on pass from 45 degrees left or right, breaking away to the same side as that from which the approach was made. Follow through the circle and swing ahead for another pass. The squadron should hold together as long as possible, but if enemy fighter interference forces a change in the manner of breaking away then it will be up to the flights to make their attacks independently.

Another form of attack which works out quite well is the side attack from 90 degrees high, coming down and breaking away when the angle of approach narrows to approximately 45 degrees. This keeps the attacking planes out of the arc of fire of that potent 20mm stinger in the tail of Japanese medium bombers and it is also easier to keep the squadron together.

As long as you can make passes on the bombers, don't engage enemy fighters. Fighters can do no damage to the target, and the enemy's air strength is weakened far more by the loss of a bomber than by the loss of a fighter. Individual scores may not mount rapidly, but the net profit will be substantially in our favor if you shoot down or drive off the bombers and deal with the fighters only when they cannot be ignored.

Light bombers and dive bombers. It may be varied to head-on or from the side under appropriate conditions, but the best attack against the Japanese light bomber or dive bomber is the attack from dead astern. Light bombers are not often encountered, but the wheels-down dive bombers are so familiar that our pilots have almost a friendly feeling toward them. These slow-moving, poorly armed, unarmored planes are the nearest things to sitting birds as will be found in modern warfare, and their strategy in action appears to be designed to have as many of them shot down as possible. Starting their dives from 15,000 to 18,000 feet, the Vals reach a maximum speed of 300 to 325 mph, drop their bombs, and go right on down to the deck, where they break formation and scoot for home in all directions. A P-38 can follow them nicely in their dives, and with any sort of luck can force them to jettison their bombs before they can release them on the shipping, which is their usual target. Having pulled out of the dive, the Val slows down rapidly, skimming low over the water, and the pursuing P-38 closes in for the *coup de grâce*.

Enemy fighters protecting their own bombers usually hover well above the formation in one large, loose group like a swarm of gnats. They do not make coordinated or combined passes and they cannot stop a determined interception. Unless they greatly outnumber the intercepting force, the Japanese fighters prefer to hang around the edges of the combat, picking on individuals completing passes or perhaps making an occasional surprise attack from the clouds, then pulling up into cloud cover again as soon as possible.

When escorting dive bombers, enemy fighter pilots almost never follow them down to protect them, seemingly acting as a decoy rather than protection against our fighters. The Zekes, Oscars, et al; stay up in hopes of having our men join combat with them there, being reluctant to make themselves vulnerable by going to low altitudes. Don't oblige them—follow the dive bombers and you will rarely find that the fighter pilots will try to stop you.

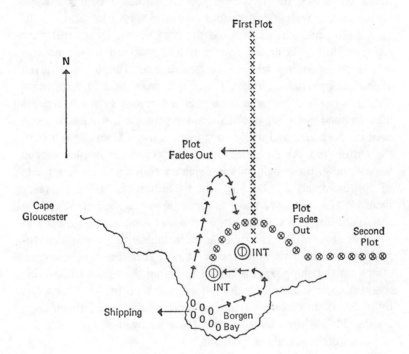

DIAGRAM 3

Japanese Tactics on 26 December 1943

The above diagram shows an interesting example of enemy tactics used on December 26, 1943 when a force of dive bombers made an attack on ships engaged in landing troops on Cape Gloucester. One of our squadrons on patrol was ordered to investigate a plot, but when it reached the area no enemy aircraft were sighted. Shortly after the squadron had returned to the area in which the shipping was concentrated, another plot was given which disappeared entirely. (Radar personnel said that it "faded out.") What had happened was that a force of Japanese fighters had dropped plates of tinfoil suspended from small parachutes to confuse the radar and to lure our fighters away from the center of the patrol area. As the squadron again returned to its place above the shipping, these fighters were sighted coming in at an altitude of approximately 23,000 feet. The squadron climbed to intercept them. While climbing, another force of enemy fighters dived on the squadron. The squadron turned under the enemy fighters and began a slight dive. At this time the squadron leader sighted approximately 30 dive bombers at 18,000 feet, just beginning an attack on the shipping. Instead of engaging the fighters above his squadron, the squadron leader led an attack on the dive bombers, following them down and forcing most of them to jettison their bombs. Meanwhile the Zekes and Oscars stayed at high altitudes to engage other squadrons of P-38s.

The first squadron kept after the dive bombers at minimum altitude, making passes from dead astern, and shot down 14 of them without interference by enemy fighters. (Other squadrons accounted for the remaining dive bombers.) Had the squadron been taken in by the deception and tried to fight with the Zeros, the dive bombers would have been successful in their attempt to slip in at a lower altitude and would no doubt have done great damage. Quick thinking and a knowledge of Japanese tactics enabled the squadron leader to take the best action possible. He knew he would not be endangering his squadron by exposing it to attack by enemy fighters because he was sure the fighters would not follow to low altitudes. He also knew that it was better to break up the dive-bomber attack before the Vals reached the point at which they could release their bombs most effectively. A successful combat is not evaluated by the type of opposition you choose to meet, but by the amount of damage you prevent or inflict.

JAPANESE PLANES, PILOTS, AND TACTICS

Japanese fighter planes. The only Japanese fighter which can be outmaneuvered by a P-38 is the twin-engine Nick. Whether pursuing or pursued, you must keep to the shallow dive, climb or turn, because there isn't a trick maneuver in the book that can't be done better by a Japanese plane than in a P-38. In making passes, hold your lead in deflection as long as you can, but just as soon as you lose that lead, roll out of the turn and keep going straight. Never pull up beyond 30 degrees when pursuing because your loss of speed will permit the enemy to loop over onto your tail. Break combat when it is to your advantage to do so; don't wait until you set yourself up in such a position that the Japanese will have the advantage. Make him fight on your terms; don't fight on his.

For the benefit of new pilots, a description of the more prominent characteristics of Japanese fighter planes follows. These summarizations should be supplemented by study of data available in Intelligence Memorandum 12 and the blue-covered Intelligence Summaries.

Oscar: Two synchronized 12.7s firing through the prop constitute the armament of this version of the generic "Zero." It is particularly vulnerable around the cockpit, where there is little armor to protect the pilot. The gas tanks are covered with the crudest sort of leak-absorbent material.

Zeke: Armed with 2 20mm cannon in each wing and 2 7.7s firing through the prop, this, the best-known of enemy aircraft, has a slight edge in speed and a better rate of climb than the Oscar. It is better armored, though the protection is still inadequate by our standards, and is most vulnerable around the cockpit and the fuselage directly behind the cockpit. Flown by a pilot of reasonable ability, it must be regarded as a packet of high explosives, to be approached with caution.

Hamp: This square wing-tip variation of the Zero has the same armament and the same vulnerability as the Zeke with better speed and rate of climb.

General. Unless the Zero is close with a slight advantage in altitude and speed, the best evasive tactics against Oscar, Zeke, and Hamp are the high-speed, shallow climb or dive and full speed ahead. Once you have outdistanced your pursuer you can turn and come back for another go, but make sure you don't turn too soon. If the Zero has diving speed, push your plane over, flattening out the diving angle after you have picked up to around 375 to 400 mph. The Zero's engine tends to cut out after a pushover, and that gives you your chance to elude him. It is probably better to do the pushover, but if you are a good judge of speed and the Zero doesn't appear to be coming in too fast, a shallow dive will be enough to shake him. If you have good judgment!

Tony: The usual armament of this plane is 2 12.7s synchronized through the prop with 1 12.7 in each wing. (Later models have 1 20mm in each wing.) With heavier armor and a fair quality of self-sealing tanks this plane does not have the tendency of the Zero models to explode or burn unless a very good hit is scored. An in-line fighter like our P-40s, the Tony is not an altitude fighter but makes up for this by being faster than the Hamp in level flight and extremely fast in a dive. A successful evasive tactic against this plane is, if in a dive, to make a diving turn to the right. At high speeds the Tony handles very poorly to the right and the enemy pilot has trouble turning in that direction. If you are pursued from the rear and on the level, a very high-speed, shallow climb will keep you out of range and eventually you will draw away.

One pilot found out about this the hard way. He was returning from a strike on Wewak when he was jumped by 3 Tonys. He was at 20,000 feet at the time and went into a shallow dive which ended up on the deck 100 miles farther south, with the Tonys right behind him. Forced to alter his tactics, the pilot began a high-speed, shallow climb and soon lost them. His was the original experience of this sort with the Tony, and his pioneering saved many from falling into the same error.

If you are on the deck a very sharp turn to the right at high speed may do as an emergency maneuver, but it is definitely a last resort and at best will only keep the enemy pilot from holding his lead on you.

Tojo: Too little is known about this new plane to permit positive assertions beyond the statement that it has a very good rate of climb and will make 370 mph at 18,000 feet. Those who have had contact with the Tojo have found that the best way to evade an attack is to go into a high-speed dive.

Nick: There haven't been many of these twin-engine fighters in this area and with their poor performance they are becoming scarcer as P-38 pilots and others prove that this is one Japanese fighter they can outturn, outrun, and outclimb. The Nick is structurally strong, and there will be some difficulty in diving away, but then it won't be necessary unless he gets close on your tail.

Japanese fighter pilots. Japanese fighter pilots are individualists who do not fly in set patterns nor attack by squadron or flight, although lately a few exceptions have been observed by Japanese imitating standard U.S. 4-ship flights when escorting their own bombers. The quality of the enemy pilots is unpredictable, although Navy pilots are definitely superior to Army pilots. The variation is entirely between very able, experienced pilots and very poor pilots, nothing to compare with the more uniform abilities of our own men. The only advance indication of the probable quality of the opposition is the type of plane the enemy pilot flies—silver or gray Zekes and Oscars with roundels on the fuselage as well as on the wings are Navy planes; green, brown, or mottled Hamps, Nicks or Tonys are Army planes.

In the early days of the war the enemy fighter pilots built up a reputation for skill and aggressiveness and they had little trouble keeping that reputation as long as they were opposed by ancient models of P-39s and P-40s. With the introduction of the P-38 and P-47 in this theater and the F4F and F6F in the Solomons, the Japanese learned caution, caution to the point of timidity. Even over their home bases they have shown a distaste for all-out fighting.

Offered in evidence is the Japanese reaction to the head-on pass. They don't like it, and 9 out of 10 will break first, even before they are in range. To be sure, the head-on pass cannot be recommended when flying a plane that has little armament, no convergence of lines of fire, and light armor, but what about the shout of "Banzai" and the suicide crash: Nothing about it, because the Japanese aren't living up to or dying for their propaganda. Instead they will break from the head-on pass in a vertical bank and try to come around for a tail attack. The P-38 pilot need only keep on at the same speed or go into a shallow dive to defeat this tactic, for the Japanese loses speed in the bank and turn and will wind up too far behind to be a menace. In the case of the exceptional one who does hold to a head-on pass, simply push over. The Japanese will invariably go up. One thing you must not do when committed to a head-on pass: YOU MUST NOT TURN until you are entirely clear.

It is a seeming contradiction to say the Japanese gunnery is good but the results don't show it. The discrepancy lies in the poor quality of the guns and the lack of convergence, factors which reduce the theoretical firepower and which have saved many of our pilots from being hit when the enemy had his lead and timing absolutely right. Don't underestimate Japanese gunnery!

Japanese fighter tactics. Most of the Japanese pilots rely on the half roll when pursued and almost always roll to the left. When on their tails aim slightly left and be ready to shift fire to the left. If the flight or element leader forces an enemy into a half roll, there is brief time in which an alert wingman can get in a deflection shot by depressing the nose of his plane. It isn't much more than a snapshot, but the chance is there if he is ready for it. If you haven't seen it before watch out for that half roll. A Zeke can do a half roll or split-S in from 700 to 1,000 feet and it is hard to realize that such great maneuverability is possible until you have been a witness to it.

There is another opportunity which sometimes comes to the pilot who anticipates the tactic. If the Japanese pulls up instead of doing a half roll he will almost certainly pull up to the left and stall out. Don't follow him up, but if you have altitude and see the enemy start to pull up you can be right next to him when he reaches the stalling point. It makes a nice shot with no danger of a surprise move on the part of the Japanese.

One trick employed by the enemy has worked on a couple of occasions and what is more, it has worked against pilots who ought to know better. This is the famous Lufbery and mock fight and its purpose is to suck in 1 or 2 or 3 of our men who are trustful enough to assume that a lot of milling around means a genuine fight. The mock fight takes place at some distance from the main fight and our Rover boy goes tearing across the sky all alone, eager as hell to get into it. Then those 6 or 8 fighters which have been sitting up above, probably in the clouds, come cracking down in the Japanese version of the mouse trap play. The Rover boy is concentrating on what he can see, and "out of sight, out of mind" is no motto for aerial combat. He'll never know what hit him.

Japanese medium bombers. Betty, the well-known medium bomber used by the Japanese Navy, and Helen, a less-formidable Army bomber, are the first-line enemy attack bombers and will usually make their strikes from an altitude of 20,000 to 25,000 feet, flying a tight V of Vs. (Line abreast has been observed.) Both are fast, with true air speeds in excess of 300 mph, and on occasion the Betty has been used as a torpedo bomber. Like the enemy fighter, the Japanese medium bomber is inadequately armed and armored and it's deficient in self-sealing protection for the gas tanks which stretch the whole length of the wing. The Sally, a second-line plane, is rarely used and need not be discussed.

In attacking a formation of Bettys or Helens, any angle except tail-on will expose you to the fire of 1 or 2 7.7s only, and they will be of the free-firing variety. The rear attack is dangerous, because both of these bombers are equipped with 20mm stingers in the tail. (Helen has the 20mm in a dorsal position with a 7.7 in the tail turret.) The Betty in particular commands a wide field of fire with this gun. If the tail gunner has been knocked out, that is another story, but in any event the attacks that are most likely to succeed will be those made head-on or high from the side. With so little opposing firepower, take your time and pick your spots when you have one of these planes in your sights. The wing tanks are easily ignited and the oxygen bottles around the cockpit are decidedly hazardous to the enemy pilots.

Japanese light bombers and dive bombers. The use of light bombers in this area is mainly restricted to reconnaissance and night bombing, while the dive bombers are used on occasions of great need or when concentrations of shipping demand higher precision than the mass formation can achieve. Of the light bomber types, the Lily is infrequently met, being a slow and vulnerable second-line plane. (Recently, 6 of them were caught at low altitude and shot down within 2 or 3 minutes by a squadron of P-38s.)

Dinah is the Japanese plane most used for day reconnaissance and is well designed for the job, being fast (325 to 350 mph true air speed) and having a service ceiling of 38,000 feet. Speed is obtained at the expense of structural strength and the elimination of all armor and armament. A combat version of this plane may be in existence, equipped with 3 12.7s firing forward, but the absence of armor and wing-tank protection destines it to a short life in any encounter with our planes.

Val, the most frequently used Japanese dive bomber, is the plane that helps keep alive the myth of Japanese willingness to commit suicide for the Emperor. Later models, with retractable landing gear, show increased armor and gas tank protection, but the 2 7.7s firing forward and the single 7.7 firing free to the rear, remain as a token gesture toward providing the plane with armament. After an attack these Vals scatter at deck level, attaining a speed of but 250 mph as they head for home. It is at this point that it becomes suicide to fly one.

The Japanese torpedo bomber, Kate, is little used in this theater and has the usual defects. Against it, as against Dinah, Lily, Sally, and Val, the tail approach gets the best results.

COMBAT GUIDES

A pilot's preparation for a combat mission is based on more things than ability to handle a plane. A great deal of his preparation should consist of a constant willingness to listen to more experienced men, even if it involves hearing the same stories more than once. The odd scraps of information picked up in this way are more useful than a formal set of instructions because they are related to situations you yourself are likely to encounter. Then there are the maps at the alert shack, always available to provide you with the data you will need if you return from a flight alone. Go out of your way to learn terrain—a brief glimpse of a familiar bit of coastline will fix your position when flying through bad weather. Learn what to expect in the way of weather conditions in the area. Weather is a big factor in operational losses and if you know when to turn back you are going to spare yourself some serious trouble. Don't buck weather and don't have so much faith in your instruments that you deliberately put yourself in a spot where you will have to use them.

You must know the limitations and potentialities of your own aircraft. It is very important to keep in mind all the performance data on the speed and maneuverability of the type as well as any little peculiarities of your own particular plane. You are less likely to get into trouble if you do not try the impossible, or rather, if you do try to use your plane in the best possible manner. Don't abuse the powers of the aircraft by maintaining excessive manifold pressure; save its strength for the time when you need it and it won't fail you. At the same time, don't snafu (return because of mechanical trouble) when some minor gauge fails to work properly. Any pilot who should be over the target but has returned unnecessarily leaves the squadron weaker and forces someone else to do double duty. The habitual snafu leaves himself liable to a bad reputation, ostracism, and eventual transfer.

In this area the P-38 pilot flies long missions, from 4 to 6 hours as a rule, and that is a long time to sit with a parachute strap twisted under your fanny or your emergency kit off-center on your back. Before you start, make sure you are comfortable, check your equipment not only for content but for maximum ease in the cockpit, and then you will be in condition for combat when you reach the target; your energy won't have been dissipated in fretting over a cramped position.

Check your gunsight soon after the takeoff and make sure it is working properly. Remember that you are playing for keeps and little things count when only your best is good enough.

On the way to the target don't indulge in unnecessary radio chatter. If you are in doubt whether to speak or keep still, shut up! You may miss vital instructions or warnings by opening your mouth at the wrong time. Be familiar with the calls of the fighter sectors, too. If you are flying above overcast it will be useful to know at least the area over which you are flying even if you cannot see terrain features, and if the fighter sectors pass on information you will know where it is coming from. Over the target use the clock system of calling in aircraft, adding high, level, or low as the case may be. Clearly identify yourself and the one to whom you are talking when you call in bogies or enemy aircraft. You won't help anyone by it and nothing will split a formation wider than some voice coming over the air and saying, "P-38, there's a Zero on your tail!"

As you near the target keep a close watch on cloud formations. The enemy is liable to be waiting for the chance to make a surprise attack. It is well to remember that effective use of cloud cover is as valuable for defense as for attack, since it may be the means of escape for you if your plane is damaged or in a situation calling for flight instead of fight.

This is what happened to one pilot over Rabaul. After receiving hits on the canopy, radio compartment, and left and right tanks, a 20mm shell burst squarely on the left engine of his plane, stopping one engine and setting it afire. Two Tonys and 3 Zekes came in behind this pilot but he took evasive action and headed for the nearest cloud. He made it and then, by slipping his plane, smothered the fire. The left engine was entirely burned out and then the right engine began coughing. The pilot tried to head for home on a direct southwest course, but twice left the cloud to find that the 5 enemy planes were waiting for him. The pilot thought this over and climbed to 8,000 feet inside the cloud, then took a heading due south instead of southwest. The enemy pilots weren't watching that side of the cloud and so the P-38 pilot dived to the water and flew due south for 20 minutes before setting his course for home. On a clear day he wouldn't have had a chance, but by using his head and the available cloud cover he was able to fly his crippled plane back to base, where he landed wheels-down, and turn it over to a service squadron for salvage.

Over the target keep formation. It is the wingman's job to protect his element leader even if he never gets a shot himself. Your element leader will give you whatever chances he can and it is not necessary to be leading to shoot down Japanese. (One pilot has credit for 8 enemy fighters, all of which he shot down while flying wing position and without leaving his element leader.) You are part of a team and holding the formation is a matter of life and death, if not for yourself then for someone else. The best results come with the best teamwork, and the highest individual scores are made by men who have a team spirit. Individualists don't live long enough to build up a personal score, because there is absolutely no chance to fight one against one with the Japanese and survive. American planes and formations are designed to force the enemy to fight on our terms. One of the foremost factors in the success of our planes against the Japanese in this theater has been General Wurtsmith's development of and insistence on the use of 2-ship elements in combat. Devised for the use of the P-40 pilots who made the Darwin raids so costly to the Japanese, the theory has become standard practice throughout this area simply because there is no better way to guarantee the high–low ratio of Japanese losses to ours.

Once in a fight don't concentrate on your own attack. The emphasis on looking around can't be made strong enough, for there is a tendency, a very natural and human tendency, to watch an enemy go down. Don't do it! Once you have completed your pass look around, both for another target and to make sure no enemy has slipped in close enough to make a target of your plane. Clear yourself before you put a notch in your gun.

Speed is important. Since you cannot outmaneuver the Japanese fighters it should be obvious that to have any success in a combat against them speed is essential. If at all possible, keep your speed in combat at 300 mph plus. Never slow down below 250 mph once in a fight. There have been pilots who slowed down in combat, but they are no longer capable of telling you how dangerous it is to do so.

New pilots have had gunnery drummed into them in schools, but it's not until they get into combat that they find out that a high degree of skill is necessary. Using the 70-mil sight, an enemy bomber will fill the sight at 300 yards; a fighter will fill half the sight. Unless they fill the sight to that extent, hold your fire; it just doesn't count beyond 300 yards. On the other hand, the closer you get the better. Your chances of scoring hits and the destructiveness of your fire will increase in proportion. Go in close and then, when you think you are too close, go on in closer. The majority of pilots with good scores believe in closing to minimum range, where there is no chance of missing and where firepower has its maximum effect. When you do close in, don't fire all the way. Use several bursts of 1 to 3 seconds' duration. Long bursts cause jamming and overheating of the guns. You are aiming at a target, not spraying the general area. If you take a shot in deflection, pull your sight through the enemy's line of flight. Misses are due more to shooting over or under than to improper lead. Above all, keep your flying smooth when you fire. The smoother the pilot the better his gunnery, for one smooth burst is more likely to bear results than a number of nervous, jerky bursts. Try taking a deep breath just before you press the button, or develop any psychological trick which will keep you steady through that brief moment when you have drawn a bead and are ready to let fly.

There are going to be a number of occasions when you will not be the aggressor. If you are attacked from above and to the side, wait till the enemy pilot has definitely committed himself and then turn underneath him. This forces him into a tighter turn, limits the effective length of his pass, and gives you the chance to straighten out while he is still in his turn. If a pass is made and your plane is damaged, don't be too quick to regain control. Let your plane appear to be more severely damaged than it is, let it fall away out of control and the enemy will not sacrifice his altitude just to check up. If you pull out too soon he will follow you down and try to finish you off, and he will have enough advantage to do a thorough job.

If you are fighting at low altitudes, watch out for the enemy who seems to be lagging just enough to let you close in slowly. If he is over his home base he is probably trying to lead you over the ack-ack positions, setting you up as a close-range target for small and medium ack-ack. Or he may let you follow him until you are so eager for a shot that you forget how close you are to the ground. The Japanese may try a rollover, tempting you to follow him in a maneuver impossible for a P-38 at low altitude.

When you are back at home base after a successful combat don't indulge in that last bit of foolishness—don't do a victory roll. You may easily be shot up without your knowing it and the strain imposed on your plane by the victory roll might be enough to break a partially severed control cable or damaged control surface. If that happens you will never be able to pick up that TS ticket you will have earned by taking a chance at the wrong time. If you really feel so good about a victory then land, check your plane on the ground, and take it up again. It is all right to give the ground crews an idea of just how well you do aerobatics but don't let the staging expenses for your act run to $125,000 worth of equipment and $25,000 worth of pilot training.

Finally, develop and display the aggressiveness, alertness, flying ability, and proficiency in gunnery which are the attributes a fighter pilot must have. Any man who does not possess all these qualities would do well to get out of a fighter outfit before his C.O. convinces him that he isn't the right type by requesting that he be transferred. There is not place for him among those whose faith in each other must be complete.

EPILOGUE

If of thy work thou would'st complain,
The chance to speak, eschew it;
Thou huntest now the biggest game
And hast no cause to rue it;
Thy weapon makes the surest kill,
Thou findest sport and prove thy skill,
And thou art paid to do it!

INDEX